'*Gamechangers* sets a new record for brilliant ideas per page. If you can't find inspiration from the brilliant strategies of 100 gamechanging companies, you might want to consider another line of work'

Ken Segall, author of *Insanely Simple: The Obsession That Drives Apple's Success*

'You will never look at brand building the same again. *Gamechangers* explodes with refreshing strategies and ideas to take your brand to the next level!'

Paulo Miguel Periera da Silva, CEO of Renova

'In 1940 Henry Ford said that one day somebody would combine a car and aeroplane. At Aeromobil we made that happen. You too can be a *Gamechanger* with Peter's excellent guide to disruptive innovation'

Stefan Klein and Juraj Vaculik, Co-Founders of AeroMobil

'Peter is the Einstein of marketing and has just solved the elusive theory of business success. This book is like a magical lens that will allow you to see a world in business in which you can always win. You will think differently, see links that you never saw before and play the 'game' knowing you cannot lose. Peter goes one step further by proving how ordinary people have created extraordinary businesses - it is impossible to imagine business success without this book'

Mark Pitt, CEO, Virgin Australia New Zealand

'At Thinkers 50 we aim to identify the best business thinkers. We have featured Peter Fisk because his work consistently challenges the status quo. He seeks out best practice wherever it may be and shares it with the world. *Gamechangers* is far-ranging and important. It delivers on its promise'

Stuart Crainer & Des Dearlove, founder of Thinkers 50

'Peter is able to succinctly capture the key dynamics in this fast-changing world of business and brands, and challenging one's own strategic imperatives. Through insights drawn from global brands, he is able to inspire of thinking and working, with highly relevant applications for those of us operating in Asia'

Ajit Gunewardene, Deputy Chairman, John Keells Holdings Plc

'*Gamechangers* is more than a review of the key movers and shakers in today's industrial world; it's an in-depth view of how the commercial world is viewed by the most innovative businesses, and how they make the difference'

Stuart Brooke, Founder and Managing Director, ashmei

'This book provides fascinating insights into leading businesses that are shaping their markets in their own vision and driving innovation and growth'

Lain Jäger, CEO of Zespri International, New Zealand

'*Gamechangers* are the businesses who make sense of our fast-changing world, and drive innovation in everything they do, in order to be winners today and tomorrow. In India, there is more opportunity than ever to innovate and grow. Every Indian business needs to be a gamechanger!'

Manish Sharma, Managing Director, Panasonic India & South Asia

'Captures provocative lessons from an enormous range of recent innovations, spanning many different categories and countries. The result is a highly stimulating toolkit that challenges marketers to see things and do things very differently'

Andy Bird, Co-Founder of Brand Learning

'Fisk succeeds in providing an entertaining, lucid and innovative analysis of disruptive companies that are transforming the landscape of all global industries. Highly recommended for those entrepreneurs aiming at changing the rules of the business game as well as for managers whose mature businesses are threatened by new entrants'

Santiago Iniguez, Dean of IE Business School, Madrid

'Unlike any business book you've ever read, celebrated brand guru Peter Fisk asks you "are you ready to play the game?" Fisk argues that "the best businesses go to where the future is", then he takes you on a kaleidoscopic tour of that very future, opening-up a multitude of new horizons. In a world limited "only by your imagination", *Gamechangers* invites you to stretch your own imagination, so as to advance in the competition for new ideas. Warning: while you are reading this, others are changing your game!'

Bill Fischer, Professor of Innovation Management, IMD, Lausanne, Former President and Dean, China-Europe International Business School (CEIBS), Shanghai

'Peter Fisk fires up a mosaic of thinking beyond business through this brilliantly enunciated century of stories. *Gamechangers* is sheer intellectual capital that everyone needs to dig, grow, store, sell and share to make this world an interesting place not just for doing business but for all of us to live'

S. Subramanyeswar, National Planning Director, Lowe Lintas, India

'Peter has captured in *Gamechangers* the essence of the future direction in business. A book to be included in all business libraries'

Labeed S. Hamid, President, Middle East Management Centre, Dubai

'A stunning book that will be 'current' for at least the next ten years. No blind theories or wild thinking, just clear and game-changing insights based on profound research'

Ward Vandorpe, Managing Director Expert Marketer Magazine, Belgium

'If you're curious about what the future could be, and would also like to be one of those that create it, then this book is for you'

Steve Gilroy, CEO of Vistage International

'We met Peter a year ago during our perpetual trip around the world. We were meeting brands with a purpose and sharing their stories to inspire other people. He asked us during that meeting: "Are you ready to change the world?" Now that we've read the manuscript… we can't wait to apply the method to our business'

Anouk Pappers and Maarten Schäfer, co-founders of CoolBrands, Netherlands and authors of *Around the World in 80 Brands*

'This is the most original and practical book. Any marketer who skips this book is missing a huge opportunity to get "genius" ideas from the father of 21st century business thinking'

Handi Irawan D, CEO of Frontier Consulting Group, Indonesia

'A great framework that is insightful, colorful, simple, and easy to put into practice. A must read for any ambitious executive'

Tanyer Sonmezer, CEO, Management Centre, Turkey

'Peter Fisk is one of the great marketing polymaths of our age. *Gamechangers* is the latest brilliant episode in his crusade to transform the way marketing creates sustainable business and brand value. A tour de force and a must for every self-respecting CEO'

David Haigh, Founder and CEO of Brand Finance plc

'A veritable alphabet of brands that are changing the world as we know it. Peter is one of the very few who really changes our understanding of business rather than simply observing it'

Shaun Smith, co-author of Bold: *How to be brave in business and win*

'*Gamechangers* is an inspiring must-read for organizations who are facing transformational change to their business model and are seeking practical ideas which can be easily executed to drive positive results'

Peter Hardwick, SVP Sales and Marketing, Canada Apotex Inc

GAMECHANGERS

ARE YOU READY TO CHANGE THE WORLD? **CREATING INNOVATIVE**
STRATEGIES FOR BUSINESS AND BRANDS

PETER FISK

WILEY

This edition first published 2015
Reprinted May 2015, January 2016
© 2015 Peter Fisk

Registered office

John Wiley and Sons Ltd, The Atrium, Southern Gate, Chichester, West Sussex, PO19 8SQ, United Kingdom

For details of our global editorial offices, for customer services and for information about how to apply for permission to reuse the copyright material in this book please see our website at www.wiley.com.

Wiley publishes in a variety of print and electronic formats and by print-on-demand. Some material included with standard print versions of this book may not be included in e-books or in print-on-demand. If this book refers to media such as a CD or DVD that is not included in the version you purchased, you may download this material at http://booksupport.wiley.com. For more information about Wiley products, visit www.wiley.com.

Designations used by companies to distinguish their products are often claimed as trademarks. All brand names and product names used in this book and on its cover are trade names, service marks, trademark or registered trademarks of their respective owners. The publisher and the book are not associated with any product or vendor mentioned in this book. None of the companies referenced within the book have endorsed the book.

Cataloging-in-Publication Data is available from the Library of Congress

A catalogue record for this book is available from the British Library.

ISBN 978-1-118-95697-7 (paperback)   ISBN 978-1-118-95695-3 (ebk)
ISBN 978-1-118-95696-0 (ebk)   ISBN 978-1-119-06533-3 (ebk)

Cover Design & Image: Parent Design Ltd.

Set in 10/12pt Rockwell Std Light by Aptara, New Delhi, India
Printed in Great Britain by Bell & Bain Ltd, Glasgow

I AM A GAMECHANGER

I believe in the **future.**
A world of infinite possibilities.
I see **opportunity** when others see impossibility.

Thinking bigger, reframing my perspective.
Seeing things differently, thinking **different** things.
I explore. I challenge. I risk. I venture.

Rethinking. Imagining. Reinventing. Igniting.

We are all in the **ideas** business.
Creating, designing, innovating, together.

I embrace my childlike **wonder** and curiosity.
I take flying leaps into the known.

Playing the game. **Changing** the game. Playing
   to win.

I want to **contribute** to something bigger than
   myself.
I want to make **life** better, the **world** a better place.

Change is my opportunity, to seize and **shape**.

Aiming higher, with a purpose beyond profit.
Harnessing the power of **brands**, the potential of
   people.
Digital **networks**, technologies and business
   models.

Fusing the best ideas. **amplifying** the potential
   of others.
Mobilizing people with a cause, **enabling** them to
   achieve more.

I don't want to live somebody else's life.
To live in the shadow of somebody else's vision.

Imagination is my pathway to a better **future**.
Ideas and brands are my guides.
Partners make them real.

Most of all, I **believe** in me, and in being more.
To achieve what I never thought possible.
To put a ding in my universe.

I am bold, brave and brilliant.
I am a **gamechanger**.

CONTENTS

INTRODUCTION...ARE YOU READY TO CHANGE THE WORLD?

CHANGE THE GAME, DON'T JUST PLAY THE GAME

'Gamechangers' are disruptive and innovative, start-ups and corporates, in every sector and region, reshaping our world. They are more ambitious, with stretching vision and enlightened purpose. They see markets as kaleidoscopes of infinite possibilities, assembling and defining them to their advantage. They **find their own space**, then shape it to their advantage. Most of all they have great ideas. They out-think their competition, thinking bigger and different. They don't believe in being slightly cheaper or slightly better. That is a short-term game of diminishing returns.

1. **Play ... the game, change the game**
   Today's brands and businesses are playing a new game. They recognize that the steady state has been replaced by a zigzag world where ideas shake up every market and winners create the future in their own vision.

2. **Change ... world-changing, game-changing**
   Discontinuous change in markets requires disruptive action. Power shifts and global trends drive exponential change and new possibilities. Incrementalism is not enough to win this new game.

3. **Win ... the Gamechangers and what they do**
   There is a new breed of business, changing the world right now, but thinking bigger and smarter, winning in new ways. Do you have what it takes to change the game? Are you ready?

This book is about you, and how you can change your game. In Part Two we explore the 10 dimensions in which you can achieve this by thinking differently. In Part Three we look at the 100 companies, chosen by you, who demonstrate these new practices. In Part Four you'll find the action canvasses, the toolkits for your success.

HOW WILL YOU CHANGE YOUR GAME?

Gamechangers think and act differently. They fuse digital and physical, global and local, ideas and networks. They win by being smart, fast and connected – rather than through scale and efficiency.

They capture their higher purpose in more **inspiring brands** that resonate with their target audiences at the right time and place, enabled by data and technology, but more through empathetic design and rich human experiences. Social networks drive reach and richness, whilst new business models make the possible profitable.

They collaborate with customers and partner with other businesses, connecting ideas and utilizing their capabilities. They look beyond the sale to enable customers to achieve more; they care about their impact on people and the world. Ultimately they want to create a **better world**.

4. Think ... Change your future
Out-thinking the competition with audacious ideas that can change the world ... possibilities limited only by imagination, guided by an inspiring purpose, daring and ingenious, forged in your own ideas factory.

5. Explore ... Change your market
Making sense of the kaleidoscope to shape markets in your own vision ... tectonic shifts in power, from masses to niches, average to individual, looking east and south, millenials and entrepreneurs, to find the best opportunities.

6. Disrupt ... Change your strategy
Finding your own space, with a strategy that shapes markets in your own vision ... choosing your future, reframing your context and audience, rewriting the rules, then having the agility to pivot from mediocrity to magic.

7. Inspire ... Change your brand
Building brands about people not products, about making life better ... more than a name or logo, brands are built through platforms and propositions that are relevant and engaging, bringing people together with shared aspirations.

8. Design ... Change your business
Innovating the whole business, from business model to customer experience ... design thinking to look beyond products, open and collaborative, simple and frugal, to make the best ideas happen profitably.

9. Resonate ... Change your story
Turning into the customer's world with real-time and relevant content ... engaging them in more relevant, topical and meaningful ways, at the right time and place, collaboratively creating content that is built around contagious stories.

10. Enable ... Change your experience
Delivering customer experiences that enable customers to achieve more ... going beyond the sale to support and enable, educate and entertain people, through digital and physical experiences, big data and mobile technologies.

11. Mobilize ... Change your relationship
Growing further and faster through networks and collaboration ... connecting people with people, trusting and loyal to each, sharing and co-creating ideas that matter to them through social communities, and even spark a movement.

12. Impact ... Change your results
Delivering and sustaining a positive impact, human and financial ... value creation is about more than sales, it is about sustained profitable growth underpinned by a circular economy, social and environmental, and leaves a legacy to the world.

13. Amplify ... Change your potential
Leaders amplify the potential of their people and organizations ... which starts with you, changing your brain to think differently, to win as a speedboat or a supertanker, to redefine your potential, by being bold, brave and brilliant.

WHO ARE THE GAMECHANGERS?

From Alibaba to Zidisha, Ashmei to Zilok, Azuri and Zipcars, a new generation of businesses are rising out of the maelstrom of economic and technological change across our world. These are just a few of the companies **shaking up** our world. Over 12 months I asked around 500 business leaders from across each continent to nominate the companies who they see as shaking up their markets. From this I identified

10 companies, large and small, in every sector and learnt how they are developing their businesses, innovating and competing, growing and winning.

14. Futurestore ... changing the game of retail

From branded boutiques to online marketplaces, digital walls and mobile marketing, retail connects physical and digital experiences.

- Amazon
- Fab
- Positive Luxury
- Aussie Farmers Direct
- Ekocycle
- Etsy
- Rackuten Ichiba
- Inditex
- Trader Joe's
- Le Pain Quotidien

15. Futurebank ... changing the game of finance

Financial services need to go beyond transactions and management, to help people to achieve more with their money.

- Moven
- Umpqua
- Zidisha
- Square
- La Caixa
- Commonwealth Bank
- Fidor
- Itau Unibanco
- First National Bank
- M-Pesa

16. Futurehealth ... changing the game of healthcare

Healthcare is increasingly personal, predictive and positive. It harnesses technology to enable more individual and intelligent wellbeing.

- 23andMe
- Epocrates
- Narayana Hrudayalaya
- Aravind Eyecare
- Genentech
- Organova
- Intuitive Surgical
- PatientsLikeMe
- Scanadu
- Second Sight

17. Futuregadget ... changing the game of consumer products

Products will embrace smart design and service to provide more connected experiences that are intelligent and personal.

- Renova
- Method
- Nike
- Apple
- Godrej
- Lego
- Natura Cosmetics
- Oculus Rift
- Pebble
- Philosophy

18. Futuremedia ... changing the game of content and media

As networks become ubiquitous, media is about relevant and distinctive content, bringing stories to life through real-time, immersive experiences.

- Coursera
- Spotify
- Netflix
- Al Jazeera
- Future
- Pledge
- Ushahidi
- Red Bull
- Supercell
- Pixar

19. Futurefashion ... changing the game of fashion

Fashion captures culture, be it current or heritage, aspirational or fun, or harnessing technology and data to enable high performance.

- Toms
- Ashmei
- Threadless
- Gilan
- Desigual
- Editd
- Kering
- Rapha
- Patagonia
- Shang Xai

20. Futuretravel ... changing the game of travel and hotels

Travel will grow rapidly as the new middle classes grow, and also driven by new business models, new categories and extreme experiences.

- Zipcars
- Airbnb
- Virgin Galactic
- Aeromobil
- Air Asia
- Emirates
- Kulula
- Pipistrel
- Red Bus
- Starwood

21. Futurefood ... changing the game of food and drink

Food brands will focus on delivering more rich and authentic experiences, supported by premium brands and new business models.

- Juan Valdez Cafe
- Zespri
- Mayrig
- Yeni Raki
- Aerolife
- Beauty'in
- Graze
- LA Organic
- Moa Beer
- Nespresso

22. Futuretech ... changing the game of technology and networks

Technologies have most impact when they empower people through intelligent interfaces, supported by smart devices and enabling networks.

- Samsung
- ARM
- Raspberry Pi
- Alibaba
- Bharti Airtel
- GiffGaff
- Google <X>
- Huawei
- Tencent
- Xiaomi

23. Futuremakers ... changing the game of manufacturing

Manufacturing has become smart and on demand – responsive to global aspirations of connected markets, and customized to local needs.

- Tesla
- GE
- Syngenta
- Corning
- Tata
- 3D Hubs
- Braskem
- Space X
- Dyson
- Local Motors

Case studies for other categories, updates of the brands in these categories, plus winners of regional 'Gamechangers' competitions to find the best local innovators, can be found at www.Gamechangers.pro.

ARE YOU READY TO GET STARTED?

At the end of the book you will find the 'Gamechanger Labs'. These consist of 16 canvasses, practical toolkits and workflows to apply the best ideas to your own business.

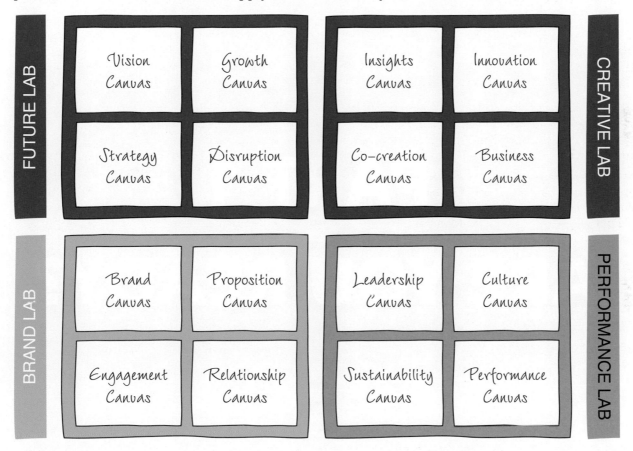

PART 1
ARE YOU READY?

Next generation businesses win by changing the game. They don't want to be a little better, they think bigger...they see things differently, and think different things...they define and shape markets in their own vision. They combine all the tricks of 21st-century business to engage and inspire people...to enable more, to make life better. And to win.

1 PLAY ... THE GAME

THE GAME, CHANGE THE GAME

'Moonshots' are the incredible, seemingly impossible, ideas that can change our world.

Google <X> is a **moonshot factory**. Full of creative thinkers, optimists, seeking out the big opportunities and most challenging problems, that with a little imagination and a lot of **innovation** might just make our world a better place. From intelligent cars to augmented vision, the <X> team fuses technological possibility with human need, to create more audacious, inspiring **futures**.

This is how we move forwards.

From **Galileo's vision** to da Vinci's mechanics, Ford's cars to Bell's phones, Apple's devices to Dyson's cleaners. They enrich society, and make life better. Markets emerge out of new possibilities, seeing things differently, thinking different things. Brands capture big ideas, innovation turns them into businesses and future growth.

We live in the most **incredible** time.

Days of **exponential change** and opportunities limited only by our imagination. A world where impossible dreams can now come true. A period of **awesomeness**. From Alibaba to Zespri, Ashmei to Zidisha, Azuri and Zipcars, a new generation of businesses are rising out of the maelstrom of economic and technological change across our world.

'Gamechangers' are more ambitious, with stretching vision and enlightened purpose. They see markets as kaleidoscopes of infinite possibilities, assembling and defining them to their advantage. Most of all they have **great ideas**, captured by brands that resonate with their target audiences at the right time and place, enabled by data and technology but most of all by rich human experiences. Social networks drive reach and richness, whilst new business models make the possible profitable.

Our challenge is to make sense of this new world, to embrace the new opportunities in innovative ways, and to be a winner.

WHAT'S YOUR GAME?

Branson flashed his trademark grin, flicked his shaggy, maverick hair.

'Business is like **the best game** you could ever **imagine**.'

We talked about his multi-billion dollar investments in financial services, media and telecoms, airlines and space travel. He described his responsibility to hundreds of thousands of staff, and millions of customers.

And he was calling it **a game**.

He was having fun now, challenging the notions of conventional strategies and structures, especially in the biggest companies. The essence of Virgin, he said, is to do things significantly different and better.

He talked about his admiration for kids and for the **next generation** of entrepreneurs – especially those in fast-growing markets who have hunger and passion, and how he was inspired by iconic revolutionaries, Nelson Mandela and Steve Jobs.

'You've got to **think different**, uninhibited like a child, never give up, have an ambition that you really care about, take more risks, be ingenious, make a bigger difference to people's lives, have incredible fun, but also **play to win**.'

I asked him what keeps him going. 'Doing things different, unexpected and a bit crazy,' he said. 'It's about playing the game. But the best way to win is to **change the game**.'

Whilst he says he's not too old for an all-night party, Branson loves a game of tennis, and that's after he's swum for an hour each morning along the coast of his own Necker Island.

From his earliest venture, launching a student magazine, he would always do things differently. He launched his first airline with no knowledge of the travel industry, but he had a **big idea**, to provide low-cost travel that was modern and fun. And he had a brand that at least some people loved. He could see an opportunity to disrupt the market, to be on the customer's side. When he launched mobile phones, he piggy backed on somebody else's network to grow **further** and **faster**, and targeted a new generation of consumers.

Even **Virgin Galactic**, his latest and craziest business, is not all it might seem. He had no experience of space travel. But he got together with glider designer Burt Rutan to do things differently, launching his spacecraft from the back of a mother ship, eventually to be fuelled by his algae farms on the Carribean, hugely reducing costs and carbon emissions and enabling daily departures and landings.

Perhaps the most surprising revelation is that space is not really the frontier. Branson's real ambition for Virgin Galactic is inter-continental travel. Imagine a one-hour flight from Rio to Jakarta, or Cape Town to Beijing. It could get a little weightless on the way, but could transform the way we think about the world.

Whilst Branson was still playing, it was already evening in Beijing.

Li Ka-Shing was sitting down to a dinner of his favourite snake soup. The Chaozhou-born, Hong Kong-based chairman of **Hutchison Whampoa** is the richest man in Asia, worth around $30 billion according to Bloomberg.

Yet he lives a relatively frugal existence, wearing simple clothes and a $50 Seiko watch on his wrist, and has donated much of his fortune to education and medical research.

This is a man who sees business as an ancient game, rooted in Chinese culture's **'Wu Xing'** where the five elements – wood, fire, earth, metal and water – come together in a mutually generative sequence.

You can see these phases in Li's business investments which include construction and energy, mining and technology, shipping and banking. Together they account for over 15% of the market cap of Hong Kong's Stock Exchange.

Li loves a game before work too. In fact you'll find him at 6 every morning teeing off at the Hong Kong Golf Club with his playing partner, movie mogul Raymond Chow.

Whilst Asia rises, the old is still important. And that great old 'Sage of Omaha', investor **Warren Buffett**, still knows how to play too.

Twice as wealthy as his Asian peer, Buffett loves to surprise his shareholders when they gather at 'the **Woodstock of business**', Berkshire Hathaway's annual meeting. Forget slick graphics explaining the complexities of financial markets, this is different.

GAMECHANGERS

As the lights dim, there's a roar off stage, and 80 year-old Buffett rides on, dressed in a leather jacket, on the back of a shining **Harley Davidson**. He grabs a guitar and starts playing a song. His review of the year. His shareholders love it.

In fact it's interesting how playful the world's most famous entrepreneurs are.

Mark Zuckerberg began writing software at the age of about 10. As his father once said 'Other kids played computer games, Mark **created them**'. Whenever he came across somebody else's game, he would hack into the code, and change it to make it better.

Facebook itself started out as a game. Enrolled at Harvard to study psychology and computer science he was quickly distracted, famously creating a game called **FaceMash** which invited fellow students to vote for the hottest girls (and guys) on campus.

Soon he changed the game, under pressure from some of his peers and University administrators. Facebook was born. And a billion people followed.

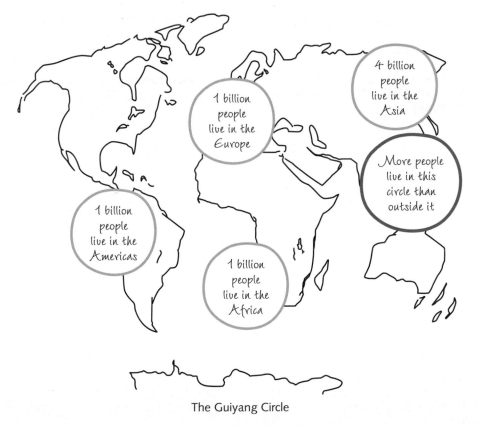

The Guiyang Circle

LIVING IN THE ZIGZAG ZEITGEIST

More than **half the world** live inside a circle based 106.6° E, 26.6° N, and within 4100 km of Guiyang, Guizhou Province, in southwest China. A quick snapshot of our changing world demonstrates the dramatic change that are, or will disrupt every business:

- **Middle world** ... Global population has **doubled** in the past 50 years, with a shift from low to middle income groups, a new consumer generation (OECD).

- **Young and old** ... As life expectancy has boomed, now at over 70, and births have declined, from 5 to 2.5, we live longer, with different priorities (UN).

- **Mega cities** ... Urban populations will grow from 3.6bn in 2010 to 6.3bn by 2020, representing 96% of the global population growth (World Bank).

- **Flood warning** ... By 2050 at least 20% of us could be exposed to floods, including many cities, an economic risk to assets of $45 trillion (World Bank).

Brands come and go with much more regularity, products are built across the world, small businesses work together in networks:

- **Business life** ... Over 40% of companies in the Fortune 500 in 2000 were not there in 2010; 50% will be from emerging markets by 2020 (Fortune).

- **Made in the world** ... 55% of all products are now made in more than one country and around 20% of services too (WTO).

- **Small is better** ... 70% of people think small companies understand them better than large ones. The majority of the world's business value is now privately owned.

- **Corporate trust** ... While 55% of adults trust businesses to do what is right, only 15% trust business leaders to tell the truth (Edelman).

Technological innovation is relentless, currently digital and mobile, but rapidly becoming more about clean energy and biotech:

- **Always on** ... 24% of the world's population has a smartphone, typically checking it 150 times per day, spending 141 minutes on it (Meeker).

- **Digital markets** ... 80% of websites are US-based, 81% of web users are non-US based, 70% of the value of all e-commerce transactions are B2B (IAB).

- **Instant content** ... Content on the internet tripled between 2010 and 2013; 70% is now video. The half-life of social content is 3 hours (bit.ly).

- **Future energy** ... By 2017, there will be close to $11bn in revenue from 35-million homes generating their own solar or wind power (GIGAom).

Customers feel increasingly ambivalent about brands and companies. In a world of infinite choice, their priorities and preferences have changed:

- **Bland brands** ... 73% of people say they wouldn't care if the brands they used disappeared; 62% say they are not loyal to any brands (Ad Age).

- **Customer emotions** ... 70% of buying experiences are based on how people feel, loyal customers are typically worth 10 times their first purchase (McKinsey).

- **Service costs** ... 7 times more to acquire customers than keep them, 12 positive experiences to make up for one unresolved negative experience (IBM).

15

- **Family life** … The amount of time parents spend with their children continues to go up, fathers spend three times more than 40 years ago (Meeker).

THE END OF THE WORLD AS WE KNOW IT

When Henry Ford launched his Model T in 1908 his Detroit assembly line, his innovative product and his pioneering marketing machine transformed an industry. His efficient mass-production methods reduced prices, improved quality and created vast wealth. He dominated the market, and by 1918 half the cars in America were Fords.

It was the third wave of the industrial revolution.

The first wave of the industrial revolution had been about **invention** – from the forging of iron in the Shropshire valleys, the spinning jenny for making textiles, and James Watt's steam engine. The second wave was about **application** – Robert Fulton's steamboat on the Hudson River, Alexander Bell's telephone, and Thomas Edison's light bulb.

The third wave was about **transformation,** when the innovations take on a scale and can change the world – from the mass production of cars, railways and airplanes, to huge factories and modern medicines. This transformed people's lives, improving health and education, the growth of cities and international trade.

Whilst the industrial revolution had begun in the north of England, making Britain powerful and wealthy, it soon spread across Europe and to America, and in later years beyond, particularly to Japan. It was 250 years of disruption, after 7000 years of a society based around agriculture.

First wave is about invention

Second wave is about application

Third wave is about transformation

Industrial age began with the mass production of iron, textiles and steam engine

Industrial innovators changed people's lives, from telephone to light bulb

Industrial age changed the world with railways, cars, aircraft, and medicines

Digital pioneers develop transistors and circuits leading to computers

Digital innovators embrace the internet, mobile devices and content

Gamechangers unlock global connectivity and collective intelligence

Waves of Digital Revolution

Now, as that age closes, we are in the midst of the **digital revolution** – embarking on the third wave of a new age that will change the world again, even faster.

The first wave, about invention, started with transistors that led to integrated circuits, the rise of **computers** and the miniaturization of machines ... from video games and mobile phones through to 1990 when Tim Berners Lee introduced the World Wide Web.

The second wave, about application, is well known to us today. Internet and mobile **communications** pervade our lives: shopping on Amazon with our Apple iPads, a world of knowledge through Google and Wikipedia, a world without borders through Facebook and Skype. First distracting us, now embraced as the way we live.

The third wave of the digital revolution is when everything changes, when digital is transformational, when power really shifts.

Whilst the last 20 years of technology has inspired us, it is only **now that the game really changes** – when the 'gamechangers' shape the future. Mass production is rapidly becoming obsolete, 3D printers are already replacing factories, companies work in virtual networks, products are bought on demand and customized by default, whilst personal channels are replacing stores which used to second guess what people wanted.

In the past we created **average** products for average people. We made the products ourselves in big factories that absorbed significant capital investment. We needed to sell on a huge scale to secure a return on investments. Markets were largely homogeneous because every competitor was close to average, therefore we could measure results by market share.

We used mass-market, broadcast advertising with average messages, at times to suit us, pushing people to buy more of what we wanted.

This game **doesn't work anymore**. That was the industrial age. Soon we will see the end of factories, shops and advertising.

Digital is by its nature not about size or geography, capability or experience. It is **borderless and democratized**, enabling anyone to have an impact. Mikael Hed sits in Espoo creating games like Angry Birds that entertain the world; Eric Magicovsky could be anywhere raising $10 million from 69,000 people on Kickstarter to launch his Pebble smartwatch; Vicky Wu flies between LA and HK building 'prosumer' demand for her latent fashions with ZaoZao.

This is the third wave of the digital revolution, where ideas can **change people's lives**, where anybody can change the game.

WHERE THE FUTURE BEGINS

The value of business lies not in what it does **today**, but in what it seeks to achieve **tomorrow**. That might seem a little idealistic, given the short-term obsession of many organizations with operational performance, yet it is the future that most interests investors and private owners who now dominate the business world, hoping to see their investments grow through future profits.

Most business leaders are 'heads down' in a relentless battle to survive, to hang onto the status quo. But that can only lead to diminishing returns. The more enlightened leaders are 'heads up' looking at where they are going, making sense of how the outside world is changing with every day, identifying the new needs and expectations, the new competitors and challenges, opportunities and possibilities.

The best businesses **go to where the future is**.

They disrupt before they are disrupted. They sell before they are worthless. They recognize that existing success is increasingly driven by out-dated beliefs, a once-profitable niche that has now become the mainstream, a previous innovation that has been widely imitated, an economy of scale that has become irrelevant, a temporary monopoly that is no more.

As we explore the shifts and trends, the white spaces and technological breakthroughs, the new attitudes and behaviours, we need to learn to think in a different way.

The **change is exponential**. So we need to jump on whilst we can. Catch the new wave, or better still, learn to ride with the successive, and ever more frequent, waves of change.

When we look around us at the companies who are challenging established positions, shaking up conventions and waking up tired consumers, they are not the big companies but the small ones. They are the **speed boats**, fast and flexible, rather than **supertankers**, steady and stable.

The challenge is extreme. It demands that we rethink where we're going, and how to get there, rather than hanging on to what made us great before.

In a fast and connected world, complex and uncertain, a winning business cannot hope to keep doing what it does and do better. It has to do more, or different.

WE ARE ALL IN THE IDEAS BUSINESS

In Hong Kong there is a great 100 year-old business that explains our future potential. For much of the last century **Li and Fung** was focused on low-cost manufacturing of textiles.

That was until salary levels grew, and places like Indonesia were able to achieve much lower cost bases. The business reinvented itself as a **virtual resource** network, helping brands to find the right partners for the business, in terms of expertize, quality and price.

Walk into a Li and Fung office in Sao Paulo or Istanbul, Barcelona or Toronto – or any one of their 300 offices in over 50 countries – and the small team of **sourcing experts** will help you find the best designers, manufacturers and distributors for your brand. Every pair of Levi jeans you buy is made with the help of Li and Fung, and around 40% of the world's textiles. If you need finance, they'll find you an investor, and if you need merchandising, processing or customer service they can find the right partner for that too. Their business model can be based on fees, on commissions, or on an agreed mix.

Actually, all you need is a **good idea**. Take it to Li and Fung and they can make it happen with you.

Those ideas are not the product of years of experience, of big organizations with thousands of employees, of rigorous 'big data' analysis and scientific labs. Those things can help, but they can also hinder. Fresh perspectives beat conventional wisdom, youthful insights connect with millennial markets, right brain intuition is an equal to left brain intelligence, and collaboration can achieve this even better.

And we haven't even started on Steve Jobs. From the revolutionary Apple Mac that transformed computing. The iPod, the iPhone, the iPad. Not just incredible products with beautiful designs, but new business models creating entirely new markets, **changing the world**.

Or James Dyson, with his bagless vacuum cleaner. Ratan Tata, with his dramatically affordable Nano car. Amancio Ortega with his ready baked Zara clothes. Or further back in time ... Henry Ford, Marie Curie, Thomas Edison, Pablo Picasso, The Beatles, Nicolas Hayek, Ted Turner and many more.

Great ideas are the result of **better thinking.**

We need to think – to see things differently, and do different things – to open our minds to new possibilities, to outthink the new competition.

- **Think bigger** ... redefine the markets we are in, reframe our brands in more useful contexts, recreate the strategies for success.

- **Think smarter** ... refocus on the best customers and categories, reinvent every aspect of our business, realigning with new partners.

- **Think faster** ... reenergize people with new ideas, resonate with customers' new priorities and aspirations, and achieve more together.

Beyond the connectivity and applications, the social networks and artificial intelligence, we now live in a world that is **more equal and accessible**, where people are more knowledgeable and capable, than ever before.

It really is a world limited only by our imaginations.

Back at the moonshot factory of Google X, they have a mantra which says 'Why try to be **only 10% better**, when you could be **10 times better**?'

Ten times better provides much more than a temporary competitive advantage, it has sufficient capacity to change the game. The effort required to think in a bigger frame, to innovate things more radically, to deliver them faster, is relatively small compared to the benefits.

But that requires one more thing. To **think different**.

Apple, or rather its ad agency Chiat Day, conjured up that phrase, but it matters more than ever. The best companies today don't just play the game, they think bigger and better, smarter and faster, in order to **change the game.**

2 CHANGE...CHANGE THE GAME

WORLD-CHANGING, GAME-CHANGING

WORLD CHANGING

The future is not an extension of today, it is wild and unpredictable, diverse and **discontinuous**. Business cannot extrapolate the success of today, and hope to win tomorrow. Even if you did, you would be swamped by a world of imitating competition all seeking to play the same game.

Just like the world changes at an **incredible pace**, in fantastic and unexpected ways, so too must businesses learn to change – to play the new game, or better still to play their own game. To shape markets in their own vision, to create business models that suit them, to engage and enable customers to achieve more. This is what it means to change the game.

The turmoil of financial markets, collapsing banks and defaulting nations, are the dying cries of a changing world; a **reordering** of markets and power that we are slowly recognizing. Amidst the shake-up there are new winners and losers. In 2014, China's real GDP grew by 7.1% compared to 0.9% in Europe. Markets from Colombia to Indonesia are thriving.

As Samsung launches its smart watch, Beijing is recognized as the world's leading city for renewable energies, **Shenzen** becomes the new Wall Street, the best web designers are in Hyderabad and fashion designers in Buenos Aires, we realize that the best ideas in business are shifting rapidly too. No longer are these **fast growth markets** the source of low-cost supplies and low-budget consumers. They have youth and education, investment and disposable income – and most of all ambition – on their side too.

Every market is driven by change, fundamental power shifts and global trends, heightened expectations of customers and new sources of competition. The shifts in power are economic and political, but also demographic and cultural. In a connected world, trends and expectations cross boundaries instantly. Even the most local or traditional markets are not immune. African children want the latest computer game just as much as those in California, Arabic consumers want global fashions and ready meals, whilst local market stalls in Europe focus on fresh, organic and exotic produce.

Technologies fuel and embrace this change. Computing power continues to grow exponentially, an iPhone smarter than a **Space Shuttle**, mobile devices supported by **Cloud** storage transform where and how we do business, whilst the most significant technical breakthroughs are in genetics, robotics and nanotech.

The current decade will be unique in its tectonic shifts. As the global population accelerates to **7.7 billion** before slowing, power will shift, the G7 will be replaced by the E7 (that's the BRIC nations, plus Indonesia, Mexico and Turkey). Even more dramatic is the growth in global wealth, a combined GDP almost doubling from $53 to to **$90 trillion**. But the shift is not

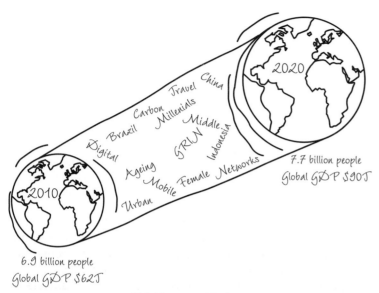

6.9 billion people
Global GDP $62T

Kaleidoscope Markets

(image labels: Digital, Brazil, Carbon, Travel, China, Millenials, GRIN, Middle, Indonesia, Ageing, Mobile, Female, Networks, Urban, 2010, 2020, 7.7 billion people, Global GDP $90T)

linear, not an extension of today, but a fundamental reordering – think of it like a kaleidoscope. Making sense of this global maelstrom, and seizing the opportunities within it, will separate winners from losers.

○ **West to East** ... the shift is intellectual and cultural, as well as economic. It will also be North to South (the rise of Africa), local to global (no borders), and global to local (staying real). Compare the fortunes of Air Asia with American Airlines, the growth of Tata with the decline of GM.

○ **Big to Small** ... the shift favours the fast and agile, not the slow and stable. Small businesses beat large ones. And people trust small businesses more too. Just look at the changing format of hotels, from Sheraton and Hilton to Aloft and Airbnb. When Facebook acquired Instagram for $1bn in 2012, it only had 13 employees.

○ **Scale to Focus** ... the shift from success through volume and market share, to being able to target the profitable niches, treating customers as different and special, not a mass of averages. Consider the fragmentation of media into specialisms and multiple platforms, more relevant and profitable.

○ **Skills to Ideas** ... the shift from the industrial to digital age means that capabilities can always be found, it is ideas that make you different. As a result we are more human in a tech world. Think about the most admired leaders, like Branson and Buffett, smart but staying real.

○ **Me to We** ... the shift from individual to collaborative, embracing the value of diversity and engagement, connecting and collaborating to think smarter and act faster. Time to get connected to platforms like Alibaba, networks like Linked-In, crowd-funders like Kickstarter.

○ **Push to Pull** ... the shift from surplus demand to surplus supply, the power to customers, and empowerment of consumers. Different is not enough, we need to be intimately relevant, in context and on demand. Think about Amazon, Google, or even pizza delivery.

ACCELERATING EXPONENTIALLY

The speed and impact of change is not only fast and relentless, but also exponential. It **keeps multiplying**. Familiar with the continual doubling of computing power, the never ending search for better and faster, and the ongoing obsolescence of devices, innovations keep building on each other, each growing exponentially, each magnifying the next.

Networks have the most exponential impact of all, proliferating ideas and capabilities, power and potential.

GAMECHANGERS

Whilst the future will be more **volatile** and uncertain it will also be more **vibrant** and unreal. The impact of change in a connected world is fast and far-reaching, as the advance of technology opens up new **opportunities** hard to imagine. **Complexity** is the norm as we learn to make sense of limitless information, discontinuities will be frequent, frictions will be **displaced,** and change will be **exponential.** Whilst ambiguity might seem disconcerting, paradox is the source of amazing possibility.

When **astronauts** return from space, they marvel at the new perspective they gain of our planet – how small it seems in the expanse of space, and how unique and fragile its life-enabling ecosystems really are. It can transform **attitudes** about what matters, how to solve problems, about the scale of our ambitions and potential impacts.

We need to learn to **think bigger**, to reframe our sightlines, to think in a connected way, to understand the cause and effects of systems.

Global GDP is estimated to grow from $62 trillion back in 2010 to over **$90 trillion** by 2020, according to the World Bank. The economies of **China and India** will triple in that period, with China replacing America as the world's largest economy. Looking further ahead, by 2050 the old G7 of advanced nations will be collectively half the value of the **E7 nations** (also including Brazil, Indonesia, Mexico, Russia and Turkey).

As economic power shifts east, political influence and military capability will follow. As global citizenship mushrooms to **7.5 billion**, it is the new lower- to middle-income consumers that will have most impact on markets. Accelerating demand for **oil and gas**, food and fresh water, metals and land, will create price volatility and political tensions. Peak oil in 2021, after which it is expected to dwindle in supply, will exasperate the problem, whilst **carbon emissions** and sea levels continue to rise.

Huge population shifts from countryside to cities, farms to factories, transform landscapes and demographics, putting enormous strain on **infrastructure**. Baby boomers live on, as the **ageing populations** of advanced nations need more healthcare, whilst youthful populations of growing economies will demand better education. They will also embrace technology faster, hungry for innovations and entrepreneurial wealth.

Of these forces, **GRIN** (genetic, robotic, intelligent and nano) **technologies** will be most disruptive. However, perhaps an even a bigger driver of markets and brands will be the dreams and expectations of consumers, alongside the imagination of the next generation entrepreneurs to fulfil them in novel and profitable ways.

Making sense of the future requires a leap of imagination. In the past we drew trend lines to understand smooth evolutions into the future. We cannot predict the future of smartphones as an incremental journey from today's models, as the devices jump to our wrists and clothing, to become embedded in our vision or minds. Nokia has learnt that a dominant market position can lead to irrelevance within five years.

EXPLORING NEW POSSIBILITIES

The idea of extrapolating the past to understand the future, even in a non-linear way, no longer works. The speed of change, the step change of capabilities, creates a future that is seismically different, and better, than our past.

Innovations emerge at incredible pace. I still struggle to remember life just 10 years ago when I couldn't order my shopping online, read the newspaper on my tablet, hire a funky car for the day, or listen to limitless free music. The emergence of new materials like graphene, the upgrading of networks to superfast bandwidth, the miniaturization of semiconductors are all quietly converging to create amazing futures, fast.

The '**internet of things**', where physical objects from beer bottles to street lights are digitally connected, will make our environment more intelligent, personal and convenient. Already smart thermostats control the temperature of our homes without a thought, cars can alert each other of traffic jams ahead, drone aircraft are deployed in warfare, and plants can text or tweet that they need watering.

By 2020, research firm Gartner believes there will be more than 30 billion 'things' online, a $15 trillion market. Darpa, the defence innovators, have developed **AlphaDog** that can walk for 20 miles without resting, Google's glasses will drive actions based on eye movements, Samsung are developing phones that have a sense of touch and computers that can smell. The stories of new possibilities are endless, 'gamechanging' is about **making them real**.

Mobile solutions – whether it's banking, shopping or healthcare – will be worth $4.5 trillion by 2020, according to Bain. However this will demand better and faster network coverage. Rethinking wi-fi based on much smaller and frequent transmitters in urban areas is one option, popular in dense cities like Seoul and Tokyo. Meanwhile Chamtech have developed a more radical solution – **spray-on wi-fi** – a liquid containing millions of nano-capacitors, that can be sprayed onto any surface, like clothes and cars, creating local, satellite-enabled, hotspots wherever people are.

Air travel is expected to **double** in the next decade, according to IATA, driven by the demand of emerging middle classes. Significantly more efficient planes will be needed, to reduce time, costs and emissions. Slovenian aircraft maker Pipistrel has developed an **electric aircraft** that also benefits from smarter navigation systems that allow it to find shorter routes, sensing thermal flows and negotiating complex paths. Meanwhile NASA has developed a twin-cylinder engine that can be mounted at the back of the plane, thereby requiring 50% less fuel and significantly reducing noise too.

Gadget-mad people are always looking for **power** sockets. And the biggest component in the **devices** is usually the battery. Miniaturized capture of solar power will transform gadgets. They will use **micro-batteries** mimicking photosynthesis, using metal oxides heated by the sun, to split sea water into hydrogen and oxygen. **Hydrogen**, clean and abundant, could then power a whole array of micro-machines, from the next generation phones to nano-tech medical implants.

The sun really is our best source of energy. It's obvious really, but we haven't yet been able to harness the obvious. **Desert wastelands** soak up more energy in six hours than the world uses in a year. Desertec seeks to harness that potential with hundreds of square miles of wind and solar plants feeding the world's electric grids with clean cheap and reliable **solar power** provided it can get nations working together: 90% of the world lives within 1800 miles of a desert, and 1300 square miles of Saharan desert, for example, could power 20% of Europe. It could transform the fortunes of **Africa** as well as solve the world's fossil fuel crisis.

PLAYING A DIFFERENT GAME

In the 1968 Mexico Olympics, **Dick Fosbury** stood alongside his competitors, no taller or fitter than all the other fine athletes. But he had a significant advantage. He thought differently. Whilst every other competitor followed the conventions established over the years, that a high jump involved straddling the bar feet first, Fosbury tried a different approach, leaping backwards over the bar. The biomechanical explanations would come later, all that Fosbury knew or cared about was that he had out-thought his competitors, and won gold.

20 years later **Nicolas Hayek**, a Lebanese-born Swiss actuary, was asked by a group of bankers to oversee the liquidation of two traditional watch-making firms who were in turmoil due to competition from Japanese manufacturers like Seiko. Instead he reorganized the businesses and acquired a young start-up brand called Swatch, who made cheap, plastic watches from minimal parts. He rapidly scaled the business, focusing on the potential of plastic for colour and design. The Swatch brand did not seek to emulate other watch-makers, but instead to be in the fashion business. 'Why buy one watch, when you can have three or four, a different colour for each outfit?'

Ten years later, **Jeff Bezos**, a Cuban American, left behind his job as vice president of a Wall Street investment bank and headed for the West Coast, with little more than his car he drove, with his wife alongside him. He could see how the internet was starting to change industries and consumers' lives. A year later he launched Amazon from a garage in Bellevue, just outside Seattle. Within two months he was selling $20,000 of books a week. He dubbed it the world's first online bookstore, choosing the name Amazon because it started with an A and sounded a little exotic and different. Innovation for Bezos is about '1000 small ideas coming together to change the world'. Over the last two decades he has achieved that, building the world's largest retailer.

The opportunities for change are all around us, what it takes is people. People who are prepared to do things differently, to put their hands up and say they believe there is a better way, and to start making it happen.

HOW WILL YOU CHANGE THE GAME?

Entrepreneurs are natural gamechangers. They have chosen to play their own game, driven by ambition and uninhibited by function or hierarchy. Large businesses have advantages too, assets to apply in new ways, existing brands and customer bases on which to build. Gamechangers can be anyone, business leaders or strategists, innovators or marketers, somebody on a shop floor or in a call centre. They can change the game because they think differently.

Gamechangers typically **innovate** in one or more of the following dimensions – the why, who, what and how – of the whole business, or any part of it. They might apply this thinking to the business strategy, but it could also apply to a brand or service experience, leadership style or organization process.

○ **Change the 'why'** (the purpose, application or benefit) – for example, from maximizing profits to enhancing people's lives, from being the biggest to being the best, from enabling communication to providing entertainment. When Coca-Cola changed its purpose from the more functional 'refreshment' to more emotional 'happiness' it was able to engage people much more deeply.

○ **Change the 'who'** (the geography, customer or context) – for example, from 'home' markets to selected markets worldwide, targeting older people rather than everyone, or women, or a different decision maker in a company. When Fiat 500 changed its target audience from low-cost owners to funky young things, it stepped out of its old peer group, and became affordable, urban fashion.

○ **Change the 'what'** (the category, product or experience) – for example, combining products to solve problems, personalizing products on demand, offering 24/7 service, making the experience fun, or extending to

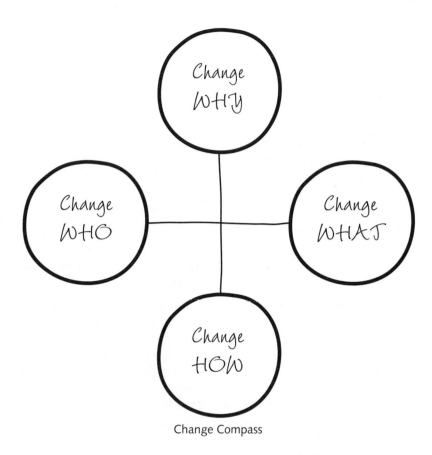

Change Compass

support people in their application. When Rapha realized it was not its clothing but togetherness that mattered to cyclists, it opened cafés and became the cult place to hang out.

○ **Change the 'how'** (the business model, service style or participation) – for example, from transactional pricing to membership fees, prices that change by time of day, reduced price in return for new ideas, or sold through new types of partners. When Zipcars wanted to be different, it didn't charge per week like other car rental companies, but created a membership club and then charged a much smaller fee per minute and mile.

The four dimensions are a simple compass by which to stretch your thinking. Some of the best innovations change in more than one dimension, or even all of them. Gamechangers then need to think about how they turn their disruptive ideas into a practical strategy for business success – what it means in terms of market and brand, innovation and marketing, business model and customer experience, resources and metrics. But all of this comes later, and often flows easier, once you have found a big, inspiring idea.

BE A REALITY DISTORTION FIELD

Steve Jobs provokes and inspires in equal measure. From his early days as a 'silicon kid', the geek in the garage that loved Bob Dylan, making games for Atari and a gadget to make illegal phone calls, to a visit to Xerox PARC where he was inspired by their graphical interface, set up his Mac **team of pirates**, and soon got fired.

But entrepreneurs don't give up. From the super computers of NeXT, he was soon in dreamland at Pixar and $1 billion richer. From Toy Story emerged his **jelly bean iMacs**, iPods and iPhones with the help of iTunes and AppStore, Leerjets and Coldplay, and $400 billion.

Love him, or hate him, he changed the world … visionary and obsessive, pedantic and dismissive, inspiring and impossible … distorting reality, disrupting possibility.

Most strategies in business search for **absolutes** – the perfect vision, defining priorities, setting limits. But markets are dynamic, volatile and unpredictable, and plans are never perfect. Businesses rarely implement the strategy they agonize over. But for Jobs, there were no straight lines, **passion and intuition** were better guides, making sense of complexity. Keep looking left-field, embracing every experience and seeing the bigger picture.

Innovation processes seek to codify a human, **creative experience**. Processes improve efficiency, maybe even speed, but they rarely deliver the right answer. Market research delivers average insights. Apple believed different. People don't know what they want, so innovation is a human, intuitive discipline, nurturing creativity and bringing ideas together in new ways. **Design** is much more than look and feel, it is about how things work – simpler, better, magical.

Brands are the **identity systems** that make you stand out from the crowd, articulate your difference and superiority. From ads to adwords, social media and relationship marketing, brands seek to build awareness, interest and demand. Steve demanded that Apple's brands should do more. Brands must **enchant** people – aesthetically, emotionally, and inspirationally. They sell dreams not products, create unconditional desire, enable people to achieve more, and reflect who you want to be.

Leadership is typically about **inspiration**, but in a positive way – bringing people together, respecting and encouraging, supporting and developing – building teams that are stronger than their parts, empowering them, and sharing rewards. There is no space for compromize in business – for less than the best people, and performance below greatness. Social niceties, and compromize, do not change the world. With really great teams you can be direct, difficult and brilliant.

Steve Jobs was at his most inspiring on 12 June 2005, in a rare public address to graduates at Stanford University, and at a time when unknown to others he had been diagnosed with terminal cancer. **'Stop spending your time** living someone else's life, and live your own. Decide how good you really want to be, and commit yourself to absolute excellence. Spend each day, as if it were your last.'

Make the change, but also, **be the change**.

3 WIN...WINNING AS A GAMECHANGER
THE GAMECHANGERS AND WHAT THEY DO

CHANGING THE WORLD, RIGHT NOW

'Gamechangers' are the **next generation** of brands and businesses who are seizing the opportunities of change, not to do things a little better, or a little different, but to change the game. **The game** of how the market works, who the customer is, what they really want to achieve and why, how to make money, and create a lasting **positive impact**.

What makes gamechangers more **significant**, numerous and influential today is the breadth and diversity of change in our world. They ride with the shifting power and new technologies. They reach across a flatter world, but selectively focus on the fragmenting niches that emerge. Whilst many of the products and services we buy have become more similar, because of the **ubiquitous** supply of components and speed of imitation, they know they have to work much harder to **stand out**, to engage the **best customers**.

This is why gamechangers **win**.

From **Alibaba** in China to **Al Jazeera** in Qatar, **Air Asia** in Malaysia to **Ashmei** in England, **Ashoka** in Canada to **Azuri** in Kenya, we searched for the businesses who were shaking up their markets. We asked peers to nominate others in their sectors, we stretched out across the world to ensure we covered every sector and continent.

What emerged were 100 fabulous stories. New start-ups, small businesses, local incumbents, global corporations are all learning to change the game and play a new one, to adapt and respond, anticipate and innovate.

Let's meet some of them … famous people, and others just like you … who are making and **shaping markets** in their own vision. At a time of relentless change, the winners know that every day counts. Here are just a few, at one moment in time:

06:00 **Los Altos, California, USA**
Anne Wojcicki, the scientist-entrepreneur, is up early in Los Altos to see how many **23andMe** 'spit tests' have arrived in the morning post. With that DNA sample and $99 she can tell you all about your ethnic heritage, and future health.

08:00 **Bogata, Colombia**
Luis Genaro Muñoz sips his first **Juan Valdez** coffee of the day whilst meeting with leading Colombian coffee growers to explore the international expansion of the brand which they created together, including their quirky, distinctive coffee shops.

08:00 McGregor, Texas, USA

Elon Musk, founder of PayPal, champion of Tesla electric cars, and dreamer of the Hyperloop between LA and San Francisco, is out early. He's preparing for the next launch of his **Space X** spacecraft destined for the International Space Station, making space travel work in a way in which NASA never succeeded.

09:00 Buenos Aires, Argentina

In 2006 **Blake Mycoskie** wanted to help the thousands of street kids he saw running barefoot around the city. He got the local factory to make simple *alpargata* which he branded **Toms** and shipped to the USA. For every pair he sold, he gave a pair to the local kids. He has now given over a million pairs to kids in 40 countries.

10:00 New York, USA

In his Upper East Side apartment, Australia's Bank 3.0 author and entrepreneur **Brett King** is pacing the floor, working on the next phase of launching his innovative online banking concept, **Moven**, innovating at break-neck speed to make his ideas happen in reality.

10:00 Sao Paulo, Brazil

Cristiana Arcangeli sips from her **Beauty'in** lychee and white tea whilst enjoying the morning sunshine in Ibiraouera Park. Having trained as a dentist, she is now an entrepreneur and TV presenter. Her range of 'alimetic drinks' and candy bars, tea and chocolate promise to make you more beautiful and feel better from the inside out.

10:00 Rio de Janiero, Brazil

Brazil's **GraalBio** is busy converting the mountains of waste built up outside the nation's sprawling megacities into new sources of energy. **Bernardo Gradin**, CEO, is talking with investors, describing his vision of a circular economy for South America.

13:00 Aylesbury, England

Stuart Brooke is just heading off for a lunchtime run, in his own super premium **Ashmei** brand running gear, developed out of his frustration with the likes of Adidas and Nike who he feels compromise quality in pursuit of mass market price points.

13:00 Cambridge, England

Up the road, **Eben Upton** is in his engineering lab at Cambridge, working on the **Raspberry Pi** circuit boards that sell for £20 and enable kids to program, and entrepreneurs to tinker without risk, empowering the next generation of Apples and Googles.

14:00 Torres Novas, Portugal

Paulo Miguel Pereira da Silva, CEO of **Renova**, has a passion for toilet paper. Maybe not the most conventional of executive pursuits, he is seeking to bring creativity and colour to a neglected aspect of everyday life.

16:00 Nairobi, Kenya

Julia Kurnia is working on **Zidisha,** her online peer-to-peer financial service, helping Kenya's small but ambitious farmers and industrialists to find loans for their new business ventures in a market where there is little support, but growth is rapid.

16:00 Beirut, Lebanon

Aline Kamakian is busy cooking in the kitchen of her award-winning **Mayrig** restaurant in the Lebanese capital, Beirut. Her passion is to preserve and promote Armenian culture and, thinking bigger, she's just launched new restaurants in Dubai and New York.

18:00 **Mumbai, India**

Buses are chaotic and popular across India, but **Phanindra Sama** is making sense of the 10,000 routes with **Redbus**, the nation's first computerized booking system, with integrated timetables and a customer rating system driving up service standards.

21:00 **Beijing, China**

Lei Jun is still at work, finding it hard to keep pace with the huge demand from young Chinese for his **MiPhone**. He's particularly focused on content, which is where his low-cost smartphones will deliver most returns. Just don't mention Apple.

02:00 **Mount Maunganui, New Zealand**

Up on the northern peninsula, **Zespri**'s CEO **Lain Jager** is checking the latest orders from around the world for his kiwifruits. In a world of wellness, his superfood anti-oxidant specialities are in high demand, as are speed and quality.

A snapshot of some of the world's vibrant marketplaces … with **ordinary** people like you, doing quite **extraordinary** things.

Aline and Anne, Eden and Elon … just a few of the '**gamechangers**', the next generation of innovators and leaders who are shaking everything up. They have their **heads up** seeing the opportunities of incredible change, **heads down** changing our world.

HOW DO THEY WIN?

As you explore the 100 'gamechangers' across geographies and categories, you will notice how different – and innovative – their approaches are. Some win through deeper customer **insights**, others by building more engaging **brand** platforms, typically embracing social **networks**, but to create more personal and human **experiences**. Some underpin this with collaborative **innovation** and others with new **business models**, and to make this happen requires new **structures** and **leadership** styles.

What is interesting is how they connect these ideas together – how social networks can turn brands into movements with shared passions, or sustainability can spark new ideas for innovation, leading to new growth opportunities whilst also doing good.

Together, key words emerge to describe what gamechangers do, for example:

○ **Fuse** – connecting unconnected ideas generates more creative solutions, connecting people with people, customers and business, customers and customers, to innovate together.

○ **Amplify** – brands amplify the perceptions of products and prices, networks amplify the reach and richness of brands, advocates amplify the reputation of business, and leaders amplify the potential of everyone.

○ **Enable** – brands enable people to achieve more, business models enable new sources of revenue, and partners enable businesses to seize opportunities far beyond existing capabilities, to enable agility and faster growth.

○ **Mobilize** – giving people a stage to do more together, to collaborate and create, propelled by a common purpose or passion, more powerful and confident, a stronger voice together and more impact than a brand on its own.

○ **Enrich** – bigger ideas are more fulfilling, to employees and partners, customers and investors, who profit collectively and individually by achieving more, making a difference locally, and the world becomes a better place.

10 Ways to Change Your Game

If we then apply these principles to each of the typical activities of a business, strategic and operational, then we get a big picture as to how they think and act differently. By breaking this into 10 sections, we then get more specific detail on what changes, or where the opportunities are for you to change and win.

ARE YOU READY TO CHANGE THE WORLD?

'Changing the world' can mean lots of different things – for 23andMe it's about decoding life, with Zipcars it's about finding a new business model, for Ashmei it's about creating a technically better product, at Renova it's about creating the world's most colourful toilet paper. They are all **shaking up** their markets in different ways.

'Gamechangers' therefore can have different levels of focus. From strategic through to operational, holistic to functional. If you like, there are three types of gamechangers:

- **Market Makers** – They explore the **future world**, global markets and emerging categories. They look through their kaleidoscope to make sense of ambiguity, connecting emerging trends and dispersed ideas, to **create their own space**, to seize and shape markets in their own vision, and to change the world.

- **Business Innovators** – They explore the business potential, creating better ways to succeed in the new markets, guided by stretching and inspiring purpose. They think creatively in systems, how to design new **business models**, applying creativity and innovation to every aspect of the business.

- **Brand Builders** – They explore the **customer** world, diving deep into chosen markets to understand what really matters to existing and future customers. They seek emotional **resonance**, sharing ambition, engaging and enabling people to achieve more, collaborating and connecting them to make life better.

Whatever your focus, gamechangers are **bold and brave**, with the ambition and **audacity** to believe that they can make a fundamental difference. Whether they are start-up entrepreneurs or part of large organizations, in Abu Dhabi or Vietnam, seeking to maximize profits or to enhance the common good, they share a number of characteristics.

Not every gamechanger will become as famous as Mark Zuckerberg or Li Ka-Shing, create the billions of Jeff Bezos or save lives like Dr Shetty, but in their own ways, in their own worlds, everyone – **every one of us** – can change the game, to achieve more, more than we ever thought possible.

Gamechangers **think bigger**. Like Cristiana Arcangeli, they reframe their markets with more opportunities for growth and innovation, and they compete by out-thinking their competition with better insights and ideas.

Like Eben Upton, they **learn faster** and act different. They embrace the best new business ideas and ways of working. They harness every aspect of their business model as opportunities to innovate and stand out.

Most of all, just like Elon Musk, they **change the game**. They shape existing and future markets in their own vision. And because they see further, they win better. They find their own space to grow, to realize their personal and business potential.

"I am a gamechanger"

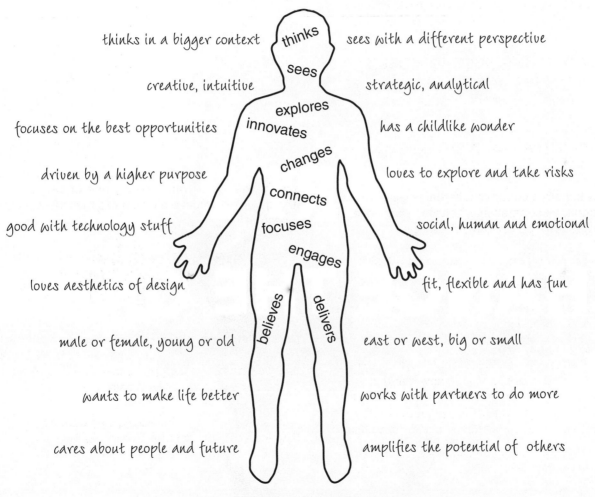

thinks in a bigger context — thinks — sees with a different perspective

sees

creative, intuitive — strategic, analytical

explores

focuses on the best opportunities — innovates — has a childlike wonder

changes

driven by a higher purpose — loves to explore and take risks

connects

good with technology stuff — focuses — social, human and emotional

engages

loves aesthetics of design — fit, flexible and has fun

believes   delivers

male or female, young or old — east or west, big or small

wants to make life better — works with partners to do more

cares about people and future — amplifies the potential of others

believe in myself, believe in better

PART 2
CHANGE THE GAME

Gamechangers fuse and adapt the best ideas to shape markets in their own vision...

They inspire, connect, enable, amplify...

They unlock the power of brands to make life better...

They integrate the best ideas for more impact: design thinking to business models, social media to sustainability...

Creating more value for every person...

4 THINK... IDEAS THAT CAN CHANGE THE WORLD
CHANGE YOUR VISION

Gamechangers see things differently, and think different things. They search for new possibilities with intelligence and imagination, articulating ideas that are disruptive and contagious in their markets, and change the attitudes and aspirations of people.

- More **ingenious**... *from making things... to creating futures...* They innovate within a bigger frame, rather than just improving the current model.

- More **audacious**... *from good ideas... to daring disruptions...* They go beyond incremental change, to imagine the bigger, even impossible ideas.

- More **purposeful**... *from making money... to making a difference...* They make a valuable contribution the world, and potentially more profits too.

4.1 IDEAS ... THE POWER OF IMAGINATION

Ideas matter. They are personal, hopeful and inspiring. They express our belief in better, provoking the consideration of others, to be stretched and shaped, combining passion and practicality. Ideas enrich society, and make life better. Markets emerge out of possibilities, seeing things differently and thinking different things. They can be powerful yet fragile, challenging or enabling. They push us forwards, making life or even the world a better place.

Markets are built around ideas – the **aspirations** of consumers, the **imagination** of brands. The scope of markets, and success in them, is limited only by how we think. In the past we defined markets by the products we made, today we articulate markets based on richer, broader concepts.

Ideas are not limited by budgets or resources. Success depends on our ability to think bigger, to **out-think** the competition, to develop better ideas, and find smarter ways to make the best ideas happen.

Thinking is the new competitive **advantage**. The ability to out-think your competitors, and to engage employees and customers in big, audacious ideas. To '**change the world**' might seem like a hollow phrase, but that's what winning is all about. The world never moved forward by playing small. In markets of exponential change, it requires big ideas to create a significant, and sustainable, difference and to win.

We create **value** by making new ideas happen. Philosophically we do this by extending the capacity of our planet – newness that adds to the sum of the wealth of everything on Earth. Commercially we do this by investors having confidence in the future potential of the business, measured in terms of the quality of its strategy and confidence that it will deliver future growth and return on investment.

> ### i·de·a [ahy-dee-*uh*, ahy-deeuh]
>
> - a thought, concept or notion ... 'that is an excellent idea'
>
> - a point of view, opinion or belief ... 'his ideas were revolutionary'
>
> - a purpose, intention or plan of action ... 'our idea is to go to the moon'

Ideas come from **everywhere**. They come from our imagination, but that requires stimulus and stretch. The stimulus comes from outside, from the direct appreciation of how to make something better, or the more abstract application from another place.

Whilst success is in making ideas happen, the most difficult part is in finding the **great** ideas. In the past we moved based on what we had done, because this was the nearest measure of what we could do. Today, with unlimited reach, it is likely we can find a partner with the capabilities to make the best ideas happen.

What makes a **great idea**?

- **Better** – the idea solves a problem, or seizes an opportunity, in a way that is distinctive and better than the current and alternative solutions.

- **Valuable** – not only does it do something better, but there are sufficient people who potentially want it, and would pay for it. It makes their life better.

- **Achievable** – it can be done, even if it requires new capabilities and processes, at costs and risk reasonable given its perceived benefits. It can be commercial.

What we shouldn't do is kill an idea too quickly. New ideas are fragile, a **glimpse** of future possibilities, and need to be worked on, stretched and strengthened. When we evaluate it, we need to consider the criteria together. First the perceived benefits and value, and then the cost and risk. First the difference it would make, and then the effort required to achieve it.

4.2 AUDACIOUS ... CREATING IDEAS WITH ATTITUDE

Elon Musk, the South African entrepreneur, had already made his fortune by the time he was 31, selling PayPal – the payment system he had started three years earlier and grown at a prolific rate through viral marketing – to eBay in 2002 for $1.5bn.

Like most entrepreneurs who sell up, he missed the excitement of his start-up. One year later, he co-founded **Tesla**, the electric vehicle company that promised to make sports cars sexier than Maserati but with zero carbon emissions. It progressed rapidly, but ran out of cash after five years. Musk rolled his sleeves up and took on the day-to-day business of making ideas happen. As CEO and also chief product architect, he has reshaped the business into a market innovator and growing business.

But sports cars are just not enough; he looked around him and saw his new peers, people like Jeff Bezos and Richard Branson, investing in '**the next big thing**' ... space travel. Musk needed his own space programme. His aim was to reduce the cost of space travel 10 times. In 2008 **Space X** won a $1.6bn contract from NASA to transport cargo to the International Space Station. Asked by *Esquire* magazine why he needed to have a space business, Musk says he was inspired by Isaac Asimov, and sees it as 'expanding, and preserving, the consciousness of human life'.

You might think rocket fuel was enough for Musk, now with a personal net worth of $8.8bn and still only 42, but his thirst was for more. In 2013 he unveiled a proposal for the '**Hyperloop**' an underground travel machine that he plans to operate between Los Angeles and San Francisco. With $6bn investment, and a solar-powered system that uses a partial vacuum to reduce aerodynamic drag, he envisioned how commuters would be able to travel the 350 miles in 30 minutes. **Audacious**.

What does it take to **change the world**?

In a world of reality television, digital grazing and instant celebrity, changing the world seems like hard work. But every new generation needs people determined to move things forward – how we think, live and work. In today's world we need more of them, to move further and faster. From Alibaba's Jack Ma, **Haim Schoppik** at Etsy, to Fangfang Wu of Greenbox, these are the factors that stand out amongst the gamechangers:

- **Be passionate**: innovators do this for more than money or power, they seek to create change and innovation that has even more value, that makes people's lives better, but also because they have a desire to explore what is possible. When **Ravi Shetty** founded his Narayana hospitals he had just taken retirement, it was meant to be a hobby that gave something back, instead it revolutionized healthcare in India.

- **Be rebellious**: innovators challenge the current world, and in particular those who are against change and progress. As an entrepreneur it's easy to rebel, to do things differently, to show little respect for today's leaders; in larger companies it's harder. But it's often the revolutionaries, like Pixar's John Lassiter or **Mark Parker** at Nike, who rise to the top because they can play the game, and change it.

- **Be optimistic**: innovators never stop believing, searching for a better way, and in their own ability to find it. They have to fight against the status quo, against being satisfied with a partial solution, and against the typical scepticism of people towards anything that is unproven or certain. When **Perry Chen** launched Kickstarter he had no idea whether crowd-funding could work on such a large scale, but he believed it would.

- **Be resilient**: when innovators are knocked down they come back stronger, the more people who say its impossible the harder they try. Like **James Dyson**, who developed 5127 prototypes before finding the right solution for a bagless vacuum cleaner that could change his world. He put it down to his youthful stamina as a long distance runner.

- **Be yourself**: innovators have an ego, not always in an irritating 'I'm better than you' way, but a belief that they are a bit special and can do extraordinary things. Of course there are plenty of innovators who you'd want to hang out with, but they do have to put themselves out there, to push themselves forward, to have an inner confidence, to believe in themselves. Look at **Will.i.am**, with a huge ego but still a nice guy.

Ideas are not the result of a quick brainstorm. Such an approach kills creativity before it gets started. Ideas need time and space to develop. They need attitude – the ability to look beyond the context of today, to challenge the assumed rules we all accept, and to ask the impossible questions.

4.3 FORESIGHT ... THINKING FROM THE FUTURE BACK

The future is a much **better place to start** thinking. It is unhindered by the limitations of today, the long list of real but often mental barriers why an idea could not happen. There are no absolutes, no right and wrong answers. However there are possibilities and likelihoods based based on our understanding of patterns and trends.

Creating multiple **scenarios** of the future, based on the relative likelihood of certain events changing the course of evolution, helps us to consider the range of possibilities. 'If Africa emerges without significant conflict then ...' 'If m-commerce accelerates at the same pace in India then ...' 'If the 2016 Rio Olympics sparks an investment boom in Brazil then ...' Scenario planning is a structured process through which to articulate potential futures, to evaluate ideas, and to make choices today about where to head.

Wellbeing Happiness Caring Tribal	Authenticity Collaboration Lifetime learning Empowerment

Agelessness Creative class Digital natives Women	Mobility Open education Cloud intelligence Entrepreneurship	Sustainable living Culture fusion Localness Storytelling

Globalisation Turbulent markets New economies New business models	Biotech Internet of things Clean energy Nano tech	Healthcare Resource shortages Transparency Travel	Climate change Urbanisation Bio diversity Population growth

Change Drivers to 2020

Whilst 2050 might seem a little fanciful, **2025** is a practical starting point because it is close enough to define real possibilities but far enough to not pre-judge them. Consider what is **possible** in your world in 2025 in terms of customer needs, major competitors, driving technologies, core solutions, likely business models, distribution networks, price points and brand differentiators. Stretch these to find extremes, and then start to connect them to explore how the market is **likely** to change. What will be the change drivers? What are the new opportunities?

Google's futurist in residence, Ray Kurzweil, believes in setting milestones to stimulate ideas but also manage expectations. Here are just a few of the key moments ahead:

2017	Driverless cars
2023	Immersed games
2033	Solar energy
2040	Forever young

Once you have described these **future worlds**, then you can evaluate which are most attractive, which are most likely, and which are most dangerous. Future thinking is not abstract. It is about the choices we make today, the directions we choose to follow, the foundations we need to lay and investments we need to make in order to win tomorrow.

The trick is to connect 'future back' with '**now forward**' so that strategy and innovation are not made staring ahead into a vacuum, but with an informed view of the future we want to create and how we will create it to our advantage.

4.4 AMBITION ... FINDING YOUR PURPOSE

Successful businesses have a **higher purpose**, one that stretches and guides them through changing times; one that aligns and galvinizes their culture and keeps them striving for better.

Economist Milton Friedman famously said that 'the social responsibility of business is to increase its profits'. Of course, value creation is an excellent measure of business effectiveness, although the moment of truth comes in how that value is shared between stakeholders. Does it all line the pockets of shareholders, or is it more evenly distributed between everyone inside and out, both financially and in terms of future investments?

Most entrepreneurs have a **bigger ambition** than their exit strategy, and most business leaders are driven by more than money, with which they are already well compensated.

Yet, too many organizations, particularly large corporations, seem happy to pursue the commodity of money. Legally executives are employed to create the best long-term return for their shareholders, and this can be an incredibly useful metric to guide decisions and measure performance. But it misses '**the why**'. The 'why this organization is likely to create a better return than another', and the 'why people as employees and customers will care'.

Indeed the new forces in business – from **Generation Y** to Eastern cultures – tend to have a different view. Rising stars of Asia, like India's Tata for example, have a different outlook on success. **Two thirds** of the equity of the company, that makes everything from steel to Range Rovers, is held by philanthropic trusts that are set up to support education, healthcare and performing arts. Tata also provides social welfare support to communities local to its operations.

Similarly, the 'millennial' mindset of young people across the world is much more about improving society, making life better, caring and sharing more. **Innocent drinks**, for example, still give 10% of all profits to charities, even though their principal shareholder is now Coca-Cola. It is part of the psyche that creates the distinctive brand and internal culture, which is why even Wall Street-minded owners are supportive.

But purpose goes beyond philanthropy. Purpose is about why you come to work each day, why people engage with your brand emotionally, and why you have a more enduring impact, despite the rollercoaster of economic performance.

A higher purpose is a '**north star**' to navigate complex and ever-changing markets, like early sailors used to stay on course as they crossed the vast oceans. It is a really big idea around which the business can align all it does over time, to focus strategy, inspire creativity and measure success. It defines the role of business in society, why it exists, its added value, how it contributes to a better world and makes life better.

Business can be full of words – missions and visions, slogans and taglines, values and goals. A higher purpose sits above these. A vision describes how we see the future world, a mission defines what we want to achieve in it. Values are the distinctive cultural attributes, and goals are strategic objectives. Slogans and taglines are creative ways to capture all of this, usually in a way that expresses the benefit to people.

P&G says that its purpose 'unifies us in a common cause and growth strategy of improving more consumers' lives in small but meaningful ways each day' whilst also recognizing how it inspires employees to look beyond a machine that makes money. The P&G purpose is to 'provide branded products and services of superior quality and value that improve the lives of the world's consumers, now and for generations to come'. It also says consumers will reward them with sales, from which come profits and value creation, which enables everyone inside and outside the business to prosper.

John Mackey, founder of **Whole Foods**, believes that business should be based on a purpose deeper than making money. 'Our motto *Whole Foods, Whole People, Whole Planet* emphasizes that our brand reaches beyond food retailing. In fact, our deepest purpose as an organization is helping support the health, wellbeing, and healing of both people – customers, team members, business partners, and the planet.'

Here are some examples of companies with a 'higher purpose', and how articulate what more they seek to do for people, their role in society, how they make life better:

- **Coca-Cola**: 'To refresh the world. To inspire moments of optimism and happiness. To create value and make a difference.'
- **Nike**: 'To bring inspiration and innovation to every athlete* in the world (*If you have a body, you are an athlete).'
- **Starbucks**: 'To inspire and nurture the human spirit – one person, one cup and one neighborhood at a time.'
- **Swarovski**: 'We add sparkle to people's everyday lives.'
- **Walmart**: 'If we work together, we'll lower the cost of living for everyone, we'll give the world an opportunity to see what it's like to save and have a better life.'

Other purpose statements, whilst still directional, are less inspiring because they are more functional, about the business and what it seeks to become:

- **Amazon**: 'To be earth's most customer centric company; to build a place where people can come to find and discover anything they might want to buy online.'
- **Audi**: 'We delight customers worldwide' through four actions 'We define innovation. We create experiences. We live responsibility. We shape Audi.'
- **Bare Escentuals**: 'To be a force of beauty … the belief that products can actually be good, makeup can be fun, business can be personal and companies can behave more like communities.'
- **Dunkin' Donuts**: 'Make and serve the freshest, most delicious coffee and donuts quickly and courteously in modern, well-merchandised stores.'

- **Tiffany & Co**: 'To be the world's most respected and successful designer, manufacturer and retailer of the finest jewellery ... committed to obtaining precious metals and gemstones, and crafting our jewellery in ways that are socially and environmentally responsible.'

The best purpose statements are simple and uplifting. They have an intent '**to be**' and '**do more**' rather than asserting their achievement. They are about people, and making their lives better, which is more engaging and memorable and also creates space to shine and grow.

4.5 RETHINK ... SEE THINGS DIFFERENTLY

The best way to develop better ideas is to change your **perspective**. When you look from the future back we have already explored how ideas look less intimidating and impossible. When you reimagine yourself as a challenger brand, you would do things differently. If you are sitting in an emerging market, with limited resources and customers with low budgets, you might be more resourceful. As a scientist or technologist you might approach a challenge differently, maybe within more knowledge of the possibilities, as well as technical discipline.

Each perspective adds richness, stretching and shaping the ideas.

Taking a **customer perspective** is perhaps the most obvious, useful and enlightening option. Customers, or better consumers if you are in a consumer market, see things quite differently from most businesses. Most businesses think that their products are everything; that people sit around all day studying the APR on different credit cards, or understand the subtleties of one computer's configuration over another.

Customers live in a bigger world. They want a credit card so that they can buy the car of their dreams, or at least not worry about the payments for some time. They want a better computer so they can study, or work, or play games. The detail of processing speed seems irrelevant compared to being able to win a new deal, or immerse yourself in the latest 3D game. By understanding what motivates customers, business can engage people much better, as well as finding much bigger opportunities to do more, sell more, and even charge more, if the perceived value is greater.

Similarly, you can see from other perspectives too. How do investors see opportunities in terms of risk and reward? How would employees see them? Competitors? Customers of competitors? Local communities? Technologists? Environmentalists? Governments? Journalists? Award givers? Children? Future generations?

4.6 QUESTION TIME ... DEFINING THE RIGHT PROBLEM

Albert Einstein is often quoted saying 'If I had 20 days to solve a problem, I would spend 19 days to define it ...' This is why innovation rarely starts with technology. It rarely starts with an opportunity either. It most effectively starts with a **question**. Defining the right question is at least half of the challenge.

Apple's iPod didn't start with 'let's make a really cool MP3 player', it started by a problem framed around 'How can I carry my **1000 favourite songs** in my pocket' which both guided the technical solution and how it was marketed. The more focused the challenge, the easier the innovation.

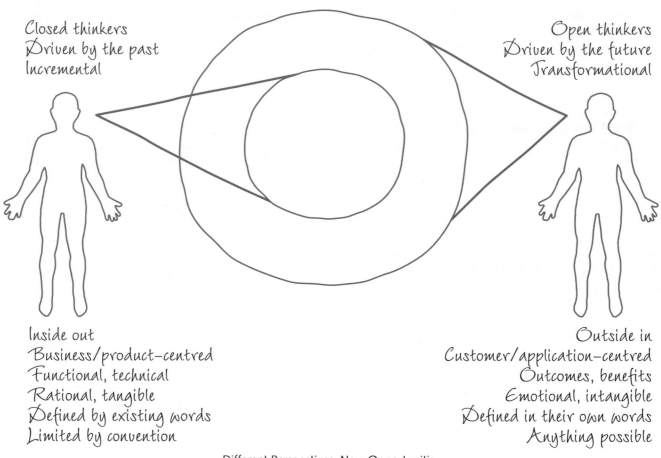

Closed thinkers
Driven by the past
Incremental

Open thinkers
Driven by the future
Transformational

Inside out
Business/product-centred
Functional, technical
Rational, tangible
Defined by existing words
Limited by convention

Outside in
Customer/application-centred
Outcomes, benefits
Emotional, intangible
Defined in their own words
Anything possible

Different Perspectives, New Opportunities

Once you have framed the problem in the right way, by asking a question that is focused but open, disruptive and distinctive, then you can start thinking about how best to address it. For the iPod, it would clearly take somebody who understood compact data storage, but also how the music industry works and the aesthetics of gadgets.

Here are some more **questions worth asking** yourself:

- Who is the primary **customer** and what do they really want? It's easy to get confused by multiple customers, and a long list of needs.

- How can we use the **assets** we already have in smarter ways? Often, the most effective solutions are about using brands, relationships, and stores better.

- What is the **benefit** we are trying to deliver, and how else can it be achieved? Forget products, think about how you can achieve the benefit better.

- How can we achieve our **purpose** in a way that our customers love, and that no other company can? A better way of finding your difference.

- Why has nobody **done this** before? Understanding the reasons, be it costs and risks, demand or brand, capability or complexity, will help innovate.

- What if customers were **in charge** of our business? Think about what they would do differently, where they would innovate, what success would look like.

- How would we do it if we only had **one tenth** of the budget? Frugal thinking helps you focus and be more resourceful.

- What things should we **stop doing**, before creating more things to do? This is hard, people hate stopping things more than starting.

4.7 BE CREATIVE ... CURIOUS AND CONNECTED

Filmmaker and deep-sea explorer James Cameron is accustomed to pushing frontiers – be they in the beautiful movie **Avatar** that portrays a human yet technological future, or in his diving expeditions to the deep unexplored trenches 10 km under the Atlantic Ocean. This is what he sees as the creative ingredients of a great script, or an audacious adventure:

- **Have your antennae on**: inspiration can hit you anywhere, anytime – and most likely when you are not looking for it – the challenge is to observe, remember and apply it in a relevant but interesting way.

- **Embrace diversity**: surround yourself with interesting people, looking at art, listening to music, hanging out with people from other walks of life, or watching a TED Talk on YouTube.

- **Find your headspace**: whilst stimulus is good, at some point we have to make sense of it all, stand back to see the patterns, to connect the unconnected, to formulate newness. This is individual and requires isolation.

- **Catch the wave**: we've all been told that our ideas are 'ahead of their time', sometimes this means waiting for other factors to line up, other innovations, social trends, people's desires. Ride waves, rather than trying to make them.

- **Stay real**: it's easy to get seduced by your own ideas, to love everything that you create, to immerse yourself in your world. But sometimes you need to see it all cold, fresh and impartially, ready to change, reject or improve your creation.

- **Never give up**: fight for your idea, believe in it and defend it, nurture and protect it, particularly when others, investors or partners, want to modify it in ways which you think will compromize the magic of what you have created.

There are thousands of creative techniques to spark your thinking. From challenging yourself to read a different magazine each week, to deploying a structured methodology for creativity in your business. Sometimes it's just about a great challenge:

How would **Steve Jobs** have innovated your market and business?

It's a fun question, but we all know Apple and the cult of Jobs. What would be the iPod of your market, aesthetic and desirable, that does everything intuitively better? What would be the iTunes, the business model that makes it work together in a new way? How would you design and innovate, add content and colour, myth and magic? What would you call it? How would you change the way you market and sell?

How would you resolve the **biggest paradox** in your world today?

As P&G's CEO, AG Lafley challenges his people to turn an 'or' into an 'and' … to find the big dilemmas, the big trade-offs which consumers have to make in their lives, and find ingenious ways to solve them. Washing powder that works better but doesn't irritate your skin. Packaging that allows you to buy in bulk, but doesn't take space in a small urban apartment. Pure water that is great to taste, but is free to the people who need it most.

How would your competitors seek to **destroy your business**?

Thinking like a challenger is always liberating. When Jack Welch was at GE he would periodically encourage all his people to 'DYB' … to destroy their business before somebody else does, and in so doing replace it with something better. People start thinking entrepreneurially, liberated from conventions and culture. The opportunity is to destroy, and improve, your business before somebody else does.

For gamechangers, the most useful sources of creativity are:

- **Insights**: the 'new, penetrating discoveries' about your customers, turning research and data analysis into useful ideas about what matters most, and how to address their frustrations and aspirations better.
- **Assets**: considering all the distinctive attributes of the organization (e.g. customer base, patents, reputation, brand, partnerships), and exploring how you can use them in different and better ways.

- **Competitions**: people love to win. From commercial space travel to electric cars, oil clean ups to digital healthcare, the 'X Prize' foundation sets audacious challenges, and finds sponsors to put up the million-dollar prizes.
- **Parallels**: learning from companies who have successfully addressed similar challenges in other industries, banks from retailers, cars from airlines. What did they do? How did customers respond? How could you apply it?
- **Co-creating**: bring together more people, with different skills and experience to solve problems better. Be it 'open' innovation with partners, working with customers or crowds, a range of brains will usually beat the lone genius.
- **Random**: sometimes it's just about finding a new starting point – click on Google's 'I feel lucky' button (Have you ever done that?), open the dictionary at a random page, watch a quirky TED talk and see what you can take from it.
- **Concepting**: you've hopefully got lots of ideas, but together they could be much more powerful. Explore how to combine disparate ideas in creative ways, clustering them like a molecule into richer 'concepts'.
- **Simplicity**: perhaps hardest, but most inspiring, is making things simpler. Describing an idea in 10 seconds, drawing it as an iconic diagram, explaining it to your mother or kids. Cutting out all the complexity to find a beautiful idea.

The 'opening up' process of idea generation is fun and exciting, the hard part is in making them happen, practically and profitably. Creativity can be applied at every stage of the innovation process. Creatively shaping ideas into solutions, creatively developing pricing and distribution channels, business models and customer support.

More than anything, creativity is about being interested in the world, being curious and believing in possibilities.

4.8 LESS IS MORE ... WHAT TO DO WITH TOO MANY IDEAS

Mark Parker, Nike's CEO, says the biggest challenge is having too many great ideas, too many problems to solve, and too many opportunities to seize. In a flat and connected world, everything is possible, so it is easy to want to achieve more. It's also easy to keep exploring, finding more insights to embrace, more ways to change.

Ideas need **focus.** We need bigger and better ideas from which to create our futures. A clear and stretching purpose helps us to filter ideas, and also to cluster, fuse and shape ideas into richer concepts. Creativity needs a process, which initially opens up, stimulating and stretching ideas beyond the normal thinking, and then closes down in a way that brings focus, but without eliminating the abnormal ideas.

These criteria should be distinctive to each challenge. Yes there will be commercial factors, a judgement about investment and risk, speed and returns, although these will always be difficult to estimate in new markets and addressing unmet needs. But without also considering how well it might move the business forwards, inspire customers, achieve good and help to change the game, financial results are not enough. Most significant of course, is that the business model can be innovated too, to find a way in which a concept that might at first seem difficult to monetize, can be.

Ultimately it is about having a **balanced portfolio** of ideas, opportunities and innovations. A business needs cash in the short-term to support breakthroughs in the long-term. We need a spread of small, medium and big ideas, which will impact in the short, medium and long-term. Even long-term investors want to see some early evidence of potential, to sustain their interest or secure more money. And these different levels of ideas need to be nurtured and protected in different ways, in order to maximize their eventual impact.

4.9 IDEAS FACTORY ... BUILDING A WORLD OF IMAGINATION

In Roald Dahl's children's classic, **Willy Wonka** built a chocolate factory to make the best candy bars and gobstoppers in the world. The doors were locked, the methods were different, and oompa loompas happily worked. Back at the moonshot factory of Google <X> you'll find real people. They are inspired by the biggest challenges, applying technology in distinctive ways. They make sense of the future by telling stories about it, fictional but possible, they are motivated as much by the journey as the end goal.

Across the world, in big companies and small, ideas are emerging through more creative approaches. This is not so much about research and technology labs, but more through environments and cultures that support more radical and disruptive thinking.

Coca-Cola prides itself on being in almost every country in the world, yet also recognizes that scale as a limitation on developing great ideas. Size and complexity can become the enemies of creativity and, even more so, the **entrepreneurial spirit** to make great ideas happen. Large companies have a vested interest in hanging on to an 'old' winning formula, and find it hard to disrupt successful revenue streams.

Coke wants more entrepreneurs in its business – people who have both succeeded and failed in their own start-ups, to bring their attitudes, behaviours and courage to the business. '**Up Global**' includes start-up weekends and are 54-hour idea-fests, encouraging teams to think differently, including how they can use existing assets in new ways. Coke, for example, has a bigger fleet of vehicles than FedEx, UPS and TNT combined, so how could it use these better? They explore new concepts, business models, develop rapid prototypes, involve real customers, and make their pitch to internal investors.

From **AT&T's Foundry** to Ferrari in Maranella, each approach is distinctive; the common theme is the search for better ideas. AT&T's Palo Alto-based 'foundry' brings together thought leaders from different fields to create FutureCasts, where academics and journalists, inventors and investors, entrepreneurs and executives mash together their brains and ideas to create possible futures. In Maranella, **Ferrari** people live and work together, encouraged to explore the arts and learn new languages. Not just for their own wellbeing, but to stimulate new ways of thinking and better innovation.

IDEO is perhaps the best known innovation company. David and Tom Kelley believe in design thinking as a methodology to solve problems in both function and form. At the heart of their approach is **human-centred design**, which makes people, and in particular social issues, the starting point of making things better. Talent Garden from Italy is an example of achieving this through a global network of innovators, and in particular bringing digital innovators together.

Innolab provides an accelerated innovation process, facilitating in-house teams to bring their own expertize and ideas together with energy and discipline. **Innocentive** and Invention Machines are collaboration platforms, bringing together external sources of ideas. Other external incubators provide processes and resources, Ashoka focused on sustainable projects, and Y Combinator as a financial investor.

In an ideas world there is no shortage of ideas, it is the ability to select and shape, apply and implement them that enables ideas companies to win.

CHANGE YOUR GAME

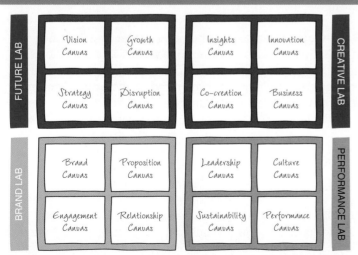

Practically apply the concepts in this chapter to your business with the relevant tools in the Gamechanger Labs:

- **Vision** canvas
- **Strategy** canvas
- **Leadership** canvas

Practical examples can be found in the 100 cases studies. Also see more details at Gamechangers.pro

5 EXPLORE...MAKING SENSE OF THE KALEIDOSCOPE

CHANGE YOUR MARKET

Gamechangers explore a bigger world, looking beyond the defined boundaries of today's markets to find the new emerging spaces, to fuse existing domains, or to reconstruct markets in their own vision.

- More **expeditionary** ... *from existing markets ... to emerging spaces* ... They look beyond the geographies and categories of today, to find new opportunities.

- More **contextual** ... *from conventional borders ... to daring disruptions* ... They redefine their markets in their own vision, typically a bigger, richer space.

- More **insightful** ... *from average needs ... to making a difference* ... They look beyond masses to niches, averages to individuals, needs to dreams.

5.1 KALEIDSCOPES ... MAKING SENSE OF CHANGING MARKETS

One of my favourite childhood toys was a **kaleidoscope**. I was captivated by the multitude of never-ending patterns produced with every twist of my hand, astounded that such a small number of components could reappear in so many ways.

In some ways, today's markets are just like that. Every way you look at them, you see different **opportunities**. And the next time you look, they have changed again. The diversity of customers and competitors, geographies and categories, products and services, channels and propositions, **mixed up**, reassembled, again and again.

Finding and focusing on the best market opportunities is the **starting point** for driving and sustaining profitable growth. In the past we developed strategies based on existing capabilities, **extrapolating** the past as a linear future, developing budgets and targets based on previous years. Markets, and business, don't work like that anymore.

Markets are kaleidoscope of diverse and dynamic opportunities. Geographies and categories are irrelevant; people think and act in more individual and human ways. Find the best market for you, define it to your advantage, shape it in your own vision.

Markets used to be stable and predictable, clearly defined in both constituents and borders, usually by category and geography, with a focus on your 'home' market. Today's markets are **volatile and dynamic**. Boundaries blur, categories converge, local and global, digital and physical, a composite of millions of niches across geographies.

Winners see the future better. Instead of heads-down, obsessed only with today, they have their **heads-up**, making sense of changing markets, finding the new opportunities, and ensuring that the choices of today lead to a better tomorrow.

From west to east, big to small, business to consumer ... the hot fashions are in Buenos Aires, the best green tech is in Shanghai, the top web designers are in Mumbai, and the most venture capital is in Shenzhen.

Are you **focused** on the big opportunities?

Over the next five years, female consumers will grow faster than China ... by 2020 there will be 50 billion devices, creating an intelligent cloud accessible to everyone anytime. By 2025, renting will replace buying, water will be the new gold ... and so on ...

Too often, we have our heads down in our spreadsheets – trying to optimize what we do, reducing the costs, improving the margins, enhancing the product or service levels.

Doing things right, but are we doing the right things? As a scientist I appreciate the quest for optimization ... the precision of segmentation, the productivity of supply chains, balancing portfolios and scorecards, budgets and service levels, net promoter scores and stock prices.

5.2 REORDER ... TECTONIC SHIFTS IN MARKETS

Lei Jun leapt onto the stage in Beijing, rock music and big words, jeans and black turtle neck. The **Xiaomi** CEO knows that he lives in boom times. His young Chinese fans adore him, and are desparate for his MiPhone. In October 2013 the first batch of 100,000 devices sold out in 83 seconds. In his first year of business he sold 7.2 million devices, and Xiaomi is already regarded as a $10 billion company.

Of course, there are many predictions as to how the world will evolve in terms of population and power, economic and political, and how this will play out in terms of our individual prosperity, lifestyles and consumer behaviours.

The **shift in power** from the G7 (global seven economies of USA, United Kingdom, France, Germany, Japan, Canada and Italy) to the E7 (emerging seven economies of China, India, Brazil, Mexico, Indonesia, Russia and Turkey) was accelerated by the global financial crisis.

In 2007, the GDP of the G7 was still around 60% larger than total E7, but had shrunk to around 35% by 2010. This gap will continue to accelerate, the E7 outgrowing the G7 by 2020, rising to 44% ahead by 2030, and doubling its size by 2050.

Whilst these new leading markets will grow fastest, much of the wealth will still be in Western markets. Goldman Sachs estimates that by 2050:

- China will have 1.4 billion people, creating $45 trillion GDP, that is $31k per capita.

- India will have 1.6 billion people, creating $28 trillion GDP, that is $17k per capita.

- The USA will have 0.4 billion people, creating $35 trillion GDP, that is $84k per capita.

- The EU will have 0.4 billion people, creating $19 trillion GDP, that is $50k per capita.

Technology has lowered boundaries, connected isolated people, democratized knowledge. The advantage of Western markets has fallen, whilst the emerging economies, with their larger populations, seek to benefit from the inflow of ideas and capital. More than 70 million people are joining the new 'middle class' each year, virtually all in emerging economies. By 2020, around 40% of the world's population will be in the **middle-income** group, twice as many as today.

Hotspots lie beyond the E7. Whilst these are vast and fast growth economies that are set to turn global trade on its head, other smaller economies offer great opportunities too, such as Vietnam, Indonesia, Taiwan, Singapore as well as South Africa and Nigeria.

Indonesia is the largest at about 229 million, while South Korea is the smallest with around 48 million, and their populations are growing – not shrinking as is the case in many developed nations.

Yet this **'reorder'** of global markets is in our hands. Markets are malleable, and can be shaped in our own vision rather than left to chaotic progress. Their uneven composition, of widely differing needs and potential, means that we must look beyond the averages, and be selective. Ongoing change means that any advantage is temporary, and markets need to be innovated like business.

5.3 EASTWARDS ... REAWAKENING THE ASIAN TIGER

Flying into Mumbai from Colombo, I was amazed by the huge, sprawling, twinkling city below me. An Indian software engineer in the seat next to me pointed out the new tech playgrounds of the megacity, and how it would take him three hours to get home, despite living 'in the city'. Whilst Mumbai airport is still very 20th century, this is a 21st century metropolis. It made me think ...

Chinese and Indian consumers are the new drivers of the global economy, the trendsetters. They have fast-changing tastes and appetites and they are transforming the world with their consumption. Consider these snapshots of opportunity for the decade ahead:

- There will be nearly **1 billion middle-class consumers** in China and India by 2020 – demanding 'more, better, now' for themselves and their children.

- Asian billionaires are growing rapidly: in 2001, China had 1 billionaire and India had 4; today, there are **115 billionaires in China** and 55 in India.

- China and India will give rise to some of the world's **most powerful companies**. China already has three of the world's top 10: PetroChina, China's ICBC bank, and China Mobile.

- **80 million Chinese** and 54 million Indians will become **college graduates** over the next ten years. Over the same period, the USA will see just thirty million new college graduates.

Whilst power has fundamentally shifted East, it is the rise of new generation attitudes, new technologies, new approaches to business that really sort the winners from the losers.

- **China** is transforming its economy **10 times faster** than the industrial revolution, with a 100 times more people (and therefore with potentially 1000 times more impact), most significantly changing the lives and businesses at incredible pace in China itself.

- Consumption in the 'emerging' (fastest growing) markets will grow by **$18 trillion** between 2010 and 2025, compared to $8 trillion growth in developed markets. Are we focusing most of our future on these markets?

- When the USA becomes self-sufficient in **oil by 2020**, the dynamics of **the Middle East** will fundamentally change. China/India's new dependency will transform global trade, and the influence of new markets.

- The biggest **impact** of the re-balance of economic power from West to East is the decline of public and rapid re-emergence of **private ownership**, particularly families, with different strategic purposes and priorities.

- Google, Microsoft, Facebook (plus emerging networks like **Alibaba and QQ**) will become the **'platforms'** for next generation consumers, brands and businesses. Are we thinking of 'platform' markets, and how to use them?

- The Chinese beer **Snowflake** is already the biggest brand in the world, based on sales volume. 'You've never heard of it, and don't think it's relevant to your market ...' Time to redefine/reprioritize **'your market'**, the space in which you compete.

- If you consider that 6 billion people in the world have mobile phones, and only 2.5 billion people have **bank accounts**, then that is a huge opportunity for mobile banking (and for new businesses like Monetise).

5.4 SOUTHWARDS ... AFRICA AND LATIN AMERICA

In Rio de Janiero, Jorge Paulo Lemann is concerned about the strategic plans for his latest investment, the $28 billion acquisition in partnership with Berkshire Hathaway of H J Heinz, and how to ensure tomato ketchup and beans keep growing around the world. The Swiss-Brazilian banker, ranked as one of the 40 richest people in the world, is keen to see the business embrace more regional variants, whilst continuing to build its iconic brands. He recently snapped up Burger King for $4 billion, which might help.

Meanwhile across in Cape Town, **Naspers** has become one of the world's leading media companies. Diversifying beyond its heritage in South African newspapers, it is the largest shareholder in **Tencent**, the Chinese technology business that is rapidly turning QQ into the world's largest social network. With interests in the likes of Souq, the leading ecommerce portal in the Middle East, and Mail.ru, Russia's instant messaging network, it is building a global network of digital media.

Yet in South Africa **Mxit** is bigger than Facebook, which started as a mobile app rather than migrating to it. Indeed it is the mobile phone that has revolutionized, undistracted by fixed line internet which never happened. With a billion handsets, mobile solutions emerged out of necessity. Services like **M-Pesa**, the mobile payment solution, are being exported to other markets like India. Similarly, the dual-sim card has been a big hit, enabling customers to switch between providers depending on the type of call.

The Masai farmer uses his phone to work smarter too, tagging and tracking his cattle, monitoring the weather and saving water. Egyptian schools regard **mobile phones** as a vital learning aid, helping children and women to read and study for exams. Where electricity is scarce, dropping into the red battery zone is a disaster and can mean walking 20 km to charge it, making solar-power charging a huge industry.

Nairobi's iHub, an office offering fast broadband speeds to entrepreneurs, is a meeting place for mobile app and software developers. The World Bank has estimated that the African mobile IT industry will be worth $150bn by 2016, with 5 million jobs and contributing 7% of Africa's GDP.

5.5 TRIBES ... REDEFINING MARKETS BY ATTITUDE

23andMe's revolutionary DNA profiling business is transforming the world of healthcare, drug research and insurance. But what people find most interesting about the profiles they receive for $99 is not their future health prognosis, but where they have come from. Almost every one of us will find that we have a DNA sourced from **across the world**.

There are more similarities between like-minded people across geographies, than there are between people within a country.

Yet most companies, for their own convenience, think of markets in terms of geography, of category, and segment. Some of us even defining markets based on our own groupings, based on business units, products, or channels.

Geography is perhaps one of our greatest misnomers. Many great American companies, great in the sense of their innovations and performance, still insist on seeing the world as USA and International. Most European companies still see each part of Europe as separate markets. Whilst customers within a geography have some similarities, and the rules of business are standard, physical distance and state boundaries are increasingly meaningless. People are more similar in niches across geographies, than within them.

The very notion of a **home market** is distracting too. It suggests that markets physically closest to your head office are in some way better, easier or come first. Whilst there are some advantages, in terms of local knowledge and physical convenience, most companies might find their best markets elsewhere, or even scattered across the world. That's not a problem, more an opportunity to service the right people better.

Categories too are blurred and limiting. In the world of technology we see a fundamental blurring of many domains. Gone are the days when one company made content and another distributed it, one company made the devices and another sold them. Communication is about content, media and entertainment, work and play. Or consider the blurring of pharmaceutical companies and healthcare, wellbeing and beauty. Whilst you could seek to pigeon hole every company into one box, the reality is that most companies play in multiple categories.

Stock markets still group companies into classic boxes, with a different view of the financial potential and risks with each. Sometimes companies can significantly boost their market valuations by declaring, like **Time Warner** did, that they are now in a different sector. But this is a superficial game; what matters is how you see your future.

Markets are about people, who are individual and different. Gone are the days when we could cluster huge audiences

into one box, create average products that met their average needs, communicate with and serve them in average ways. Such an approach symbolizes the lazy business that cannot think through how people are different, focus on groups with more distinctive needs, or create modular solutions that can be flexed and customized for each individual.

Research has typically treated customers as individuals, and then sought to group them into **segments** of similar characteristics for efficient targeting. An alternative view is that people are more social, not only similar, but influenced by each other. They are **tribal**. They are influenced by the desire to imitate others, and their consumption is about being part of something bigger. And their loyalty is to each other, rather than any brand.

We see tribal customers everywhere – supporting one team at a football match, bike riders admiring each other's bikes, online gamers comparing scores and tactics, Tupperware parties. These people don't come together rationally, but around deeper, profound needs such as kinship, passion and identity.

Sometimes brands tap into the passions of these tribes and facilitate their communities, like Apple or **Harley Davidson** or Nike, but more often customers have a higher calling that no brand has yet responded to beyond providing transactional products and services.

Communities of enthusiasts often have their own languages, symbols, and rituals. As tribes move activity online, netnography (online ethnography) allows us to understand people better. Value for these people is less about product benefits, but they co-exist and achieve more together.

5.6 MILLENNIALS ... THE SHIFT TO GEN Y

Two age-based groups of consumers are perhaps more influential in our markets than any other – millennials and boomers. Whilst age is a broad classification, it has some relevance because similar people grew up at the same time, influenced by **changing society** trends, they progressed through life in similar phases in terms of their outlook, their priorities, their financial spending power, and their aspirations.

Each generation has its own attitudes and values, shaped and absorbed by the world as they grew up. '**Boomers**' (born 1946 to 1964) are very different from their parents. They revolted against conservative morals, protested at the meaninglessness of wars, and created a new set of values, from sexual freedom to feminism, that eventually dominated culture.

The generation now most influencing, and changing, our culture are the '**Millennials**' (born 1980 to 1995). They have grown up in a digital age, established their identities and social circles on Facebook, and communicate through text speak and photo-based snap chats. They live in a fast and connected, diverse and always-on society where the folk heroes are internet entrepreneurs and reality TV stars. Before they even reach their teens they have opted out of family norms, although often continuing to live at home, watching time-shifted TV on demand, defining themselves with global brands and with different values.

Millennials are also known as **Gen Y**. They sit between the Gen X who are increasingly the business leaders of today, and Gen Z, the kids of today. Gen Y are therefore likely to shape markets and business over the coming years. They represent 25% of the world's population, and whilst less wealthy than older segments, they are more influential because of their outspokenness and connectedness. Their differences are more in attitude and outlook, driven by technology and also by an acceptance of a new world order. This shapes how they think, who they trust, what they want and how they get it.

'Boomers' are at the other end of adulthood, but have some surprisingly similar characteristics. With kids having left home, and more time in retirement, they often have more disposable income than they have had in years, and with decades of good health still ahead of them, have great aspirations to see the world, learn new skills and enjoy life to the full.

It's an incredible fact, but if you have made it to 60 years old today, you have are more likely to make it to 100 than not. They are the wealthiest demographic. By 2017 they will make up half the US population, and control 70% of its disposable income. By 2050 there will be 62% more over 60s than today, and 82% of them will be in emerging markets. Euromonitor estimate that they will be a $15 trillion market by 2020.

Whilst boomers will inevitably have more healthcare needs, they are also ambitious to see the world, improve their communities, give back and achieve more for themselves. Not afraid of technology, they spend more time searching out products, reading small print, finding the best solutions and sharing ideas. Marathons see huge increases in mature participants. Business schools are refocusing on 40–60 year old re-education. Banks are redefining financial portfolios, helping people rethink investments.

Brands are slow to catch up. How many ads do you see for older people buying fashion or food, travel or technology?

Gen X

Born
1965–1980
50 million

Influenced by fall of Berlin Wall, capitalism, Live Aid

Open-minded, practical and pragmatic

Self-reliant, reject the rules, what's in it for me

Career professionals, but also seek work-life "balance"

Computer adopters, emailers, but like face to face

Gen Y

Born
1980–1995
75 million

Influenced by 9/11, reality TV, and social media

Ethnically diverse, realistic and optimistic

Self-inventive, rewrite the rules, make the most of life

Seek freedom and flexibility, work "with" not for company

Digital natives, big texters and social media users

Gen Z

Born
1995–2010
100 million

Influenced by economic and climate crisis, Arab spring

Global minded, caring and opportunistic

Collective, don't know the rules, "in it" together

Seek security and stability, multi-takers, project workers

Digitally immersed, driven by mobile and crowd behaviour

Gen X and Gen Y and Gen Z

5.7 WOMEN ... THE SHIFT TO FEMALE

Globally women control around $25 trillion of consumer spending. Whilst they earn slightly less, around $15 trillion, they influence much more of shared money, and inherit the majority of wealth. In most places they are now equals in the workplace, through to senior management roles. This is particularly the case in developing markets where many family-owned businesses are led by females.

Educationally, girls have largely caught up with boys in schooling, whilst socially there is much more respect and equality between men and women in terms of earning and spending. Collectively they represent a bigger **growth opportunity** than China and India combined.

Women make more buying decisions. US research shows that they make around 85% of all consumer decisions, including 92% of vacations, 80% of home improvements, 60% of cars and 51% of electronics. They are an important segment for every brand, For example, 10% of Harley Davidson customers are female, prompting the brand to create bikes with lower seats.

Women are big **online shoppers**, responsible for 58% of ecommerce purchases, including two thirds of shoes and fashions. They also spend much longer making purchases, understanding brands and considering options. Women are most frustrated when they cannot find help when they shop physically, whereas men care most about how close the parking is to the store.

In China, female earnings will grow from $350 billion in 2000 to $4 trillion, a tenfold increase in 20 years. India's voters elected a female prime minister (Indira Gandhi) and president (Pratibha Patil), but there is still great inequality; around 30% of women work and earn 25% of men's wages. Yet the economy could still grow to $900 billion by 2020.

Most brands are slow to catch up. Gamechangers think different.

5.8 INSIGHTS ... FINDING WHAT REALLY MATTERS

It's amazing how many brands spend fortunes trying to **understand people**, and then analyse the results in terms of **averages**. The average needs or expectations of the average consumer, based on asking questions developed with existing assumptions and prejudices. Most market research tells us nothing more than average trends and aspirations, specific and potentially relevant to nobody.

Yet consumers are more **diverse**, different and **discerning** than ever. Clustering them within defined markets doesn't help as they tend to be more similar in niches across markets than within them. Globalization, and economic crisis, have opened their eyes to new aspirations and expectations; changing what is valued and matters most.

They don't passively accept sameness or mediocrity; they are not logical, consistent or average. People want to achieve more. In fact the notion of customers who are transactional partners is not enough. They are individual and emotional with high expectations.

The **customer world**, be they clients or consumers, is a much more **inspiring world** full of richer opportunities to do more. **Thinking customer** and benefits, rather than product and features, is still tough for many organizations, particularly when large and technical. Gamechangers see **customers as partners**, riding the waves of change together.

Newness typically emerges in the margins, not the mainstreams. Gamechangers are naturally driven by customers. In a world of ideas, where you have little but your brain, you don't start with products or capabilities. You start with a potential audience, their wants and aspirations, frustrations and needs. Not just what they want, but how they want to do things too.

One of the brand manager's most frequent questions today is 'What do customers really want from our brands?'

Insights are **'penetrating discoveries'** that understand 'what' but also 'why' people have certain attitudes or aspirations. This is not achieved through superficial research; it requires a depth of inquiry – asking why, and why, and why again. Insights require more questions and are by definition more anecdotal and interpretive. Quantitative analysis is still helpful – identifying where to enquire and then seizing the emerging knowledge.

Insights usually emerge from the combination and interpretation of multiple sources of information – data analytics and observational anecdotes, parallel situations and extreme users, singular perspectives and crowd-sourced aggregations.

Insights are most often found at the heart of a **dilemma**, a paradox which the customer struggles to resolve. They must be fresh, or at least a new interpretation. And they are most effective when they are expressed in the first person.

5.9 TRENDS ... THE SHIFT IN PRIORITIES

Trends are observed behaviours, patterns in the zeitgeist that rise above fashions and fads. They are the factors which most influence the needs and priorities, aspirations and expectation of customers. Whilst we recognize the trends in markets – demographics, disposible income, etc. – it is the trends in what people want that drive innovation.

Emerging trends are like **earthquakes**. They build slowly based on tensions between cultures, generations, outlooks and

possibilities. Like the early tremors of the earth, trends can be initially spotted **on the fringes**, controversial and disruptive. As they build to a critical point, they eventually explode in the market, with ripples across everyone. They influence customers broadly too, creating new expectations across every market.

Increasingly the trends work across categories, or even types of business. They are about how people want to live their lives, what they believe in, and how they therefore want to choose and engage with brands.

- **'Me to We'** … whilst still wanting individualization, consumers will work together, trust their friends rather than companies and support each other.

- **'Statement to Stories'** … people engage in real stories about how you can make their lives better – the end of promotional 'push' and trivial slogans.

- **'Consistent to Deviant'** … the end of 'sameness' – people want to see more variety (for example in packaging), and to express themselves in their own ways.

- **'Selling to Enabling'** … people are much more interested in how you help them to use the product, not just buy it – to improve their home, to get fit, to look good.

- **'Passive to Participating'** … don't just make products and push them out – actively involve people in designing, making and selling products 'made by people like you'.

- **'Products to People'** … people are human, emotional, artistic and alive – brands are much more about what people do, who they connect with, where they are.

- **'Good to Great'** … embrace sustainability, not as a 'reduction' challenge, but as a 'boing better' opportunity – natural, local, helping consumers do more good.

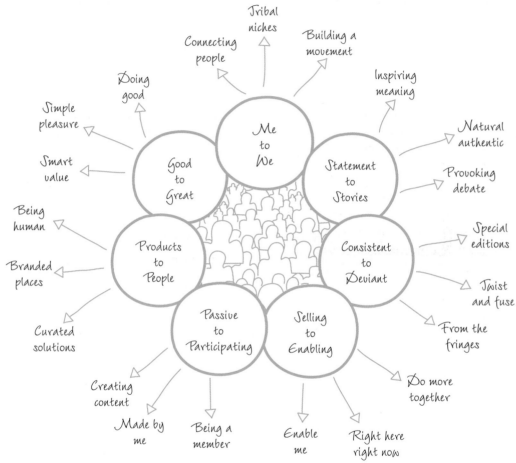

The New Customer Agenda

of these trends, perhaps the most significant is that of **collaboration**. People are naturally social. They like to participate, to contribute, to share. For too long business has not appreciated this as a benefit, or known how to achieve it. Technology changed that.

As individuals, empowered and enabled, the **best brands** give us the power to achieve much more than we could otherwise. They increasingly give us the confidence to dream bigger and take bolder actions, to compete in sport or start our own business. They also give us the capability to achieve more, through the products they bring and the support as we use them.

But brands do more. They **bring us together**. The best brands allow us to find people like us, who share the same aspirations and passions. They create platforms through which we can

participate in the brand – thinking, making, supporting – but also through which we can do more together. These brands facilitate communities, giving them an identity, momentum and voice, to achieve more together.

Incredible me. **Irresistible we**.

CHANGE YOUR GAME

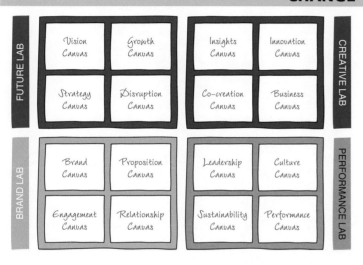

Practically apply the concepts in this chapter to your business with the relevant tools in the Gamechanger Labs:

- **Growth** canvas
- **Strategy** canvas
- **Insights** canvas

Practical examples can be found in the 100 cases studies. Also see more details at Gamechangers.pro

6 DISRUPT ... CREATING YOUR OWN SPACE IN THE WORLD

CHANGE YOUR STRATEGY

Gamechangers seek to out-think and out-play their competitors by changing the game ... they envision and articulate their market, then change the dynamics of competition, with new expectations and impacts ... shaping markets in their own vision.

- More **disruptive** ... *from playing the game ... to changing the game ...* They outwit competitors by creatively rethinking the market and the whole business.

- More **focused** ... *from mass and average ... to selectively different ...* They look beyond masses to niches, averages to individuals, needs to dreams.

- More **agile** ... *from unchanging direction ... to strategic jazz ...* They ride the waves of change, flexing and adapting, whilst making the future happen.

6.1 GROWTH…FINDING THE HOTSPOTS AND WHITESPACES

In 1940 Henry Ford famously said 'Mark my word, a combination of airplane and motorcar is coming. You may smile but it will come.'

When I was launching Gamechangers in Central Europe, I asked business leaders across the region to nominate the brands and businesses who they thought were most shaking up the region's markets. Some amazing concepts were nominated – from Rimac's million-dollar supercars in Croatia, to the incredible Ukrainian digital gloves that turn sign language into spoken words – but I was not expecting a winner like **Aeromobil**.

Stefan Klein grew up in Bratislava, the beautiful capital of Slovakia, just a 30 minute drive across the border from the much larger metropolis of Vienna. His father and grandfather had infused in him a love of flying small planes, but his career had taken him to the car industry, becoming the head of research for Volkswagen and BMW. But for the last 20 years, the academic and artist had pursued his dream to create a **flying car**.

Three days earlier in Montreal, Canada, Klein had been showcasing his new Aeromobil flying car prototype to Boeing and NASA. He drove it through the city, a stylish looking sports car, but when it reached the airport, it sped straight past the car park and onto the airfield. The wings spread out, a propeller emerges, and it's all **James Bond**. Down the runway he gathers speed, and lifts off. Incredible.

On hearing that he had won, Stefan called me from 400 km away. He wanted to be there to share his vision, to meet the audience. Within a few hours he arrived, a quiet unassuming guy, but bursting with pride and ambition. 'To be called a gamechanger in my home country is a very special moment' he told me. Still awaiting certification, but with a top speed of 200 km/h and range of 700 km, and some help in scaling and commercializing the design, Aeromobil really could change the game.

The **definition of markets** is constantly evolving. Time Warner recently declared itself a media rather than technology company, whilst Virgin Media shifted from communication to entertainment, and Disney declared itself to be about experience rather than entertainment. Whilst some of these statements are for financial gain, the premium the stock market places on media companies being much greater than technology companies, for example, it is also about convergence and customer thinking.

You can define markets however you want – nobody controls the boundaries or words you use – start with possibilities, explore a wide range of ideas and insights, and then focus down on the best opportunities for you. This becomes your space, defined on your terms, and to your advantage.

6.2 DISRUPT...BREAKING THE OLD RULES

Paulo Miguel Pereira da Silva thinks that toilet paper is the most boring product in the world. So he decided to change it. 'Why shouldn't your bathroom be colourful and sensual? It is one of the most intimate places you spend time' he says. His company, **Renova**, makes toilet paper in pink, fuscia, black, lime. Anything but white.

Creating a new game typically involves **breaking the 'rules'** of one game to set the rules of a new game. 'Rules' might be accepted ways of working, established business processes and customer practices, setting expectations of service and perceptions of value. 'Rules' might also be legal regulations or ethical practices, which have been set based on one way of working and may need to be evolved or redefined.

A **disruptive innovation** changes the possibilities for people, enabling them to achieve more, often in a different way. The change is dramatic and unexpected, it creates a new market, addresses a new customer segment and displaces competitors – low-cost airlines, car-sharing clubs, modular clothing. Prof Clay Christensen is most associated with the concept of disruption, using the example of how floppy disks were disrupted by CDs (and subsequently by USBs, external hard drives and clouds).

Disruption dɪsˈrʌpʃn
noun

- disturbance or problems which interrupt an event, activity, or process.

In contrast a 'sustaining' innovation is incremental, does not create a new market, is mainly about better products or services, often through technology improvements and beating competitors. Early cars were innovative but not disruptive, because most people continued with horse and carts. However Ford's mass produced Model T was disruptive because it prompted the end of horses. It was not just the technology, but the business model which made it powerful and profitable.

Whilst it might feel like a disruptive world, few large companies **dare to be so bold**. The need to reduce risks and ensure short-term returns typically work against more radical pioneering ideas. Christensen said at a Thinkers 50 seminar that 'Japan is a perfect of example of disruptions that made it great, and then the lack of them which led to its decline'. Entrepreneurs and long-term private owners are more motivated by the future, and are likely to make better disruptors.

6.3 VISION...IMAGINING A BETTER PLACE

Bill Gates often says 'We overestimate the amount of change that will happen in the next 1 or 2 years, but underestimate the **huge change** that will happen in the subsequent 3 to 10 years.' The future is exponential, non-linear, and not predictable.

'**Futurizing**' lies at the heart of what gamechangers do. It doesn't require big documents or long presentations, it requires stretch vision and clear choices, often so simple yet compelling that they take the form of the famed 'napkin diagram' or a digital doodle. What emerges is a strategy, a **market strategy**, a gameplan to change the world.

Most markets converge to **sameness**. They are defined by the needs of the average customer and the solutions of the average competitor. Most brands target everyone. Whether they admit it or not, they hate to narrow their focus, to boldly state who they are for, and not for. Most market research tells us about average trends and aspirations, specific and potentially relevant to nobody.

Add to this, most companies don't want to change the market, they want to fit in. To win by playing the existing game slightly better. Given the speed of imitation, this usually results in a price contest, a spiral to lowest cost, and profitabilty through efficiency rather than innovation.

Business **vision** is about having a clear view of the future, or at least the possible futures, and how you want to play in it. It is typically set **10 years ahead**, maybe longer in some industries like energy and pharma where decisions are made over a 20–30 year frame. It should be a **creative process**, engaging participants in the scale of ambiguity and choices they will need to make. The value is as much in the discussions, understanding the drivers and likely disruptors, as it is in creating a perfectly formed, but impossibly perfect, outcome.

Whilst scenario planning is a powerful technique to understand how your market might evolve, the likely drivers of change and inflection points on the way, and thereby create a range of possible scenarios for which you can prepare, a vision is of your making. It is the world you want to see. Most likely it is a better world – maybe where disease or poverty have been eradicated, where carbon emissions are zero, or cars are driverless. It shows what companies and people do, and the benefits to them. It is a better place.

Once you have clarity of your desired future world, you can engage other people in this. It makes purpose more real. It demonstrates in black and white the difference you seek to make, compared to today. It inspires employees to say 'Yes, I want to work there!' and customers to say 'Yes, I want to be there!'.

Strategy is then about setting a course to get there.

It is easy to get confused about purpose; vision and mission, values and culture, strategy and priorities, goals and metrics, all fit together. Purpose is the most enduring aspect, a north star giving an organization direction as it evolves and innovates. Strategy is more agile, making choices for the future, but being flexible about how to get there.

6.4 CHOICES...DEVELOPING A WINNING STRATEGY

AG Lafley is fond of describing strategy as a game. 'It's about **playing to win**, it's all about making better choices' he said on his return to P&G as CEO in 2013. Whilst some companies use strategy to make sense of what they currently do, or to justify a financial budget, the best strategies are creative, directional and transforming.

What strikes me about the gamechangers is how **focused** they are. They know where they are going, what they are trying to achieve, and will give everything to get there. They have an intensity, clarity and energy, driving them forwards.

Strategy is not in vogue. It requires choices, making sense of complexity and uncertainty. It requires focus, deciding what to do and what not. It requires commitment, to allocate resources and reputations in some directions, but not others. It means letting go of the past. Too many people prefer to keep their options open, to mitigate the risks, to hang on to fading success, and avoid big decisions. And to close their eyes to their future.

There are five big questions to answer in developing a winning strategy, and the choices we need to explicitly make:

- **Why are we here?** … our inspiring purpose about how we make life better, supported by a vision of what it will be like and our role in this future.

- **Where will we play?** … our target markets, in terms of sectors and categories, as well as geographies and customer segments.

- **What will we do?** … our primary activities, the brands we will build, products and services, experiences and support.

- **How will we win?** … our choice of business model, including competitive advantages, costs and revenues, how we will create and share value.

- **What will it take?** … our essential resources to make this happen, people and partners, assets and investments, and the business operating system.

The biggest challenge to strategy is to make it agile. Strategy doesn't require 100 pages of dense text; it requires one page of definitive clarity. Strategy is increasingly a **frame** in which to operate, defined by its boundaries – where to focus, and where not – rather than the detail within. Strategies typically have a one, three and five year time frame, constantly evolving to keep pace – or rather keep ahead – of relentless market change.

6.5 FRAME … DEFINING YOUR OWN SPACE

Framing is about defining the space in which you want to play.

It's about you articulating what market you are in, or want to be in. This might be a standard definition, or it might be entirely your own creation.

The labels of industry sectors are entirely arbitary. No customer lives entirely within one sector. Few businesses cover an entire sector. Consider yourself a telecoms brand, you could equally 'reframe' yourself in the worlds of communication, entertainment, media, publishing, technology. It's your choice.

Framing is about **establishing context**, and positioning, in people's minds.

It's about establishing the way in which you want your brand to be considered, the benefit it seeks to address, the competitors – or alternatives – which you want customers to consider, and the perceived value which you want them to associate with you.

It's also about finding **a better way to stand out**. In the torrent of mass markets, the noise of competitors, it's about finding a distinctive place from which to be seen differently and heard more clearly.

Whilst 'blue ocean strategy' was all about finding new white spaces, moving beyond the competitive 'red oceans' to find uncontested markets, there was one problem: there were very few customers there.

Framing is instead about defining your space in existing or new markets.

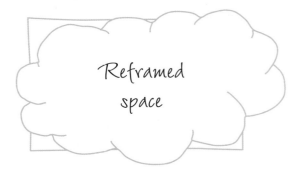

Existing space	Reframed space
Defined by industrial category, products and technology	Defined by your imagination, customers and aspirations
Established market boundaries, practices, rules and prices	Create the ways of working, and price points, on your own terms
Most innovation is incremental, immitated and commoditized	Most innovation is transformational, disruptive and differentiated
Customers buy, investors invest based on comparison	Customers buy, investors invest based on vision and concept
Easy to explain, accepted and regulated, and fits in	Need to educate people, encourage trial, and make established
Examples: Gillette next gen blades, Ford diesel cars	Examples: Virgin Galactic defining space tourism, Tesla electric cars

Finding Your Own Space

It is often about becoming more focused within a category, like sportswear for yoga, or about merging two categories together, like functional foods, or about redefining your space on customer terms, like meeting people.

We see **reframes** in every walk of life. Cost cutting is reframed as improved efficiency, anti-abortion is relabelled pro-life. In business, the 'personal computer' was a reframe of the computer market, iPod was a branded reframe of the MP3 market, and 'wellness' is about prevention rather than cure in the pharmacy market.

The most effective way to 'reframe' is to think like a customer. Instead of occupying a narrow market space defined by your functional product, it is about capturing the space defined by the customer's benefit, or even better by the benefit they derive from the product's application.

An airline, for example, might functionally be about schedule and service, but to the business traveller it might be much more about making new connections, finding new opportunities or accelerating business growth. The challenge is to find relevance but also focus, so that you can occupy your reframed 'space' with authority and demand.

6.6 SHAPE...WRITING THE NEW RULES OF THE GAME

Having found your space, you then have an opportunity to shape it to your advantage.

Any, or every, aspect of market and business activity could be changed to achieve this – the why, who, what and how.

When Dyson launched its bagless vacuum cleaner, it used design to express youth and modernity, it used selected retailers to establish a certain type of audience, it even used carefully chosen images and typography to be associated with a desired peer group. All of this communicated who it was for and supported the desired premium price.

As **Virgin Galactic** sets out today to shape the market for consumer space travel, it searches for ways to frame its new market. If a one-day flight into space is a once in a lifetime experience, what does it compare to? Maybe scaling Mount Everest, which on a guided tour might cost around $50k. That establishes a context for the experience. Shaping the rules go beyond this, maybe it should require one day training, include the costs of insurance and customized spacewear.

If you can **shape your market** to your advantage – in a way that makes it much more difficult for others to imitate – then you can establish customer behaviours and expectations, which are potentially difficult for others and so a barrier to their entry.

Yeni Raki is the classic brand of Turkey's traditional drink – a strong, aniseed-flavoured alcohol. In Turkey there are many imitators, but only one dominant brand. It sells not the drink but the culture of the drink. It is about slowing down, enjoying the intimacy of friends, eating traditional foods, enjoying Turkish music. It is a unique ritual.

When the Turkish brand, owned by Diageo, started to sell in new markets, like the USA, it needed to find its own space amidst the hundreds of vodka, gin and other spirit brands. It focused on selling a cultural experience, not the drink. Creating branded glasses, for example, exclusive to certain restaurants. Introducing key words, associating with certain food brands and music through channel cross-promotions, events and incentives. It shaped how, when and where people would experience the brand.

6.7 PIVOT ... MOVING FROM MEDIOCRITY TO MAGIC

In reframing, a brand can often see where it wants to get to, but has impatience or uncertainty as to how to get there. It needs to find some way to make the transition and, better, to do it fast and painlessly. This is what pivots do, like in engineering, they allow you to **turn in a new direction**, fast and easily.

Digital businesses have been most effective at pivoting, executing a sudden shift in strategy that turns hundreds of followers into millions of fans, evolving an idea into a billion-dollar company.

Pinterest started life as Tote, helping people to explore online retailers and sending them updates about prices and availability. It realized users were mainly using the site to build and share ideas lists, and soon shifted course to focus on 'pinning'. **Groupon** began as a platform for social action called The Point, before reinventing itself in the crowd-based local coupon business. Ushahida started as an African elections monitoring service, before growing into a crowd-sourced new aggregator. **Twitter** emerged out of a mediocre podcasting concept called Odeo that was outshone by iTunes.

The ability to pivot, be it a subtle shift in direction, or a radical reinvention, is essential to scaling start-ups into commercial businesses.

Fail early and cheaply is a start-up mantra. Use prototypes to learn from customers, such as a paper-based process before investing in detailed coding, a Powerpoint before a website, testing with Google Adword before spending more. And keep learning from customers – insights about why some customers don't currently get or want your idea, or exploring their real problems and aspirations more deeply.

Find well-established partners to co-brand with, reaching out to their audiences, transferring equity from their brand, or maybe creating a better solution. Watch emergent behaviour, particularly people who adapt products for other uses, like engineer codes that become texting, or scarves that become snoods. And above all, stay passionate. If you aren't truly excited about a concept, it's unlikely your customers will ever be. Find what really excites you, and the people who will be excited by you.

Even the classic brands of today had to pivot to where they are today. **Wrigley's** gave away free gum whilst selling soap and baking powder, but found people liked their incentive more than the product. **Avon** has a similar history, a door-to-door bookseller that gave away perfume samples to attract women. **HP** focused on industrial solutions before finding consumers. **Starbucks** focused on selling coffee beans until Howard Shultz visited the coffee houses of Italy and came back inspired to create his 'third place'.

These companies had the focus to find their space, the boldness to shift from their existing world to the better world, and then shaped the market in their own vision.

6.8 HORIZONS ... ROADMAP TO A BETTER FUTURE

Strategic implementation is a journey, with many horizons.

Whilst defining a new direction and potential destination is relatively easy, getting there is harder. It takes time and resources. It requires a migration from old to new worlds, changing people and actions inside and outside. Horizon-based planning is a more effective way to plan the phases of implementation in such a way that they are progressive, reducing time and risk, but also have more impact in each phase, not just at the end.

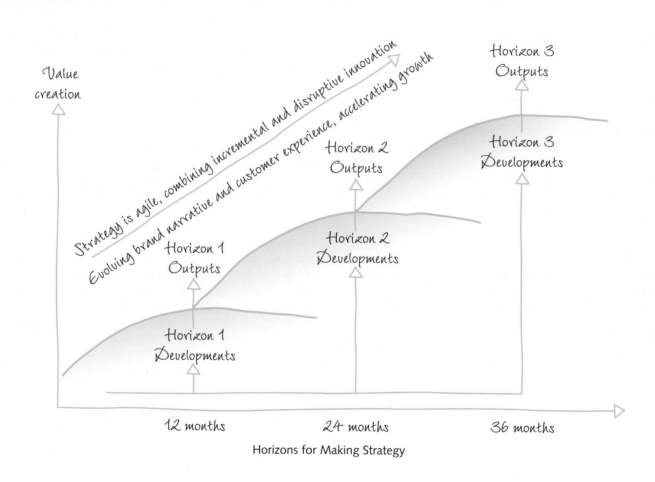

Value creation

Strategy is agile, combining incremental and disruptive innovation

Evolving brand narrative and customer experience, accelerating growth

Horizon 3 Outputs

Horizon 3 Developments

Horizon 2 Outputs

Horizon 2 Developments

Horizon 1 Outputs

Horizon 1 Developments

12 months   24 months   36 months

Horizons for Making Strategy

The horizons are progressive, in the sense that they build towards the completion of the strategy. They are similar to **'S-curves'** in some models. However the coherence of the progression is mostly external, finding a narrative that builds over time, offers more to the customer at each phase, with specific 'icons' that capture attention and imagination. These icons might be new product releases, additional parts to a bigger solution, or additional 'gestures' in terms of service or relationship.

At the same time, there is an internal coherence to get right. This is about building and evolving platforms, establishing the base for a new business or experience, and then building on it over time. It also requires **time-based thinking**. Some developments, particularly complex technology-based innovations, will take more time. Then, being able to develop future horizons in parallel with delivering initial horizons is important. The outside-in sequencing of horizons also drives new revenue streams that can either fund, or reduce the risk, of later horizons.

As an example, in **rebranding** a boutique Asian hotel chain, we explored the horizons for implementation. Some executives were keen to launch the new name quickly, and then improve the hotels and service levels later. What made more sense was develop the interior design first, which then inspired staff to deliver better service, which then led to the moment to relaunch the brand, when we could actually deliver on heightened expectations.

Similarly with a brand extension strategy for a food brand, they wanted to deliver radical innovations in new categories, but as a first horizon we chose to extend in more related categories, creating a bridge in the consumer's mind so that the authority and meaning of the brand could gradually shift from its origins to a wider meaning, rather than what might appear like a random and untrusted leap.

6.9 PLAY ... WINNING THE NEW GAME

Once you have found and shaped your space, it's about winning the new game. This is about playing to your advantages. The way you have defined the market should work in your favour – because you have the best reputation, built an ecosystem of all the best partners to source, create, deliver and complement the proposition. As a **market maker**, you create barriers to others entering your space, because the way you have designed it makes it difficult for others.

Perhaps the best way to capture your space is to become the definition of the market. Dyson became the de facto name for bagless cleaners. Not only did competitiors find it legally difficult to imitate the patented designs, but found that customers articulated their need through the brand, saying 'I want a Dyson'. The same with Lego, the same with Nescafe, the same with iPod or iPad, and many other successful brands.

At the same time, **owning your space** is an ongoing challenge. There is no rest; even the best monopolies are temporary. Being a 'thought leader' means you have to keep thinking, evolving and innovating, staying ahead of the pack, shaping the game again before others shape it. This becomes hard, as Apple has found in recent years.

In small companies, it is what entrepreneurs do. They thrive on change. As small becomes larger, subsequent managers seek to keep the founder's spirit alive, seeking to sustain the disruptive nature of the innovation rather than just harvest the established market until it runs dry. In big companies, it is typically the marketers who keep the fire burning – searching for new opportunities, making sense of change, evolving markets and driving innovation, translating new possibilities into advantage for customers.

GE's CMO, **Beth Comstock**, describes the role of marketing as 'going to where the future is, innovating with customers, telling global stories with local accents, connecting people with machines ... To be an **effective marketer**, you have to go where things are, you have to see what's happening and be a translator. You have to immerse yourself and not be comfortable sometimes.' She talks of rural doctors in China and farmers in Africa, where she sees GE making the most difference, and money.

Connecting the dots is also about making sense of fast changing markets, looking for the patterns, the opportunities. She sees marketers as the people to do this, saying a great

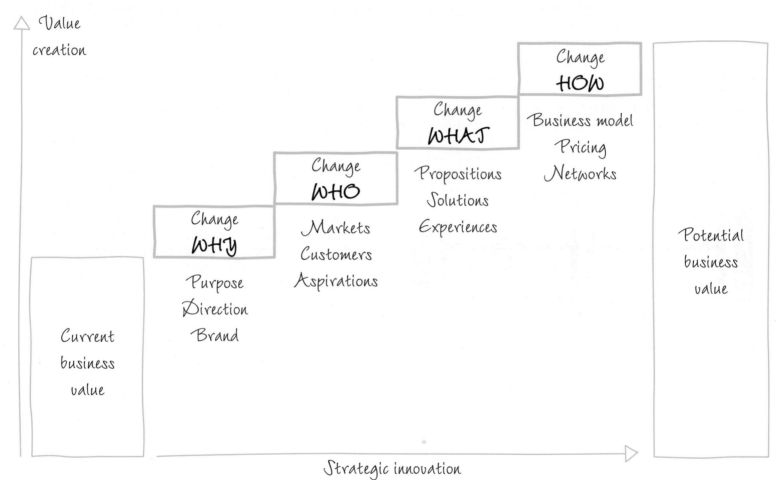

Value creation

Change
WHY

Purpose
Direction
Brand

Change
WHO

Markets
Customers
Aspirations

Change
WHAT

Propositions
Solutions
Experiences

Change
HOW

Business model
Pricing
Networks

Current
business
value

Potential
business
value

Strategic innovation

Value Impact of Changing the Game

marketer 'translates observations into insights that can move a business or product forwards'. However that is not just about brand and communicating what exists, 'Marketing is now about creating and developing **new markets**; not just identifying opportunities but also making them happen.' ... In short, marketing is about market making. Be that strategic in the sense of finding and shaping new markets, or every day in terms of owning and evolving in real-time.

Market Makers are the brands and innovators who create and shape the markets of the future. They do this through imagination and vision, insights and connections, redefining how the markets work, what inspires and enables consumers to do more, and how brands and business can win commercially too. Underpinning this is new market strategies to business models, innovation and sustainability, social media and real-time marketing.

CHANGE YOUR GAME

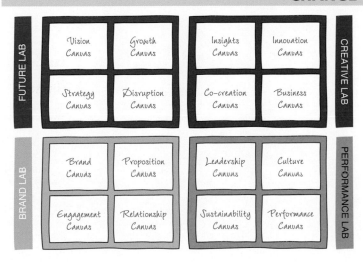

Practically apply the concepts in this chapter to your business with the relevant tools in the Gamechanger Labs:

- **Growth** canvas
- **Strategy** canvas
- **Disruption** canvas

Practical examples can be found in the 100 cases studies. Also see more details at Gamechangers.pro

7 INSPIRE...BUILDING BRANDS
THAT MAKE LIFE BETTER
CHANGE YOUR BRAND

Gamechangers build brands that capture the aspirations of their audiences, rather than promote their own egos. They represent more purposeful ideas, inspiring people to seek more, believe more and achieve more.

- More **aspirational** ... *from business identities ... to enabling possibilities ...* Brands articulate what people seek to be or become, to belong to and achieve.

- More **human** ... *from words and images ... to purposeful ideas ...* Brands are about people, not products, and so can move easily across portfolios and categories.

- More **powerful** ... *from ambient communication ... to mobilizing forces ...* Brands engage and connect people, empower and enable, a force for change.

7.1 PURPOSEFUL ... BRANDS MAKE LIFE BETTER

Brands are about **people** not products. Whilst they started out as marks of ownership, functionally describing companies and products, they have evolved to reflect the hopes and dreams of real people, emotional and inspiring.

Brands are therefore more **purposeful**. The best brands make life better, either through inspiration and confidence or by practically enabling people to achieve more. They capture the imagination of people, through contagious ideas that people seek to believe and define themselves by. They elevate products and services to a higher level, bringing together more valuable and intuitive solutions, and they connect like-minded people to do more together.

Brands have the **power to change people**, to transform attitudes and behaviours. This might be through fashions and innovations, enabling people to feel and achieve more, but it might equally be about living and doing better.

Brands can make life better. Brands can be a force for good.

However a purposeful brand has to have a purpose, to stand for something, to have a point of view. This requires attitude, boldness and clarity. It means having a distinctive, relevant and engaging concept that resonates with your audience. It also means not trying to please everyone, which is a sure route to compromize and mediocrity. As Scott Bedbury, the man who put the 'Just do it' into Nike, says 'A great brand polarizes people. Some will love it, some will hate it'.

I love Nike.

Not the company, but **the idea**. It's not about the founder Bill Bowerman and the story of his waffle iron, much more about the adrenalin and inspiraton that I felt tingling down my spine on the night when Steve Cram broke 3 minutes 30 for the 1500 m in Nice. I've worn Nike shoes and clothing for 35 years, and never considered any other brand. Products have come and gone, trends and technologies. It's not about technical quality or superficial image, it's about the confidence and confirmation that I get from wearing the iconic 'swoosh'. It's **about me** and how I feel.

Brands have come a long way. From their origins in the 'brandt' of a farmer's mark on his cattle, to the reassuring symbol of ownership, and even premium value. But today, everything is a brand. So the best ones need to be more. They are a reflection of customers, a uniquely shared value, and potentially your most valuable business asset.

People trust the best brands more than any traditional institution – more than governments, lawyers, sometimes even more than religion. Brands connect with them, shape their attitudes and aspirations, connect them with people like them to give them a platform to achieve more together. Ultimately, brands have the power to change the world – not just to sell products and make profits, but to make life better.

However this requires a more enlightened approach to branding – to challenge our conventional wisdom as to what a brand is and how to manage and innovate with it.

Brands are not about what you do, but **what you enable people to do**. Brands are about people not products. Brands are about customers not companies.

A great brand is one you want to live your life by, one you trust and hang on to whilst everything around you is changing, one that articulates the type of person you are or want to be, one that enables to you to do what you couldn't otherwise achieve.

Brands were originally developed as labels of ownership. They were factual and introspective – the best cosmetics company in the world, the most innovative technological solutions, or the original hand-made shoe company. They relied upon their names and logos, articulated through superficial taglines, and delivered through generic service.

Just like internally motivated mission statements, this does little to engage customers, it doesn't reach out to them, it doesn't describe their world, it doesn't cut through the noise of crowded markets or gain the trust of sceptics. It can also be limiting to the business, with less ability to flex and stretch into other markets and applications.

Brands are engaging to customers when they are about them, when they reflect who they are, or want to be. They define what customers want to do – or be, become, or belong to – rather than what products do. They **capture the dreams** and aspirations of customers or at least the applications and benefits.

A brand builds on the purpose of a business, articulating and visualizing it in a clear and compelling way, relevant and about customers, standing out from the crowd and touching people more deeply.

Brands can become 'anchors' around which customers live their lives, representing something familiar and important whilst everything else is changing. Yet brands must also evolve as markets and customers evolve, with the portability to move easily into new markets and **the glue** to connect diverse activities.

A great brand is not designed for everyone, but for target customers. In reflecting these people, they seek to build affinity and preference, encourage purchase behaviour and sustain a price premium. They seek to retain the best customers, building their loyalty, introducing new services and encouraging advocacy.

The brand identity, communication and experience is designed to reflect the target customer. Look at the typography of Build a Bear Workshop logo, the layout of its stores, the programme of activities – all designed to be child-like. Consider the design of Apple – from its logo to its typography, the black t-shirts of its people, and industrial design – they all capture modernity, coolness and simplicity.

Old Brand Thinking	New Brand Thinking
Brands are not just about	Brands today are more about
Image	Aspiration
Promise	Experience
Difference	Resonance
Values	Spirit
Consistent	Coherence
Awareness	Participation
Personal	Shared
Engaging	Enabling
Like	Love
Relationship	Movement

Brands Are About Me Not You

If a brand seeks to reflect its target audience, then this also means that a brand must be prepared to alienate other people.

FC Barcelona can never be everyone's favourite sports club, but it is everything to its fans. McDonalds is heaven to some, hell for others. Some people adore their Mini Cooper, other people think it is ridiculous.

7.2 ESSENCE ... FINDING THE IDEA THAT DEFINES PEOPLE

Brands capture an irresistible idea, compelling and intuitive, engaging and inspiring people in ways that companies and products cannot. A great brand captivates people emotionally and irrationally, about them and what they want to achieve, ultimately it is about making life better. Brands are also your bridge to new products, catagories and markets, to sustaining and growing your business in a world of relentless change.

Gamechanger brands capture their big ideas in more inspiring ways that resonate with their target audiences at the right time and place, enabled by data and technology, but most of all by rich human experiences.

These brands recognize that people are **more emotional** and intuitive, different and discerning than ever. They know what they like and who they want to be with. Social networks drive reach and richness, whilst new business models make the possible profitable. They collaborate with customers, and partner with other business, fusing ideas and utilizing their capabilities. They look beyond the sale to enable customers to achieve more; they care about their impact on people and the world.

Brand concepts are bigger ideas. Names and logos are just shorthand ways of representing this bigger idea. Products and services can make the ideas tangible, but so can packaging and display, pricing structures and retail displays, service style and communication stories. These are all part of the brand entity. The Apple store says as much about the brand as the iPad. The friendly Starbucks barista is as important as the coffee. The cabin scent of Singapore airlines is as distinctive as the logo on the head rests.

There are many complex models of brands. However a brand is fundamentally not about description, but enablement – what it does for people, rather than what it is. It then describes this in three components – rational, comparative and emotional.

- *Rational*: What does the brand enable customers to do? (Nike is not about great sports shoes or apparel, it's about people doing sports, such as running.)

- *Comparative*: Why does it enable them to do it differently or better? (Nike is not just about running, it's about running faster or further than you could ever before.)

- *Emotional*: How do people feel about the brand as a result? (Nike is an attitude to doing more, doing it better, and winning – just do it, no finish line.)

At the heart of the brand, connecting these different components is the **core idea**, which should be very similar to the business purpose for a corporate brand, but perhaps articulated in a more creative and memorable way.

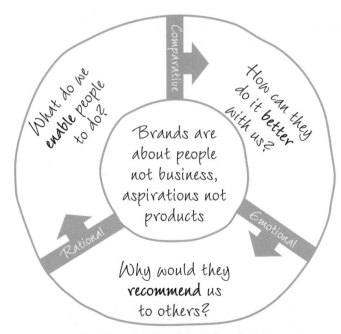

Capturing the Essence of Your Brand

7.3 ELEVATE ... ENABLING PEOPLE TO ACHIEVE MORE

Brands **'lift'** people above the noise, creating an emotional shorthand for who they are, how they are relevant and distinctive. They lift organizations above the arrogance and formality of corporate-speak, and they lift products and services above their functionality and the commoditization of competitors.

They transform needs into wants, interest into desire, likes into love.

As brands become more about people rather than products, they also become more focused on what they seek to achieve and how they do it. Vodafone used to be about the power of technology, then about 'now', which has evolved into 'power to you' ... a 180 degree change in narrative.

However **'enabling brands'** are more than a story. They need to embrace an experience which goes beyond the product and its purchase. Years ago **Michelin** had the foresight to look beyond car tyres, to talk about navigation and even restaurants. If a tech brand promises to improve your productivity, it needs to include the apps and education to help you achieve that. If a food brand promises the best meals it needs to curate all the ingredients, with a recipe to guide you, maybe even some wine and music to bring it to life. If a healthcare brand promises wellbeing, then it needs to go beyond the pharmacy, to help you get active, stay healthy, enjoy life.

Emotionally brands go even further, changing the way people feel about themselves and their lives. In the same way that strategy works, 'future back', brands should consider first the way they seek to make life better, and then design the stories

and experiences to deliver it. There are four ways a brand really emotionally enables people to achieve more:

- **Do more**: achieve more practically, eg Timberland.
- **Be more**: confirm who you are, eg Estee Lauder.
- **Become more**: achieve more emotionally, eg Nike
- **Belong more**: connect with others, eg Harley Davidson

By elevating the essence of a brand to help people achieve more, the brand becomes more purposeful. People engage with the brand at a higher level – be it in terms of perceived value and therefore pay more, or in terms of perceived ownership and therefore become more participative and greater advocates.

Brand equity was described by David Aaker as the 'brand assets and liabilities linked to a brand name and symbol', which add to or subtract from the value provided by a product or business. This radically changed the marketing function, articulating the direct impact it can have on the business, rather than as a support function to selling. In a sense it's the amount of 'positivity' in the brand to elevate a product or business beyond a commodity.

Of course a brand creates value for customers and business, and equity, and the way in which it is nurtured and grown should reflect this too.

For the business, brand equity is driven by awareness (how many people know about it), perception (how they feel about it and are they prepared to pay more for it), preference (how different is it, do people prefer it, will they stick with it) and agility (how far can it extend and evolve). For the customer, brand equity is driven by relevance (is it for me, both in terms of function and aspiration), confidence (do I trust it and feel good using it), connection (does it connect me with others) and enablement (can I achieve more because of it).

Whilst this might sound obvious, it is surprising how many businesses, and brand agencies, still see brand as a labelling device to communicate their difference. Brand 'positioning' is often seen as how visible and different you are, as opposed to focusing on the brand's primacy in an audience's mind, based on perceived relevance and value.

Brand value is often quoted as the financial outcome of this equity which has been built in a brand. Business leaders delight in telling others that they have a 'billion dollar brand'. What they probably mean is the sales volume of the brand; Diageo for example claim to have 12 such brands including Johnny Walker and Smirnoff.

However when BusinessWeek announce Apple as 'the world's most valuable brand' (worth $98bn in 2013, ahead of Google $93bn, and Coca-Cola $79bn) they are actually seeking to measure the amount by which the brand enhances the market cap of the business. In other words, the way in which a brand increases the future revenues, and within them the price premium that people will pay and the certainty of them buying.

7.4 ACTIVATE ... BRINGING BRANDS TO LIFE

Brands are about more than words and slogans, images and colours, stories and experiences. They are more than businesses and their cultures, products and their functional benefits. They are all of this, together. It is tempting to focus on storytelling, advertising and social media, which play a huge role in connecting people with brands. But that

would be a superficial, and would somewhat trivialize the brand as a communication device. What comes first is the purpose, and the many ways to capture the brand's big idea.

Lululemon Athletica was founded by surfer and snowboarder Chip Wilson, who fell in love with yoga and created a range of surf-inspired clothes good for stretching and meditating. From the first store in Kitsilano, Canada in 1998, the brand grew as a place to do yoga and buy clothes.

The brand is captured in the **Lululemon Manifesto**, which is actually 31 ideas and life philosophies for healthy and positive living including:

- Do one thing a day that scares you.

- Listen, listen, listen, and then ask strategic questions.

- Life is full of setbacks. Success is determined by how you handle setbacks.

- Your outlook on life is a direct reflection of how much you like yourself.

- That which matters the most should never give way to that which matters the least.

- The world is changing at such a rapid rate that waiting to implement changes will leave you two steps behind. DO IT NOW, DO IT NOW, DO IT NOW!

- Breathe deeply and appreciate the moment. Living in the moment could be the meaning of life.

Of course there is a great science to brand-naming itself. In the days when brands reflected ownership, national industries or founder names sought to engage us. Bank of China, British

Airways, France Telecom have clear limitations. Names of founders, like Marks & Spencer, or Saatchi & Saatchi, become increasingly irrelevant, as people care less about history or institutions. Perhaps the worst offenders are advertising agencies like BBDO and TBWA. Who are these people?

Defining the big idea, then finding a more relevant name to capture it. Apples are simple, intuitive, and Newton transformed the world. Nike wings her way to victory. Diesel is industrial and democratic. Google is complex but simple. Of course, heritage names can be recast in new ways. Nokia is a small village in Finland, Umpqua a river in Oregon state, IKEA is an abbreviation of the name and town of it's founder, Ingvar Kampfrad. Whilst this captures heritage, it can be hard work too.

Beyond the name comes **defining gestures**. This might be a symbol, like Accenture's accent, or BMW's propeller wheel. Some brands don't feel the need for a symbol, like Zara, whilst others don't use their name, like Nike. Strong brand gestures mean more, and quite often the simpler they are, the more powerfully they work. There are many other ways to convey ideas. Alessi puts a totally irrelevant but iconic bird on its kettles, Aston Martin provides owners with an ECU – emotional control unit – known to others as a key.

Gestures are increasingly emotional, often **subliminal**. Walk into an Abercrombie and Fitch store and you are immediately struck by the scent. It's a classic but youthful fragrance designed to capture the casual, west coast styling which is accentuated by the store interiors, typographies and clothing range. Walk along the mall to the chain's next brand Hollister, and it is an entirely different smell, look and feel. You are now in California. The brand logo is different, but many of the clothes are actually the same, though seeking to engage a different

audience with different aspirations. Walk a little further and another branded sensory experience awaits you at Gilly Hicks.

The brand experience is an immersion into the personality of the brand.

For a café or store, bank or airline, this is a great opportunity. To engage people in ways that product brands – like packaged goods or technology – can only dream of. It is also about joined up thinking. **Everything** that the customer experiences, hard and soft, real and perceived, is part of the brand. From the store design, decoration and ambience, to the lighting, sounds and smells. From the merchandise layout and shelf fittings to the staff dress and service style. From the typography on the store signs to the small print on the check-out receipt. This is all part of the brand experience.

7.5 PLATFORMS ... CREATING SPACE TO EXPLORE AND ENGAGE

A brand creates a platform for a wider range of products and services, with significant space to innovate, add new products and services, or even new business models. This might be at a total brand level, or more often through creating themes that are more like sub-brands, capturing a big idea, or bringing together a range of products.

IBM's **'Smarter Planet'** brand concept is a great example of a broad and enduring brand platform that allows the brand to build a rich story. It can be accessed in different ways by different audiences, making it relevant to many segments. It can support a diverse range of products and services, because it is not about them, but the higher purpose which they support. It inspires and accelerates ongoing innovation, creating a context in which to add new themes, and helps new ideas enter the market quickly.

Dove's **'Campaign for Real Beauty'** began in Sao Paulo, back in 2004. A forensic sketch artist draws several women, first based only on their descriptions of themselves, and then based on the descriptions of a stranger who has observed them. The women, seeing the resulting sketches side-by-side, realize that the sketches inspired by strangers are much more flattering than the versions from their own self-descriptions. 'You are more beautiful than you think.' The first two versions of these videos each got over 35 million views within two weeks of being posted to YouTube.

Led by Unilever's VP for brand development, Fernando Machado, the 'campaign' has many components. Advertisements showed real women, older or heavier than the 'ideal' but still beautiful. Passers-by were invited to vote on whether a model was 'Fat or Fab' or 'Wrinkled or Wonderful', and results were updated live. The brand seeks to engage 15 million girls by 2015. It partners with the Girl Scouts to promote self-esteem and leadership with 'Uniquely ME!' and 'It's Your Story – Tell It!' An annual Self-Esteem Weekend aims to inspire mothers to talk with daughters about beauty and confidence.

Dove is a brand that **makes life better**, connecting with deeper issues in a relevant way, challenging itself and its industry, building a movement amongst its customers with new attitudes and purpose. Insights came through extensive immersive research; an advisory panel guides the campaign in collaboration with consumers and specialist groups. One of the ads, 'Evolution', showed how much effort goes into

creating a 'model look' winning unpaid exposure estimated to be worth over $150 million. Dove has a broad platform about beauty, ranging from 'Nutrium' body washes and 'Weightless' moisturisers, through to Men+Care that has distributed across 80 countries.

Narrower brand platforms, like Vaio for Sony's range of laptop computers, again create a platform about smart and stylish hardware which comes and goes in its models and specifications. People engage with the idea of a Vaio rather than a specific product. Similarly car brands like **BMW's Mini** can have a diversity of models for different audiences, but be promoted together with a bigger idea.

Brand platforms are more strategic, more emotional, and more engaging to audiences. They create the 'air space' under which a wide range of products, services and experiences can evolve. These can be clustered and configured into personal solutions for each customer. Business models, through which the brand works with partners, and different price points and revenue models, can be flexed. And the overall experience can be adapted too.

Ultimately brands are **clusters** of many ideas and symbols, with a coherent 'big idea' theme. These ideas might be aspirations and stories, products and services, channels and pricing, affinity partners and distribution channels, business models and service styles, distinctive content and ways of participating. They form brand molecules. Indeed an alternative 'bottom up' way to develop a platform is to map out the molecule, and then find the richer theme in it. Different molecules can be shaped for different audiences, with the component elements coming and going over time.

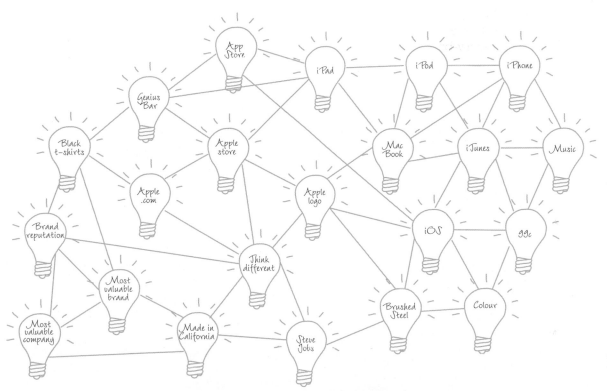

Innovative Solutions as Idea Clusters

7.6 PROPOSITIONS ... MAKING BRANDS SPECIFIC AND RELEVANT

Propositions make brands more relevant to specific audiences. They are not products, campaigns or slogans, but more focused ways of explaining the brand and its benefits to each audience. They typically capture some more rational benefits – hence, they are sometimes called **customer value** propositions (CVPs) – and competitive differences. They might be enduring, or change frequently. They might even be unique for each customer, particularly in B2B situations.

A simple example is from Nike, where the brand is more relevant to different audiences based on their sporting passions or character – Nike Running, Nike Football, Nike Golf, Nike Women. These propositions differ in the benefits and style of communication – Football is all about adrenalin, speed and success; Women is more about wellbeing, relaxation and empowerment. They become category-based sub-brands. Often the products captured within different propositions are similar, maybe with slight tweaks, or clustered into relevant solutions.

Umpqua Bank broke the mould in banking by talking about customers rather than products. They recognized that different customers have different objectives through their lives or stages of business. For personal customers, the propositions focus on 'go' (if you are just setting out),'reach' (for your dreams), 'savour' (achieving success), 'cruise' (enjoying your better years). For business cystomers, the propositions focus on 'launch' (your business), 'drive' (grow faster), 'flow' (optimize performance) and 'practice' (in a professional world). Behind these propositions are many of the normal banking products, savings and loans, credit cards and insurance, clustered in relevant ways, and augmented by some innovations for each audience.

A proposition therefore addresses the specific needs or wants of a targeted audience. It articulates the most relevant benefits to them, and how they are better. It can also consider the **benefit–price equation**, and even articulate this clearly as an ROI business case for business customers. Importantly, they start with the customer not the product, benefits not features. In that way they are more relevant and engaging, but also create new space for innovation and growth.

7.7 STRETCH ... EXTENDING BRANDS TO NEW MARKETS

A brand defined around customer aspirations rather than product functionality can stretch across categories, providing a faster, less risky way to grow your business.

Brand extensions used to follow product adjacencies, extending to categories with similar capabilities, turning product brands into range brands. Today the best brand extensions follow customer adjacencies, extending to help them achieve more, built around a coherent and relevant brand purpose.

Brand extension is a disciplined yet creative process. Caterpillar's stretch from heavy engineering to clothing and footwear was not obvious but makes sense once the core brand is recognized for its strength and durability, rather than its technical machines. Dove's extension from soaps into shower gels and shampoos worked well, but an attempted stretch into spas and clothing were steps too far.

Starbucks is a great brand story, turning great coffee into brand experience, the 'third place' between home and work. Once they'd saturated our cities, they wanted to go further, extending onto supermarket shelves and into new segments. Their Vie micro-ground coffee showed how a brand can extend with the help of an innovation, bringing a new level of performance to the adjacent category and justifying their premium gained through providing an experience. When they identified juice bars as an adjacent sector, an alternative for their health-minded customers, they had problems. Starbucks was too identified with coffee, rather than a place. Instead they created a new brand, called Evolution, seeking to create a new third place.

A **strong brand core**, built around customer aspirations is far easier to stretch into new categories than a famous but functional product brand. A brand about refreshment can easily work across drinks categories. A brand about travel can extend from airlines and hotels to travel guides and tours. Whilst it is often useful to have manufacturing capability to support an adjacent category, this can be sourced through partners and is secondary to adding to the customer's experience.

Licensing is often a more effective way to extend into non-familiar categories, relevant to the customer but not your existing expertize. **Virgin** is the ultimate licensed brand, finding partners in every sector – from airlines to space travel, banking to communications – who can deliver a Virgin brand experience effectively. This requires careful understanding of the brand equity to find a way of operating an airline, or a bank, that is true to the brand. How are Virgin phones different? What is better about its banks? It also requires a smart business model to ensure continued influence over the brand and its activation, as well as IP ownership and financial reward.

In planning brand extensions, it is essential to plan the move carefully. Whilst new categories might seem attractive, it is important to strengthen or shift the core brand concept first. Once ready to stretch, the migration needs a logical order, the right sequence of categories, and innovations to support

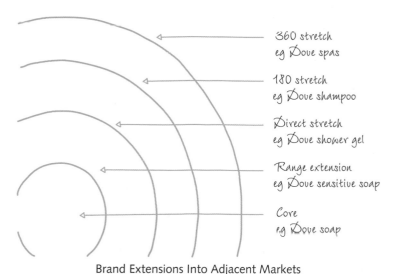

360 stretch
eg Dove spas

180 stretch
eg Dove shampoo

Direct stretch
eg Dove shower gel

Range extension
eg Dove sensitive soap

Core
eg Dove soap

Brand Extensions Into Adjacent Markets

entry into each. This is a brand and innovation **journey**, the sequence of which can ensure success or failure. Sometimes it can even mean shifting the core, as IBM effectively did, moving away from low-margin hardware into high-margin services. Whatever the strategy, it needs a structured and thoughtful execution to protect the current brand and business whilst also realizing the best new market opportunities.

7.8 PORTFOLIOS ... ARCHITECTURES AND OPTIMIZATION

As a business grows, its range of products and services become more diverse and complex. Brand portfolios need focus and brand architectures based around customers.

Different architectures emerge by design or default. **'Branded houses'** like Apple or Diesel retain a core idea, whilst a **'House of brands'**, like Nestle or P&G, contain a diverse array of product brands and sub-brands, all requiring their own support, without any overall theme. Brand architectures built around bigger ideas are more efficient to support and more effective in cross-selling and building brands that mean more.

Large companies struggle with complexity. This is mainly because they have grown through diversification and acquisition over time, adding many entities to their original theme. From a customer perspective they associate with individual brands with little understanding of the company behind them, or what more they do. In an age of transparency, people want to know where products come from. From a business perspective, the cost and complexity of building 100 product brands, is far more than say building 5 ranges or concept brands.

Some companies, like GE, seek a **'monolithic'** approach, where everything is branded under the corporate umbrella.

The difficulty with this is that the corporate brand needs to stand for something, have purpose, which is not easy with so many different technologies. Stories and propositions become important in creating relevance to different audiences. Consumer product companies like Unilever seek to enhance the **endorsement** of their corporate brand, like a seal of approval on their product brands. Others like Nestle seek to create platforms, for example around Healthy Eating, that bring together their wide range of breakfast cereals.

When seeking to **optimize a brand portfolio**, there are two distinct tasks. One is to optimize the portfolio of products – ranges, products, or variants (SKUs). The other is to optimize

the portfolio of brands – names and concepts, trademarks and designs.

When seeking to optimize a product portfolio, you will typically find the **80:20 rule** in play: 80% of the revenues will come from 20% of the products (and 90% of the profits from 10% of them). Some companies label these most important products as their 'power brands', deserving of most investment and attention. As with all types of focus, putting more effort in some areas means less in others. It is not uncommon to find that around 30% of the products are value destroying. That is, when full costs are allocated across the portfolio, a significant number of them are unprofitable, and selling more of them will just become even more unprofitable.

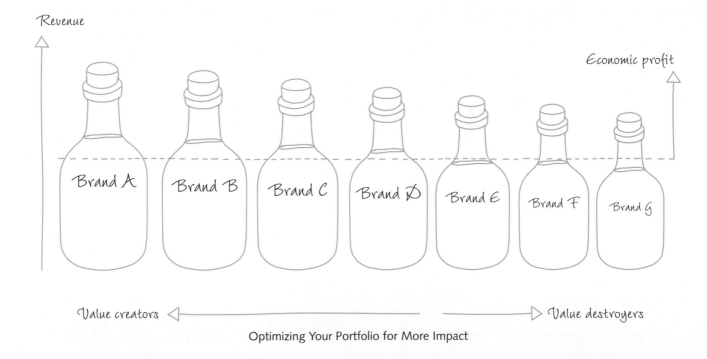

Optimizing Your Portfolio for More Impact

When drinks company **Diageo** evaluated its portfolio, it found that a number of its largest brands based on revenue actually destroyed value (they didn't deliver a sufficient return on the capital employed). One of these brands was Bailey's, requiring the business to rethink the brand from its positioning to its bottling process. They found that by refocusing the brand on a younger audience, portraying it as sophisticated cocktail with ice, and sold in miniature bottles through specialist channels, it was able to transform the image and economics of the brand.

The second challenge is the brands themselves. Consumer goods companies have huge numbers of functional brands, often with supporting ingredient brands, and usually executed differently in local markets across the world. This can create huge cost and confusion. The challenge is to find focus and coherence. Global and local branding are both good, but need to work within a system.

The biggest difference can be made by bringing together brands with a similar purpose, and for the same audience. **Volkswagen's** portfolio – from Bugatti and Audi to Seat and Skoda, is not a diversity of technologies, but a carefully planned spectrum of brands to address different audiences, each motivated differently. These technological platforms are shared across the brands and models, enabling efficiencies in design and manufacturing.

7.9 EVERYTHING ... BECOMING A BRAND COMPANY

Red Bull 'gives you wings' ... it's a brand that gives you the adrenalin to be extreme, incredible. Of course there is a functional benefit to the caffeine-maxed soft drink that is sometimes called 'liquid cocaine', but the brand is as much about emotional attitudes, demonstrated by its

connection with extreme sports, people and teams, and global events.

From the Red Bull **Air Race**, with stunt planes spectacularly flying along the Danube, to the Red Bull Flugtag, where amateur teams launch their home-made contraptions in the hope of flight, the Red Bull X-Fighters freestyle motocross and Red Bull Cliff Diving in Boston Harbour, from fun Soapbox racing to music events, to high performance F1 and soccer teams, the brand engages audiences in spectacular experiences. The brand is the event organizer and team owner, not just the sponsor; it has full control of the immersive brand experience, the enormous PR which spins out of it, and all the IP which sustains the stories further. The *Red Bulletin* magazine with 4.8 million copies sold monthly sustains the interest, as does the brand's Facebook page with 40 million followers.

It seems a long way since from 1987 when **Dietrich Mateschitz** was in Bangkok selling photocopiers. After a long flight he collapsed into the chair of a hotel bar. 'I know exactly what you need, Sir' proposed the Thai waitress. She quickly returned with a glass of *Krating Daeng* (daenq means red, krating is a guar, or very large bison). Whilst the original ingredients were said to contain bull's testicles, Mateschitz was soon energized, returning to his native Austria with a plan to modify the recipe and launch his new brand.

Of course, 'extreme' keeps going further. In October 2012 over 10 million people watched Felix Baumgartner rise 38 km above the New Mexico desert in a huge ultra-thin helium 'Red Bull Stratos' balloon, jump off, and reach 830 mph during a 9-minute fall, setting records for the height and speed of descent: 35 million have since watched the YouTube video, read news features, and watched broadcast documentaries. Despite costs of around $40 million, in one way or another over a billion people have engaged in the branded event.

In fact, Red Bull **Media House** has become a profit centre, a media company, and an interesting example of the emerging brand companies. Whilst many large brands have set up their own brand-owning companies within their corporate structures, a specialist business unit which then licenses the brand to other business units for a royalty, this was initially for tax benefits. As these diminish, the real benefit comes in building a brand beyond product, as the core business.

The **brand becomes the business**, and the business becomes the brand. It is far less reliant on external agencies for creativity, and learns to build its brand and associated properties in a far more coherent, integrated and profitable way. In a world of 'ideas and networks' business structures, brands and the ideas which they capture can become distinctive and incredibly valuable entities, and brand companies become the heart of the business.

CHANGE YOUR GAME

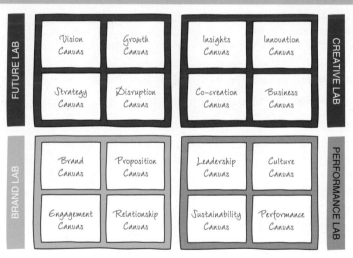

Practically apply the concepts in this chapter to your business with the relevant tools in the Gamechanger Labs:

- **Brand** canvas
- **Proposition** canvas
- **Culture** canvas

Practical examples can be found in the 100 cases studies. Also see more details at Gamechangers.pro

8 DESIGN...INNOVATING A BETTER BUSINESS MODEL
CHANGE YOUR BUSINESS

Gamechangers innovate far beyond their products, applying their creativity and design to the market and business, embracing ideas from outside and in, bottom up and top down, from simple frugality to advanced luxury.

- More **innovative**...*from product development*...*to business innovation*...They think more creatively and disruptively about every aspect of their business.

- More **designed**...*from technical invention*...*to design thinking*...They combine function and form, in everything from business model to customer experience.

- More **collaborative**...*from technical experts*...*to open diversity*...They work with customers and partners from initial ideas through to commercial impact.

8.1 INNOVATION ... MAKING THE WORLD A BETTER PLACE

Do you remember music **before Apple**? As a youth, I sat surrounded by vinyl. As an adult, piles of CDs littered my home, and when I tried to download my first MP3 file, I pulled my hair out until I looked like Steve Jobs. **My first iPod** arrived with clickwheel in translucent white. It looked beautiful, felt good, but didn't do much. But then iTunes arrived. And the industry was **transformed**. And my home, and my music, too.

Innovation, turning ideas into practical applications, is all around us. Whilst most product innovation is incremental and quickly imitated, it is the innovation of **business models** and **customer experiences** that transform businesses, industries and markets.

Whilst new **business models** stand out as the gamechanger's innovation of choice – addressing new audiences and partners, leasing and licensing, sales to subscriptions – they also focus on transforming the customer experience. Gamechangers are natural **collaborators** – connecting customers, partners and social networks with issues like sustainability and new market entry, finding better solutions out of creative **fusions**.

Whilst innovation is so often called the lifeblood of organizations – the top priority when talking to investors, the rallying call of leaders – inside the vast majority of organizations it goes little beyond the brainstorm. What amazed me as I visited many companies was the lack of disciplined innovation strategy, process and coordination. Too often it is still seen as focused only on products, a subordinate activity of marketing, a 'nice to have'. People are confused between **creativity**, and **design**, and **innovation**.

What surprised me even more is the speed of change in the outside world. Whilst Coke is tinkering with its flavours, Microsoft preparing for its next release, and even Apple preferring evolution to revolution, the world is moving ever faster.

Small companies understand the scale and direction of the changing world better than large companies, particularly in the emerging markets of Asia and South America where networks and technologies enable the tiniest businesses, with the brightest brains, to out-think and out-manoeuvre the lumbering supertankers of the last century who are caught between old and new markets, legacy capabilities and future opportunities.

But perhaps the biggest surprise was how much business can learn from other areas.

Lady Gaga might seem a youthful irrelevance to many business leaders – but consider how she came from nowhere to global dominance in 24 months. On the very week that Lehman Brothers crashed amidst financial crisis, Stefani Gremanotta, and her mentor Akon, were launching *The Fame Monster*. Bold and provocative, maybe even mind bending, she harnessed the world of social media and digital downloads to make herself a global superstar. What could your business learn from her?

Add many others to this. What could you learn from **Damien Hirst** about contextual pricing? How can you resolve a paradox like rocket man **Burt Rutan**? And when science says no, like it did to Zaha Hadid when designing the London 2012 Aquatics Centre, how can you overcome the challenge? What is the secret of fusion according to **Sir Paul Smith**? And when it comes to social impact, look east to the fabulous business model of Aravind Eye Care, or west to the social renaissance inspired by the Guggenheim.

These are just some of the more inspiring stories I came across.

8.2 CREATE ... DIVERGE AND BE DEVIANT

Creativity moves us forwards. Not always in a linear or incremental way, more often in disruptive and more dramatic moves. It challenges the status quo, assumptions and conventions. Most importantly it opens up new avenues of thinking, which we would miss in our haste to improve and optimize what is currently in focus.

Most simply, **creativity** is about making new **connections**.

Seeing things everyone has seen, but thinking what nobody else has thought. Maybe spotting a great idea in one market and applying it to another, or an unusual behaviour by the

most radical customers in your market, and bringing it to the mainstream. It might be about combining two existing ideas to create something better, or to resolve a paradox where you bring two seemingly contradicting ideas together. Creative fusions.

In neuroscience, creativity requires activating parts of the brain which don't normally connect. In the simplest form we think of **left-brain** (logical) and **right-brain** (intuitive) thinking, where creativity emerges out of using them together. Of course, it's more complex than that, with the frontal lobe most important for generating ideas, which are then edited and evaluated by the temporal lobes.

Creativity is about divergent thinking, **opening up**, exploring possibilities.

This requires new stimulus, stepping outside our normal frame of observation and experience, maybe by learning from new places, extremes and deviants. It is about being constantly curious, learning and open-minded. It is about suspending judgement, so that logic doesn't process newness as normality, filtering out the new insights and more radical ideas. It is also why the subconscious can be effective, fuelled by sleep, meditation or artificial stimulus. I have my best ideas when out running!

For business, this stretch and stimulus most effectively comes through collaboration. Engaging the minds of external people, specialists or crowds, and most importantly customers. This is about exploring ideas, digging deeper, being divergent. It is not about pre-judging by setting closed questions, or multiple-choice answers. This gives quantified averages, but little insight. Observation and immersion are ways to learn more. Listening to the small details, the language and emotion, and asking 'why?'

Whilst creativity is about divergence, innovation also requires convergence.

Creativity takes us to a better place from which to innovate. It explores more possibilities, whilst also engaging and energizing people. We see a **bigger picture**, from which to make more sense of complexity, to see cause and effects, sequence and systems, more opportunities and ideas to fuse into richer concepts.

Innovation makes creativity happen effectively. However it is not just about products but about any or every aspect of business. In fact it's not really about business, it's about customers and making life better.

8.3 DESIGN … ENGAGE WITH FUNCTION AND FORM

From coffee pots to high-heeled boots, digital user interfaces to soaring skyscrapers, wallpaper to newspaper, design is all around us. Fashion designs, graphic designs, grand designs. As James Dyson said in Ford's customer magazine 'good design is about looking at everyday things with new eyes and working out how they can be made better. It is about challenging existing technology'.

Design is the planning that lays the basis for the making of every object or system. It can be used both as a noun and a verb – a plan, a style, an object, a process. As a verb, 'to design' refers to the process of originating and developing a plan for a product, structure, system or component. As a noun, 'a design' is used for either the final solution (proposal, drawing, model, description) or the result of implementing that plan, the final product of a design process. It is about **function and form**, rational and emotional, process and solution.

Designing requires a designer to consider the aesthetic, functional and many other aspects of an object or a process, which usually requires considerable research, thought, modelling, adjustment and re-design.

Tim Brown, CEO of the world's leading design firm IDEO promotes the concept of **'design thinking'** as an essential discipline for anyone in business.

He reminds us that design, like Thomas Edison always said, is primarily about hard work – 1% inspiration, 99% perspiration. More significantly he sees design thinking as a process applicable to every aspect of business. Whilst innovation is recognized as essential to differentiation and growth, it is design that adds the real difference, adding **simplicity** and **elegance**, stimulating all the senses.

Historically, design has been treated as a downstream step in the innovation process, argues Brown, the point where designers come along and put a beautiful wrapper around the idea. Whilst this approach has stimulated market growth in many areas by making new products aesthetically attractive, design is much more than the cosmetic finish.

Looking back over recent decades, design has become an increasingly valuable competitive asset in, for example, the consumer electronics (remember those first iMacs), automotive (the iconic styling of a Porsche 911), and consumer packaged goods industries (everything from Nike Air to Tetra-Pak's drink cartons). But in most others it has remained a late-stage add-on.

Now, however, Brown believes that rather than asking designers to make an already developed idea more attractive to consumers, companies are asking them to create ideas that better meet consumers' needs and desires. The former role is tactical, and results in limited value creation; the latter is strategic, and leads to dramatic new forms of value.

Design is a deliberate, structured, thoughtful discipline, most commonly referred to as a process. As the understanding of design has evolved, so too has its scope – from products to services and experiences, and from cosmetic styling to a holistic business concept:

- 'Style' design – shapes, colours, graphics.

- 'Product' design – also includes research, engineering, industrial design.

- 'Experience' design – also includes marketing, communication, service, people.

- 'Business' design – also includes business model, organization structure, operations.

'Design thinking' has become a new business mantra, led by Tim Brown. At a TED event, he described design thinking as 'a **human-centred approach to problem solving**. It is a process built from people (inspiration gained from looking and listening to them), prototyping (making ideas tangible as soon as possible), and stories (getting things implemented by selling compelling narratives not concepts)'.

Design thinking typically has four components:

- **Customer-centricity** – understanding what customers, or consumers, really want, which is often not what they say they want, through immersion and ethnographic techniques.

- **Team experimentation** – exploring different possibilities and solutions, opening up before closing down, and then focusing on a smaller number of hot prospects.

- **Rapid prototyping** – rather than talking about it, just try building it, thereby enabling more discussion, understanding, enhancement and engagement.

- **Emotional appeal** – engaging people in the potential applications of the design through storytelling rather than glib product specifications or advertising slogans.

Jonathan Ive never made much of an impression when he worked on wash basin designs for Tangerine in London. He had design ideas that no one understood. Then he moved to California, and began work at Apple, and there he found the people who understood his passion for **'humanizing technology'**.

Ive, who after Steve Jobs, was most responsible for Apple's amazing ability to dazzle us with iPods, iPhones and iPads, believes in 'the craft of design'.

He likes to understand his challenge deeply – the user, application, materials and tools. And he cares deeply about what he creates. He combines what he describes as 'fanatical care beyond the obvious stuff' with relentless experiments into tools, materials and production processes. 'With technology, the function is much more abstract to users,' says Ive comparing Apple's challenge to what he sees in other sectors 'so the product's meaning is almost entirely defined by the designer'.

8.4 BREAKTHROUGHS ... CREATING TODAY AND TOMORROW

Innovation can therefore be defined in terms of intensity and scope.

The intensity of innovation relates to how ambitious it is – how much time and resource, cost and risk it embraces – and how great an impact we seek in the market and bottom line as a result. There are three levels of innovation intensity:

- *Incremental:* innovation as improvement, keeping pace with change and expectation, adapting designs and applications to evolving needs. In the car market we see a new version of the same car emerging frequently, maybe with slightly enhanced features.
- *Next generation:* innovation as change, moving ahead of the competition to define a new level of performance, tapping into emerging needs and exceeding expectations. In the car market, this is a significantly new model, launched every few years, with a new brand name.
- *Breakthrough:* innovation as revolution, changing the rules of the market, challenging the behaviours of customers, maybe redefining the market altogether – 'game-changing'. In the car market, this is the SUV or the hybrid engine, creating a new genre, a new category.

You need **all** of these innovations – a **balanced portfolio** of innovation projects at each level being developed simultaneously. Incremental innovations keep you in the market, little noticed and quickly imitated. Next generations get you ahead for a short time, maybe opening up a new revenue stream. Breakthroughs are what make you famous, shaping your markets. They inspire customers, attract investors, and deliver leaps in value creation.

Whilst game-changing innovations are **'breakthrough'** in nature, taking more time and effort as well as cost and risk, they need not be. Smart thinking can sometimes be fast and cheap. Telling a different story, reaching an alternative audience, revolutionizing the cosmetic appearance of products, can all break the rules and find new space, but be relatively cheap and fast to implement.

8.5 INTEGRATE ... INNOVATING EVERY ASPECT OF BUSINESS

Business innovation emerges out of two streams of thinking. Jay Doblin identified that there were many sources, beyond product, of innovation across the business. Alex Osterwalder and others have explored how their connectedness can be innovated, to innovate the business model.

Together we now recognize that business model innovation has the following components:

- **Purpose innovation**: Why does the business exist? Capturing the strategic direction of the business, and how it seeks to make the world better. **Virgin** innovates by being on the customer's side; Nike innovates by rising above footwear to wellbeing.
- **Market innovation**: Which market are we in? Defining the space in which you seek to compete, either within established categories, or a new domain. **23andMe** innovates wellbeing into personal futures. Renova innovates by focusing on bathrooms, not toilet paper.
- **Brand innovation**: How to articulate the big idea? Capturing the purpose in a way relevant to customers, through words and images, distinctive and iconic. **LA Organic** innovates by redefining Spanish olive oil. Red Bull innovates its brand through big gestures.
- **Customer innovation**: Who does the business seek to engage? Defining the customers or segments, physically or attitudinally, which are most important to the business. Alior Sync innovates by clearly stating it is a bank for Gen Y, Rapha innovates by targeting premium cycling enthusiasts.
- **Proposition innovation**: What is the distinctive offer? Articulating the unique benefits, most relevant to the

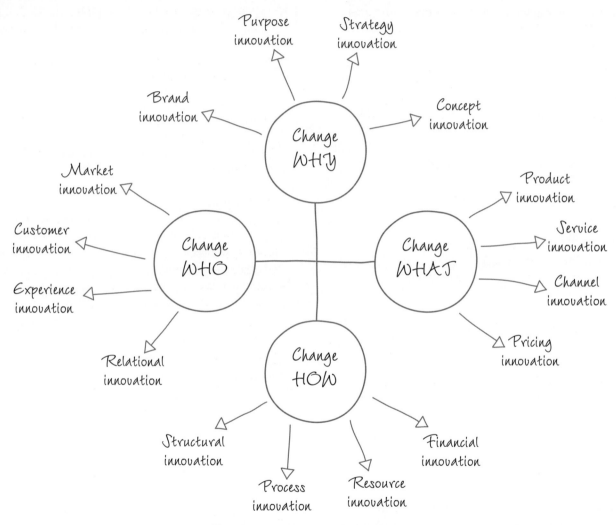

Purpose innovation

Strategy innovation

Brand innovation

Concept innovation

Change WHY

Product innovation

Market innovation

Service innovation

Customer innovation

Change WHO

Change WHAT

Channel innovation

Experience innovation

Pricing innovation

Relational innovation

Change HOW

Structural innovation

Financial innovation

Process innovation

Resource innovation

More Ways to Innovate Your Business

target customers, at what price level. **Ashmei** innovates by saying it is expensive and better. IBM innovates to explore technology in the context of a smarter planet.

- **Product innovation**: What is the solution for the customer? Defining the product or service and supporting system. Airbnb innovates by creating a global room-sharing service. **Tesla** innovates by creating high performance, premium styled, electric cars.

- **Experience innovation**: How does the customer engage? Designing the customer's interaction, from initial purchase to enabling them to use it better. **Umpqua** innovates on bank environment, Yeni Raki innovates on the ambient culture of drinking.

- **Channel innovation**: Where does the customer interact? Developing effective distribution and interaction, physical and/or digital. **Lululemon** innovates with stores as fitness studios, Safaricom turns its phone network into financial and healthcare services.

- **Service innovation**: How do you support the customer? This is about the level and style of service, not just around the purchase transaction, but throughout their experience. Kulala innovates by making the service human and fun, Square by making payments fast and simple.

- **Organization innovation**: How do your people work together? This is about structure, but also culture and what creates most value, such as IP or speed. **Pixar** innovates culturally around empowered creativity, IDEO innovates by how it helps others achieve more.

- **Process innovation**: How does the business work operationally? Lean and local, automated or on demand, from supply to delivery, process delivers the proposition. Zara innovates through incredible speed, **Kickstarter** through crowd-funded innovation and sales.

- **Resource innovation**: What resources are required to achieve this? From initial ideas, to raw materials and complementary products. Juan Valdez innovates by branding and serving its own coffee. **Threadless**, by co-creating the coolest t-shirts with a community of fans.

- **Partner innovation**: How do you work with partners? The network to make or deliver can be vast, open or outsourced, alliances and licenses. **Renault** and Nissan innovate through a cross-shareholder alliance, ARM innovate with a virtual model, licensed to device partners.

- **Financial innovation**: How do we make money? Combining the cost model (suppliers, risks, debt) with the revenue model (price, payment model and revenue streams). Together they drive profit, and long-term value creation. Azuri innovated solar panels with pay as you go, **Zipcars** innovate car rental with subscriptions.

- **Impact innovation**: What is the result long term? This about value creation for customers and investors, but also about the wider impact on society. It is about reducing negative impact through circular models, and making a positive difference. **Natura** innovates by using entirely natural ingredients, Toms innovates through a dual product giving model.

8.6 BUSINESS MODELS ... HOW THE BUSINESS WORKS

The term 'Business Model' is over used and under defined. Business models explain how organizations work – how they create value for customers, and in doing so how they create value for all other stakeholders. They can map the current business, or explore options for the future.

The approach originates from mapping 'value networks' in the 1990s, understanding the systems across business and its partners through which value (both financial and non-financial) is created and exchanged – by who, how and for whom. I remember working with Pugh Roberts to create a multi-million dollar dynamic model for Mastercard which showed how varying any one driver – such as interest rates or branding – affected everything else. And thereby being able to test new ideas and optimize the model.

Business models represent the **dynamic system** through which a business **creates and captures value**, and how this can changed or optimized.

Henry Chesbrough described business models in his book *Open Innovation* as the way in which a business applies a technical innovation in order to perform better – which market, what proposition, how it works and makes money, and why it's different. When working for British Airways and launching a low-cost carrier called Go, I remember the need to think differently about the audience, what would motivate them, and the entirely different infrastructure required to make it possible and profitable at such low prices. The business model was the real innovation.

Business models are a configuration of the **building blocks** of business, and their creative reconfiguration can be a significant innovation.

Business models became fundamental to business strategy. The strategy drives the model, although the model itself can shape the strategy. Hambrick and Fredrickson's Strategy Diamond is all about aligning the organization, achieving an economic logic between strategic choices. Working in complex organizations like Amex or Microsoft, it is amazing how often there is little 'connected thinking' between choice of customers and products to develop. They lack alignment across departments and strategically.

Business models help to **align** the business, matching the right strategies for outside and inside, using the proposition as the fulcrum, and profitability as the measure of success.

Business models can often appear very mechanical, lacking emotion and easy to imitate. In 2001 Patrick Staehler, in particular seeking to explain the new breed of digital businesses, created a business model 'map' driven by the value proposition and enabled by the value architecture, creating economic value and sustained by cultural values. The last point here is most interesting, in that it captured the distinctive personality of a business, its leadership styles and ways of doing business. This is much harder to copy, and also sustains the other aspects.

Business models are sustained through a culture that brings the logic to life, and sustains it by giving it meaning and personality.

Alex Osterwalder's subsequent **Business Model Canvas** emerged as the most common template on which to map a business model. He popularized the approach so much so that his supersized canvas now features in workshops throughout the world, always with an array of multi-coloured sticky notes as teams debate the best combination of solutions for each box. Whilst the canvas lacks the sophistication of value driver analysis and dynamic modelling, it is about testing hypotheses in each aspect, and how they could work together, and in that respect works as a thinking model.

Business models have become a practical tool for rethinking the whole business, seeing the connections and then innovating the business.

Maker models	Channel models	Crowd models	Payment models	Exchange models	Asset models
Make and distribute business model eg CocaCola Microsoft	**Spectrum retail** business model eg Amazon Marks & Spencer	**Membership club** business model eg Costco, Quintessentially	**Subscription payment** business model eg FT.com, Graze	**Buyer and seller marketplace** business model eg Etsy, NYSE	**Advertising or Sponsorship** business model eg Google, Metro Newspapers
Make and sell direct business model eg BMW, HSBC	**Niche retail** business model eg ToysRUs, Wiggle	**Crowdfunded ventures** business model eg Kickstarter, Zidisha	**Regular Replacement** business model eg Gillette, Nespresso	**Collaborative consumption** business model eg Buzzcar, Regus	**Listed or Promoted** business model eg Monster Linkedin
License to make business model eg ARM, Ed Hardy	**Curated retail** business model eg Fab, Positive Luxury	**Opensourced community** business model eg RedHat, MySQL	**Shared rental** business model eg Zilok, Hilton	**Branded Consortia** business model eg Cisco, Spar	**Network builders** business model eg Hotmail, Twitter
Demand then Made business model eg ZaoZao, Threadless	**Auction retail** business model eg eBay, Sotheby	**Multilevel marketing** business model eg Tupperware, Natura	**Freemium pay within** business model eg Angry Bird, Coursera	**Tradeable currency** business model eg Bitcoin Air Miles	**Reputation builders** business model eg Tripadvisor, PaywithaTweet
Knowledge and time business model eg McKinsey, Harvard	**Franchised retail** business model eg McDonalds, Subway	**Group buying** business model eg Groupon, Huddlebuy	**Pay as you go** business model eg AzuriTech Techshop	**Transaction facilitator** business model eg Paypal, Visa	**Customer data** business model eg Facebook, 23andMe
Certification and endorsement business model eg ISO, Verisign	**Remainder retail** business model Eg Saks, Vente Privee	**Reverse auction** business model eg Priceline Freemarkets	**Micro payments** business model eg Flattr Grameen Danone	**Dynamic pricing** business model eg Expedia, Uber	**Non-profit business** business model eg Oxfam Wikipedia

36 Types of Business Model

8.7 SIMPLER...THE ULTIMATE SOPHISTICATION

Steve Jobs loved Japan, everything from soba noodles to Sony's iconic designs. This inspired in him a zen-like ability to focus and simplify by zeroing in on their essence and eliminating everything else. 'Simplicity is **the ultimate sophistication**', he declared in Apple's first marketing brochure.

He first appreciated simplicity when working the night shift at Atari as a college dropout. Atari's games had no manual. The early arcade versions stated: 'Insert quarter. Avoid Klingons.' He was also inspired by Bauhaus architecture, which emphasized clean lines and functional design devoid of frills or distractions. So much so that having bought his first home, he refused to clutter it with furniture.

To some people there might seem to be a **paradox** – how to find simple and easy, whilst also embracing that latest complex technologies and functions. Jobs sought simplicity that conquers, rather than just ignores, complexity. He wanted to engage people in more human ways, to inspire not challenge them. 'If you can get your thinking. Simplicity can move mountains' he said.

Siegel and Gale publish a **simplicity index** that ranks brand and the impact of simplicity. 'In a world crowded with complexity, simplicity stands out. It brings clarity instead of confusion, and decision instead of doubt'. By exploring the benefit to simple brands like **Aldi**, Google and McDonalds, the index finds that people are more likely to recommend simple brands, and to pay around 4–7% more for them.

In *The Laws of Simplicity*, John Maeda, a graphic designer from MIT's Media Lab, offers ten principles for balancing simplicity and complexity in business, technology and design. He challenges our temptation to improve something by adding to it – to reduce rather than add. Better organized and faster, education and relevant context, emotional and trusted. These are all sources of simplicity, although he warns that reduction is not always possible. At the end he summarizes: 'Simplicity is about subtracting the obvious, and adding the **meaningful.**'

8.8 CHEAPER ... FRUGAL THINKING TO FIND YOUR 'JUGAARD'

In Hindi, the words 'Gandhian' or 'Jugaad' mean a **stop-gap** solution. Across India, and many other developing markets, people improvize with what they have, to make their cars work, to improve technologies, to imitate an unaffordable solution. Out of these temporary fixes can emerge simpler, cheaper innovation.

Frugal innovation is about reducing the complexity and cost of a product and its production. Removing the non-essential features might also improve its durability, and the ability to produce and maintain it locally. It often involves alternative channels, low margins but high volumes.

Unilever were one of the first to recognize frugal opportunities, creating single use sized toiletries in developing markets, thereby making them accessible to many more people. Renault Nissan CEO, Carols Ghosn, is a big fan of frugal, particularly in the sense of using less to achieve more. He acquired the tired but simple brand **Dacia** from Romania, to create cheap but reliable cars, targeting a lower income but huge potential market, backed by the investment and expertize of a leading global manufacturer.

Examples of frugal innovation include GE's portable cardiograph machines that cost only $800, and **ChotuKool** fridges made by Godrej, that use a small computer fan rather than a conventional compressor, opening up huge new markets for its chilled foods. In South Africa, SAB Miller and Diageo got together to make low-priced **Sorghum beer** out of cassava rather than malting barley, then sold in kegs not bottles. The **'Jaipur leg'** costs about $150 to make, using an adapted irrigation pipe. Safaricom's **M-Pesa** brought banking to much of Africa, using simple SMS messaging, whilst the Nokia 1100 is the world's bestselling phone, sold to over 200 million people, providing basic voice and text services, plus a torch feature.

These innovations succeed in developing markets, but can often provide a new source of innovation for developed markets too. This **'reverse' innovation**, also sometimes called a 'trickling up' stream of simple ideas, can often provide the basis of minimalist ideas which we then see on the shelves of IKEA or Tchibo. Equally Western innovators, seeking to solve developing market problems, have found more demand close to home – like the Freeplay wind-up radio, or One Laptop Per Child's XO tablet, originally designed as an educational charity item but now selling for $99 in Wal-Mart.

8.9 TOGETHER ... COLLABORATIVE, BETTER AND FASTER

Whilst some companies have hi-jacked the 'co-creation' word to redefine customer research techniques, such as focus groups and immersion, others recognize that it is a bigger approach, engaging customers as partners in a journey from ideas to implementation.

- **Co-thinking**. Working with customers to understand their needs and wants, but also to develop new ideas and possibilities, using collaborative creativity techniques.

This is similar to 'crowd-sourcing', but more personal. P&G take consumers away to hotels for weekends, or go to their kitchens, to explore better ways to do washing or cleaning.

- **Co-funding**. Once people are engaged in the initial idea, they become fans who want you to succeed, and want to be part of the journey. Kickstarter and other crowd-funding platforms allow thousands of people to be part of making an idea happen, either as a way of securing a first edition, maybe something even more unique for larger fees, or through investment that shares in the rewards.

- **Co-designing**. Problem-solving together, by better defining the issues and potential solutions, may be encouraging people to submit new designs both in terms of the business and the style of products, in the way Threadless rewards the best submitted t-shirt designs or Jones Soda prints your photos on their bottle labels.

- **Co-evaluating**. Testing ideas with customers, building advance customer networks, getting their feedback for improvement whilst also turning them into lead-user ambassadors. This might involve extreme users, for example Nike working with elite athletes to evaluate new shoe designs, or Gore working on new fabrics with emergency services.

- **Co-developing**. Customers can be as skilled and fanatical as your own technicians in being able to develop better products or specify better services. The Boeing 787 Dreamliner was developed in partnership with customers, Nike ID design studio is at the heart of Niketown, and IKEA 'allow' you to find your products in the warehouse, and build them yourself.

- **Co-communicating**. Customers can be your best, and most trusted, advocates. They might write reviews on your website or on other directory sites, such as hotel customers on Tripadvisor. They might even develop user-generated advertising for you, like those made possible with Scrmblr, and demonstrated by Converse's social ad campaigns.

- **Co-selling**. People are much more likely to buy from friends and others like them rather than some anonymous salesman. 'Customer get customer' in return for a case of wine or iPod is familiar to us all, as is the pyramid selling model championed by Avon and Oriflame, which has even turned some of their most active customers into millionaires.

- **Co-supporting**. When something goes wrong, particularly when trying to use technological devices, you need help and fast. User guides are gobbledegook, so you get online

and ask other users for help. Apple have utilized user communities to great effect, ensuring that you get an answer to your question in minutes and in a language you actually understand.

Together we can achieve more. The **wisdom of crowds** beats the lone genius, whilst also providing the momentum, in the form of confidence and stimulus, to make ideas happen. Engaged customers become more, they are fans and partners, wanting you to win and willing to contribute more. They become your storytellers, your salespeople and your support team. The result, more often than not, is a better solution, cheaper and perceived to be worth more, that develops faster and reaches further.

CHANGE YOUR GAME

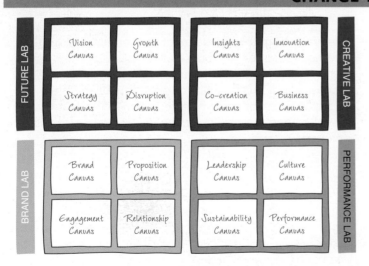

Practically apply the concepts in this chapter to your business with the relevant tools in the Gamechanger Labs:

- **Innovation** canvas
- **Co-creaton** canvas
- **Business** canvas

Practical examples can be found in the 100 cases studies. Also see more details at Gamechangers.pro

9 RESONATE...TUNING INTO THE CUSTOMER'S WORLD

CHANGE YOUR STORY

Gamechangers are more in tune with their target customers, with what matters to them at the moments that matter. They 'resonate' with their aspirations and priorities, through pull not push, in context and on demand.

- More **contextual** ... *from anytime, anywhere* ... *to right time, right place* ... They connect with people when and where it matters, putting ideas in context.

- More **relevant** ... *from timeless and passive* ... *to topical and personal* ... They connect with the zeitgeist, the customer's agenda, anticipating and reacting.

- More **contagious** ... *from passive awareness* ... *to ideas worth spreading* ... They recognize that people trust people, through storytelling and advocacy.

9.1 RESONANCE ... IN SYNC WITH YOUR AUDIENCE

Rockstars know that there is a fine line between success and failure. There isn't a set formula to be cool, for why one record will be a global **mega-hit** and another won't feature, or for what it takes to be worshiped by millions of teenagers across the globe.

Sometimes things just work. They hit on a sweet spot, they find a vibe. They **resonate**.

I first explored resonance in a physics lab; when two electromagnetic waves get '**in sync**' they start vibrating much more than normal – sonic boom, flash of light. The analogy is not scientific, it is about finding that point where, despite crowds and noise, brands and individuals are 'in sync' ... they resonate.

When I push my daughters on their swing, it seems hard work at first, but then the swing builds momentum until it finds a 'natural resonance', a frequency at which the swing moves further and easier than at any other.

Most brands find this hard to do, to find a **natural resonance**, to be in tune with their customer's worlds.

Too many brands are obsessed about themselves. They are driven by their own goals and priorities, launching a campaign to sell everyone the product they want to sell at a time when they want to. They target the TV shows we most love, interrupting them to sell us something which we are not in the mood for buying. They incentivize us with coupons and loyalty points to buy more of what we don't need.

Finding the right frequency of brand communication, proposition or narrative that '**resonates**' with your audience therefore becomes essential.

Rapha is a brand that understands resonance. The premium cycling clothing company shares a passion for the rituals of the Sunday morning cycle, as seen all across France for centuries. The name comes the aperitif drink, St Raphael, the equipment design echoes the eccentricities of Tour de France heroes like Eddy Merck. At the core of the brand experience is the brand's own bike shops, where the lycra-clad enthusiasts can be found discussing aluminium frames and road gradients. Rapha shops are primarily a meeting place, a coffee shop with the best espresso around, building community and sharing ritual passions. Resonating.

9.2 IN CONTEXT ... IT'S ABOUT MY WORLD, NOT YOURS

Finding resonance means starting from where the customer is. There are two times when I love to listen to music – when driving my car or working out in the gym. In these moments

I love to turn on a great tune, turn up the volume and be immersed. If you want to sell me a great track of music, or a better listening experience, these are the moments when it is relevant. Car dealers or filling stations, fitness clubs and sports shops would be the perfect places to sell me music. Not in a music store, even an online one.

'In context' is about time and place, enabling through associations with the related activities that the customer does.

For decades we have moaned about banks, stores and phone lines being open when we are busy, and closed when we have time. Slowly, forced by a new breed of challengers, we can do ever more when and how we want – the 24/7 call centre of the shopping mall. Store formats have changed in shape and location. Mini supermarkets on street corners or at rail stations offer premium convenience, compared to the drive out of town.

The mobile phone will eventually be more disruptive in marketing and retailing than the web has ever been because of 'solomo' – **social, local and mobile** – the ability to engage the potential customer at the points of decision making, influenced by others like them. As payments migrate from plastic to devices, offers will move from shelves to screens, harnessing the mountains of 'big data' to target and personalize each incentive.

9.3 IN TIME ... REAL-TIME, FAST AND TOPICAL

'Real-time' marketing is built around engaging customers in a way that is fast and topical, **relevant** and personal.

Whilst the old communication was about long-planned ad campaigns that pushed the brand's own messages at people, when, where and how it was convenient for the brand, real-time marketing is the **opposite**.

Real-time works across media. Whilst tweets, webpages and emails can be sent in minutes, it might equally be about news stories for TV and press, posters and videos, even TV ads turned around in hours. It is also about being more real. Real people writing **real** tweets and blogs that are more natural, location-based information and incentives to engage people in context. And images too. No more stock photos, grinning salesmen, or photo-shopped portraits.

Real-time marketing requires marketing teams to act more like a newsroom, for example creating a **real-time creative studio** in the office. It is about working across all media, to track what is happening in the world, and particularly the world of target customers, and then to connect with it in relevant ways. This might be about monitoring industry news, or twitter feeds, or major events.

The role of agencies changes too, more about providing a store of assets to be used as required. It is about having prepared message frameworks, useful assets than can be used as required, the mental agility to think fast and creatively, and empowerment to make it happen. It then needs fast and empowered decision processes, avoiding requirements to check with bosses or legal departments, having established play-books of likely situations and responses.

Symantec employees must ask themselves three questions before pushing 'send' on their real-time content:

- Am I creating unneeded risk to the brand?
- Could this impact the company or myself negatively?
- Would I want my grandmother to read this?

9.4 ON DEMAND ... WHEN, WHERE AND HOW I WANT IT

Gamechangers market with **focus and agility**. Gone are the days of product push, of interuptive communication. 'Live' marketing connects with customers **in their worlds**. They partner with other brands that are already in context. They use the tools that work best in this situation, be it search optimization, instore promos, or social media. They develop **propositions** on topics, in a language and in style that is **fresh and relevant.** They're on the customers' side, working on their terms. They know customers don't really trust brands, they trust each other. So they know the best marketing is not done by them. It's word of mouth, **customer to customer** ... and it's free!

As the nature of content moves from words to images, predictive and personal, customers will resonate with marketing that goes to the next level. They will demand:

- **Me: Specific, relevant, and personal** ... Harnessing data and context to create a customized proposition and experience that learns from previous interactions, anticipates and responds to me as an individual. Walk into a Burberry store and I see myself simulated on-screen in the latest fashions, the Starbucks barista knows my name, PizzaHut puts my photo on the box.

- **Now: Instant, anywhere, anytime** ... I expect a response in seconds, delivery within a day, to be available whenever I want it. Why queue at a cash machine when I can transfer money with a phone app in seconds? If Amazon can predict and ship my order before I even order, why should I have to wait elsewhere? Not only my expectation, but my tolerance levels are minute.

- **Easy: Fast, convenient, intuitive** ... Why don't you send me a text alert when a new product comes out, rather than waiting for me to find it? Thirty days to approve my application, why don't you trust me and check later? The product with the 30-page user guide, the insurance policy with the 50 self-serving clauses ... Try opening a new Apple product, just click and play.

- **More: Enabling me to achieve more with it** ... Don't just sell me a product, or deliver your service, connect it with whatever else I need to solve my problem or to do things I couldn't before. Commonwealth Bank of Australia's app enables you to photograph a house to buy, and immediately find the details from the agent and get pre-approval for a mortgage from the bank.

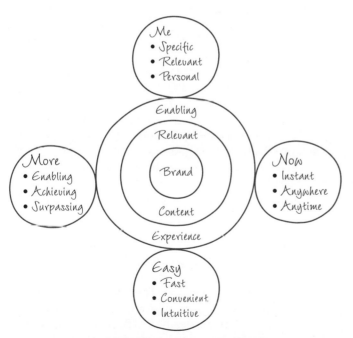

Four Dimensions of Real-time Marketing

9.5 MOMENT OF TRUTH ... THE FOUR 'RESONANCE POINTS'

In 2012, Google published a great little e-book that explored how digital customers made decisions in what they call 'The Zero Moment of Truth'. This is the ultimate moment of decision, typically as the result of a Google search, when the customer goes one way or another. When brand perceptions and loyalties are put to the test. This is partly true, and an important moment, but in a multi-channel, multi-interaction experience, there are other big moments too.

Moments of truth were first described by SAS Airline's CEO, Jan Carlson, to mean the points in a customer experience where people make choices about you: yes or no, love or hate. So whether it is Google's click path, or the physical experience, the challenge is about finding the most important moments which can then be targeted and influenced.

The reality is that there are four significant **'resonance points'** that matter most:

1. **Search**: What do you find first, the context and clarity of engagement.
2. **Choose**: How you perceive it, and then the purchase choice you make.
3. **Use**: What it's like to use, having bought it how good is it?
4. **Share**: How you tell others about it, would you buy it again, and recommend it?

With increasing importance, these are the moments where marketing investments have most return, and where revenues and costs can both be allocated. The 4th moment is somebody else's 1st moment, or if it works well, for more than just one more person.

The connections with customers become quite prolific – digital and physical, before and beyond, direct and indirect. The marketing challenge is to make that complexity a positive experience for customers and best influence the moments of truth.

Every business is multi-channel, and every channel is interactive. Forget the old mental model of parallel pipes pushing products in every direction. Instead it's the way they work together that makes the real difference – ordering online and collecting from the store, buying from a third party retailer then getting direct support by phone, joining them to co-create new products or to just be part of the brand.

9.6 CREATING CONTENT ... THAT IS 'LIQUID AND LINKED'

For more than 100 years, Coca-Cola has been a leader in 'storytelling.' From kids of every background 'teaching the world to sing', to a cheery Santa Claus wishing us 'Happy Holidays'. Trouble is, it was one way: an advertisement.

But now Coke has realized that 30-second TV slots just don't work anymore. They don't engage people. They don't interact with people. And they don't move the story on. Instead they have embraced content marketing as a much bigger discipline than advertising, or even communication, and the means by which they will double consumption of Coke by 2020. There are three pillars to Coke's new approach:

1. **'Liquid and linked' content** – instead of a thousand stories, created by multiple agencies in different formats, it is about giving content shape – being part of a bigger idea that morphs and moves forward, telling a story that keeps evolving. There's a balance to find between Liquid (provokes conversations) and Linked (relevant to the brand),

allowing and enabling the content to diffuse and evolve on its own. Whilst some of this is empowering consumers to shape and extend the content, 'viral' content only works for consumers if it has an edge to it, provocative and interesting, and for the business if it is strong enough to connect back to the underlying themes, strategy and goals.

2. **The 70/20/10 content plan** – 70% of the budget is spent on content that is expected, uncontroversial and low risk. It is easy and takes relatively less time to create. However 20% goes on content that is more innovative, it dives deeper and takes new paths, like a special report or video, requiring more effort and risk but typically resonating more with the people that matter. Then there is 10% on high-risk content, new ideas that might change the world – or the brand – or might fail. This is the stuff that moves the brand forward, excites the people who create it, and becomes the 70% of the future.

3. **Content excellence** – This is about being the ruthless editor, ensuring the result is not just confusion or noise, and that the content works across multiple channels and devices, and creates a relevant joined up experience for every consumer.

Jonathan Mildenhall, speaking at the Festival of Commercial Creativity, said that generating Liquid and Linked content starts with the consumer – telling stories through their eyes, about their lives, with them. These brand stories combine business purpose with customer aspirations. They should possess the classic elements of storytelling: compelling characters, plot, suspense and surprise, heroes and villains, beginnings and endings. The story evolves with the audience, dynamic and collaborative, unpredictable and interesting. Every day, the Coke team creatively explore where to go next. He suggests spending 50% of time on the 70% 'bread and butter' content, and the second 50% split between the more radical, and potentially higher reward, concepts.

Liquid and Linked has transformed Coke's marketing. When seeking to engage Australians to drink more Coke, the concept of local characters emerged – the first place to put popular names on the bottles, but also to get the 'Kylies and Shanes' to become real spokespeople for the brand too. During the 2012 Superbowl, Coke's polar bears took sides, reacting as the teams did good or bad, and engaging the crowd with them as much as the real game. Stuck in a traffic jam trying to cross the Bosphorus bridge in Istanbul, a Coke van started giving away free drinks. And Coke machines set up in India and Pakistan, with added webcam and screen, enabled people from the two countries to wave at each other, even hold hands.

9.7 STORYTELLING ... TURNING IDEAS INTO MEMORABLE STORIES

We all love a great story. To share a laugh, shed a few tears, enjoy a chat over a cup of coffee. Great brand stories, from **Levi's classic 501 jeans** in the laundrette to Red Bull's adrenalin-pumping extreme events, resonate more deeply and with more enduring impact.

Pixar is perhaps the greatest storyteller of our age, using lovable characters, classic stories and incredible technology to create works of art. Nike has its own chief storyteller, that keeps evolving the tale from Bill Bowerman and his waffles, Michael Jordan and his hoops, to Mo Farah and his mobots, Google uses stories of future possibilities to reframe its brand, far beyond a search engine, Puma borrows the coolness of Jamaican sprinters to stand out as a brand of urban mobility, whilst HP connects with entrepreneurs by reminding us how it all started in a garage.

For thousands of years stories have entertained and educated, connected and inspired us. They communicate ideas in more engaging ways, more relevant and memorable, connecting people. Stories have more context, helping people to make sense of new ideas, involving characters to whom they can relate, creating a parallel rather than being direct. The stories can be told, or can evolve. Increasingly a brand sets a framework through which the story evolves in real-time, in collaboration with customers, based on day-to-day events.

Stories are typically built around timeless, **enduring truths** – like myths, legends and fairy tales. Indeed there will often be a classic plot on which you can build your own story.

Leo Tolstoy said that all great literature is one of two stories: a man goes on a journey or a stranger comes to town. Some say there's only one story that matters – the quest for the Holy Grail.

Stories have a shape, a narrative arc – although many brand stories are enduring and without an end. That's what keeps us engaged. But they are unlike most other types of communication. They have drama, tension or conflict, secrets and surprises. As author John Le Carré put it: 'The cat sat on the mat is not a story. The cat sat on the dog's mat is a story.' Storytelling coach Elen Lewis suggests a simple structure for your story:

- **Someone** … (a character)
- **Wants** … (a quest, a goal, a mission)
- **But** … (a challenge, an obstacle)
- **So** … (a means of succeeding).

Relating this to a brand, think in particular about the character – feminine or masculine? Mainstream or quirky? Consider your purpose, and brand essence, what aspirations are you seeking to connect with? Think about the opportunities and challenges, hopes and fears, from your audience's view, and relate to them.

Consider the objective of the story, how do you want them to feel, and what to do, and the story's conclusion. And think about the media across which the story might be told, how the audience might interact, become involved and personalize it.

Finally think about the **words and pictures**. The language you use matters. Make it simple, emotional and aspirational. Think of words that are relevant to your audience, unusual and memorable. And also a little playful, open to multiple meanings, twistable, and make people smile. And remember that an image can capture a thousand words, be processed and recalled faster. Most of all, don't be 'corporate', be human.

9.8 CONTAGIOUS … CATCHING THE IDEAS VIRUS

Why did a crazy song by the South Korean entertainer Park Jae-sang, also known as Psy, become YouTube's biggest ever hit, with a ridiculous dance imitated by US President Obama and the UN's Ban Ki-Moon, and top the charts in over 30 countries?

Ideas don't spread by accident. The most powerful concepts, the most catchy songs, spread because they are memes – patterns that can be easily captured, coded and transmitted by the brain. **Memetics** is a science, although just like a great song, it is human and intuitive too. There are six useful factors that make an idea contagious:

- **Relevant**: We survive information overload through selective attention. Keywords, topics, images, authors, even sounds and images, are ways in which we filter the noise around us, to find content worth exploring further. Just like search engine optimization, consider the words and phrases that might be on your audience's mind.

- **Fresh**: News is the most frequently shared type of idea, because it is new, topical, edited to be relevant and quickly absorbed. Creating your own news-worthy ideas or linking your ideas to topical stories (real-time) helps timeliness. Better still is to be first with the news, which is why speculation or gossip is so infectious.

- **Practical**: We like information that we can use, that gives us some form of advantage. Education or entertainment, popularity or power. The more useful the information, the more people will pass it on to others. The social utility of information, however, is as much aesthetic and emotional (image and gossip) as functional and practical.

- **Intuitive**: Ideas have to be easy to interpret, but also easy to articulate. Otherwise they won't get repeated. Forms of clichés, mnemonics, even alliteration can help. 'Gamechangers' is not a completely new phrase, but it's easy to understand – people who change the game – who themselves are new and interesting.

- **Seeded**: Finding the early adopters, typically the most active and engaged audiences, they become good transmitters because they have passion for the topic and also like to be seen as first to know. Ideally find influencers who are respected by the audiences you seek to reach and enhance the brand's desired values.

- **Wanted**: There is no shame in asking people to pass a message on – a special offer which encourages you to tell all your friends, a member get member scheme that explicitly rewards you, or a tweet that includes the phrase 'Please RT' is more likely to be retweeted. Calls to action work, particularly in social media where sharing is the norm.

Advocacy is, of course, more than passing on a cool video. It is about people trusting people and their recommendations.

It is about customers being the ambassadors for the brands they love, the storytellers to others, in a way that is more human, more relevant and more effective. Forget the expensive advertising, the complex relationship systems, the best form of marketing really is free. However it takes thought and focus to engage the right people with brand propositions that resonate, who then share aspirations into experiences, and their stories into contagions.

9.9 EXPERIENTIAL ... FORGET ADS AND IMAGES, THINK PEOPLE

Bringing this together, you start to see a very different model of marketing – one centred around the customer, which invariably starts with a Google search on a smartphone, and is much more about triggers and influences, connections and partners not driven by the brand, but by the customer. Imagine this scenario:

- Anna is having lunch. She loves her friend's new coat, so pulls out her smartphone, and easily **connects** with the coat's embedded tag.

- Using the restaurant's free wi-fi, she brings up the coat in a range of colours, automatically overlaying her **own image** to show how she looks in it.

- There's also a list of nearby stores and prices, plus the offer of a free bottle of wine from the restaurant if she decides to buy today.

- She **tweets** the coat and options to more friends, asking them what they think, and which colour suits her best.

- She receives a text from a local store inviting her to come along and try the coat, including examples of matching boots and scarf if she is interested.

- At the store, she chooses an entire outfit from a brand she'd never even thought of buying before. The **personal** tailoring service is able to deliver next day.

- Next morning it arrives, she loves it. The store invites her to send a **'Wow!'** to her twitter friends plus a special offer for them to try the brand too. She agrees.

- The brand keeps sending regular updates to its collections, knowing her sizes and preferred style. She joins the restaurant's lunchtime shopping club too.

- She wears the coat for a theatre visit a week later. The coat's tag **detects** where she is and the brand offers her a free glass of champagne in the interval.

Marketing and brand comunication is fundamentally different in this new world. Forget interruptive ads and pre-planned blanket campaigns, it is about refocusing your time and investment, and finding better connections. From 'push' promotion to **'pull' engagement**, from messages to stories, from planned campaigns to real-time action, and increasingly from content to experience.

CHANGE YOUR GAME

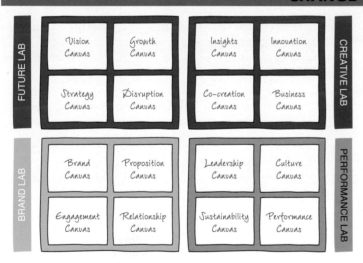

Practically apply the concepts in this chapter to your business with the relevant tools in the Gamechanger Labs:

- **Engagement** canvas
- **Brand** canvas
- **Proposition** canvas

Practical examples can be found in the 100 cases studies. Also see more details at Gamechangers.pro

10 ENABLE...CUSTOMER EXPERIENCES THAT ENABLE MORE

CHANGE YOUR EXPERIENCE

Gamechangers do more than sell products, they create and deliver an experience that immerses the customer in the brand, and goes beyond the sale to help them apply products better and achieve more together.

- More **enabling**... *from selling products... to enabling more*... They go beyond the sale to support people in choosing, buying, applying and achieving more.

- More **immersive**... *from functional journey... to emotional experience*... They look beyond the process to engage people more deeply and usefully.

- More **participative**... *from passive delivery... to valued participation*... They work with customers, from co-created products to user generated content.

10.1 EXPERIENCES ... SEE ME, FEEL ME, THRILL ME

Harley Davidson's CEO eloquently describes the experience by which he seeks to bring his brand to life:

> 'It's one thing to have people buy your products, it's another for them to **tattoo your name** on their bodies ... What we sell is the ability for a 43 year old accountant to **dress in black leather**, ride through small towns and have people be afraid of him.'

Brands and propositions are delivered through every possible medium that the organization can utilize – from names and logos to leaders and buildings, products and services to advertising and brochures, colours and packaging to uniforms and interiors, culture and behaviours to training and rewards.

Jan Carlson, the former CEO of Scandinavian Airlines, gave every one of his employees a little black book called Moments of Truth, where the few words inside spelt out, incredibly simply, how every interaction is an opportunity to make or break a lifetime relationship with that customer.

However customer **'experiences'** are much more than just consistent delivery across all the different touchpoints – it's about ensuring that the journey (not just the flight, in the airline's case, but from the first moment of need, until the mission is accomplished) is connected and coherent, consistent and complete. On top of this it's about bringing it to life, making it distinctive and relevant, and ultimately adding value at every point along the way. It's the customer's experience, not the business's experience.

Meaningful experiences are about relevant and distinctive interactions, rather than irrelevant and undifferentiated transactions. Instead of customers searching, selecting and buying, they are about helping customers to explore, play and learn. They are defined **on customer's terms**, in customer's language, by what customer's see, feel, think and do.

A typical air traveller will have around 45 interactions with the airline, real or perceived, from the time he or she decides to travel to the moment they arrive at their destination.

From dreaming of destinations to choosing flights, finding the best prices and buying tickets, car parking and checking-in, maybe visiting a lounge before the crush to get onboard, a glass of champagne and magazine of your choice, meals and drinks, time to watch a movie too, reclining your seat or going to the stand-up bar, confident words from the captain and smiles from the crew, your baggage arriving – hopefully, and then time for taxis and hotels, ready for that meeting, or to hit the beach.

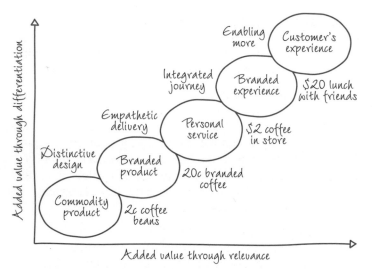

The Evolution of Customer Experiences

10.2 ENABLING ... IT'S NOT WHAT I BUY, IT'S WHAT I DO WITH IT

Experiences are more than products and services, or purchase and delivery of the goods bought. That's relatively unimportant compared to what the customer wants to **achieve**.

To achieve a personal best marathon with the new running shoes. To throw a great party with the ingredients bought. To write a novel with the new computer. To build the most amazing office with the construction materials just delivered. Clay Christensen calls these **'jobs to be done'**, the product application, the customer solution.

Whilst guiding the customer through awareness, selection and purchase is obviously important commercially, it is just the beginning for the customer. And for the brand. What matters more is what happens next – applying, using and achieving more.

Whilst it sounds obvious to say 'People don't want a drill, they want a hole in the wall' there are few DIY stores who really help people to do even the basics of home improvements.

We explored 'reframing' a proposition from product to customer. For example the pharma company that doesn't just sell drugs, but helps doctors to deliver better care, and even manage their practice better – or the IT company that doesn't just sell laptops and software, but also offers the training and support to help the client improve their productivity. The 'enabling' customer experience delivers this bigger solution.

It is also about value – the real value to the customer comes not from the product but in how the customer effectively applies and gains benefits from using it – or at least their perception of this. Aligning that with a business model to this broader sense of value can open up new revenue streams (eg education and support), payment models, and increased price.

Whilst that might sound theoretical, it **transformed IBM**. Realizing that clients valued its business advice on support much more than its hardware, IBM started charging for its consulting services. Customers paid much more for hours of support than the original product, making IBM eventually realize that it was hardly even worth making the computers, and just provide the support experience. IBM Consulting was born.

10.3 ENHANCING ... STREAMLINING AND ELABORATING

Jack Dorsey was inspired to create **Square** by small artisans like his glass-making brother, who missed out on many sales because they didn't accept card payments. The incredibly simple dongle that transforms your tablet or phone into a card reader has helped some small businesses to double their sales. Add the simple financial accounting records that come with the reader, and the bookkeeping nightmares of many creative people are eliminated at a swipe.

When mapping out your customer's experience, try creatively removing all the **value 'destroyers'** – the negative moments, the irrelevant points, the activities that do nothing for customers but are perhaps only there for the convenience or efficiency of the business. Consider whether, practically and commercially, it might be possible to still deliver this experience – now entirely consisting of positive **value 'creators'** – without the eliminated activities.

Of course, you may now have eliminated negative steps that are still important for the business, such as receiving the bill, making the payment, making the furniture, or disposing of the waste. Now consider replacing such essential steps with a different way of achieving them, that still fulfil the business need, but in a more positive way for customers. This is about:

- *Streamlining*: making interactions that are unimportant, uninteresting or irrelevant to the customer shorter, simpler and faster.

- *Elaborating*: making interactions that are important, enjoyable and desirable to the customer longer, enhanced and memorable.

American Express recognized that its main communication with customers – the monthly statement of payments – was not an entirely positive one for its cardholders. Instead it sought to make it more positive by tieing individual rewards and incentives to the transactions – 'we hope you had a good meal at your local restaurant, and we've arranged with them for you to have a free bottle of champagne on your next visit, with our compliments'.

10.4 EDUCATING ... INCREASING THE POTENTIAL IMPACT

Tech Shop is an inspiring place. As 'making' comes back in vogue, either as a hobby or business pursuit, so too is the demand for tools. Except in today's world of digital engineering and 3D printing, equipment is prohibitively expensive. TechShops are a branded network of urban workshops, where all the latest equipment is available to use, either to those with member subscriptions or who pay per hour to use the facilities.

Once in the workshop, ambitions kick in, and you most probably seek some advice in how to operate the machines, or perfect your process. Informal advice evolves into structured workshops, with resident coaches delivering educational courses. Of course this is not dissimilar from many brands – witness the 'learning space' at the back of the **Apple Store** where hourly tutorials are held, or the personal fitness coaching offered by sports shops, or the 30-day online support when you buy a new gadget.

Education is perhaps the most valuable way to enhance your customers' experience. Formal workshops or informal coaching, at the time of purchase or through the lifetime of the product; education enables people to achieve more, in a way that is valued, either as a source of tangible advantage and relationship or a shift or addition to the business model. For the brand it can be a positive enhancement too – the **Subaru Driving Experience** both captures the expertize of tuition and the credibility of the brand.

The more enlightened brand experience, and business model, therefore focuses on the 'job to be done' – the product when it is used, not when it is bought – not as an afterthought, or an additional service, but as the core to the brand, the value proposition and the ongoing experience.

10.5 ENRICHING ... ADDING EMOTION AND PERCEIVED VALUE

Whilst the benefits of education are tangible, customers are more emotional than ever. Enriching the experience is more subtle. It might be the sense of humour with which a brand communicates its proposition, the smell of freshly baked bread whilst shopping, the fun way in which a website is organized, or the premium clunk of the closing door of a well-made car. We are sensory, irrational beings, after all.

Juan Valdez Café has made the Colombian coffee growers far wealthier than if they had only ever sold their raw coffee beans to Starbucks and others. Instead they created their own packaged coffee brand, communicating the authenticity and richness of taste. Profits grew 10 times as they sold directly to consumers. But then they started building coffee shops, with local music and décor. The baristas wear ponchos and the farmer's donkey is tied up outside. This is far more than another globally franchised store brand, this is the real experience. Colombian coffee drunk as it should be. And worth 100 times what it would traditionally have been to the growers.

Entertainment in its many forms is equally human. Live music in the local restaurant, the car brand that makes short movies about driving experiences, or turning boring transactions into must-play games. **Drench** is a soft drink brand. When it launched its own branded vending machines, they were fairly similar to others. Except they included a short on-screen game which buyers played before receiving their bottle. Pay your money. Play the game. But you don't get your drink until you win. It became addictive.

10.6 INTELLIGENT…BIG DATA-DRIVEN EXPERIENCES

'MyMagic' gives Disney the ability to gather reams of personal data about the millions of people who flock to the resorts each year, tracking where they go across the resort, how they spend their money and what they eat. There are visible sensors at every location, but also remote sensors tracking you around the park. It enables visitors to plan their trips in advance, and to enjoy a more personalized experiences, eliminating queues, maximizing the magic.

How does Mickey know your name? And how come Buzz Lightyear knows my previous best score? Browse the stores,

and just wave your bracelet to make it yours. Personalized meals are waiting for you in the café, and if there is a spare moment, you might suddenly get a special offer saying there's a spare seat waiting for you.

Rather than investing huge sums in new attractions each year, Disney can simply **individualize** every marketing proposition, highlighting the rides, hotels or characters that you missed last time. With parks generating over $13 billion per year, a 10% increase in sales, of vacations and particularly within the park, would give an impressive return.

Disney has invested $1 billion in a **big data** upgrade to its theme parks. By giving visitors rubber bracelets embedded with RFID microchips and encouraging them to plan minute details of their trips weeks ahead of time, the company expects to get a larger share of their total vacation spend.

The amount of 'big data' available is quite mindboggling.

CERN's Large Hadron Collider contains around 150 million sensors, capturing 600 million collisions per second. If all sensor data were recorded, there would be 500 quintillion (5×10^{20}) bytes per day, almost 200 times higher than all the other sources combined in the world.

Decoding the human genome originally took 10 years to process, now it can be achieved in less than a week, at 0.01% of the cost, (which is 100 times faster than the reduction in cost predicted by Moore's Law, which originally suggested computing power would double every 24 months).

Walmart handles more than 1 million customer transactions every hour, which is imported into databases estimated to contain more than 2.5 petabytes (2500 terabytes) of data – the equivalent of 167 times the information contained in all the books available worldwide on Amazon.com.

The volume of business data worldwide, across all companies, **doubles every 1.2 years** according to estimates. The point of this is to enhance the customer experience. More intelligent, more personal, more effective and efficient.

'Big data' is defined by Gartner as being three-dimensional, i.e. increasing **volume** (amount of data), **velocity** (speed of data in and out) and variety (range of data types and sources). Gartner recently added: 'Big data is high volume, high velocity, and/or high **variety** information assets that require new forms of processing to enable enhanced decision making, insight discovery and process optimization.'

10.7 DIGITAL ... SOCIAL, LOCAL AND MOBILE

CEO Mark Parker sees Nike's future as much in digital experiences as in physical sports for which people buy his products. With a brand purpose to help people do better, Nike becomes more than a shoe or shirt, and an enabler of performance. **Nike+** monitors your performance, from heartbeat to running pace, tracking and analysing performance, storing and sharing it with others, inspiring and helping you to do better.

The best experiences are hybrids, combining the best of physical and virtual worlds. Whilst Nike+ is digital, the performance is physical. Whilst you can buy customized editions online, you first check out the size instore. Whilst you share running routes virtually, you then come together on the start line of real events.

In the world of retail, most online plays are seeking to become more digital and physical stores are enhanced digitally. This is partly about multi-channel, being able to buy online or instore, but also about the fusion of components within channels. Burberry's digital mirrors enable you to digitally superimpose yourself in different outfits whilst instore, whilst Net a Porter's premium packaging and glossy magazines complement a sophisticated digital experience.

Most significant of all is **mobile**. Mobile lubricates hybrid experiences, providing continuity between different interactions, whilst also storing personal data, enabling payment, adding social influence of friends, providing GPS-fuelled information and incentives based on time and place, access to support in use, and being ongoing. Mobile is less of a channel in its own right, but more the customer's navigation across a richer, continuous, personalized experience.

10.8 INTEGRATED ... THE BRAND'S EXO-SKELETON

Organizationally, the customer experience becomes the backbone of the **customer-centric** organization. In reality more like an exoskeleton, because it's the external customer's experience that then aligns the whole organization internally. Whilst product-centric structures were driven from within, working in functional silos, focused on products and selling, customer-centric businesses are designed from the **outside in**.

Delivering a seamless, integrated, learning experience requires people, processes and culture that are all aligned to deliver. It requires collaborative teams that work across functional boundaries, or even between partner organizations. It is fuelled by customer insight and information that is shared and applied to anticipate and personalize service. It requires shared purpose and rewards that encourage people to work in this way.

As the organization becomes more intelligent, it adds more value by shaping and sharpening its propositions, solutions and experiences. One of the best examples of this is through curation – reducing the complexity and increasing the relevance to customers. **Brand curators** cut through information overload and the infinite choices which we are confronted with, providing more personal recommendations and expert guidance. Whilst online retailers like Fab and Positive Luxury excel at this, it is also possible physically. Fashion brand Jaeger recently unveiled a curated mix of latest fashion designs and trends from its own and competitor collections. Whilst this might seem counter-intuitive, Jaeger is putting its customers first, and drawing them into its store.

10.9 ENDURING...DOUBLE-LOOPED EXPERIENCES

Customer experiences are conventionally mapped as a linear flow, the reality of course is that they are much more complex. Most significantly, they become continuous loops of engagement as customers repurchase and do more with the brand. As the key resonance points are as much beyond the sale – in using the product, and choosing to repurchase or recommend to others – so marketing influence has shifted.

Mercedes Benz famously focus around 90% of their entire communication spend on people who have bought their car,

rather than those just thinking about it. Think about it. What they really want is for the customer to be so convinced that they have made the right choice that they not only do so next time, but tell all their friends too. One Mercedes driver probably knows 10 others with similar values, needs and spending power. And those 10 others are far more likely to listen to, and trust their friend's, recommendation than any form of impersonal advertising.

The experience therefore becomes a **double loop** – the purchase loop and the retention loop – or better still a positive spiral – achieving more together. The 'positive spiral' experience is built on engagement, enablement and advocacy. Whilst this becomes more complex for organizations, it is fuelled by intelligence and hybrid interactions. As organizations shift from scale and average to focus and personalization, it means that they have fewer spirals to manage, but these are potentially far more profitable.

CHANGE YOUR GAME

Practically apply the concepts in this chapter to your business with the relevant tools in the Gamechanger Labs:

- **Engagement** canvas
- **Co-creaton** canvas
- **Business** canvas

Practical examples can be found in the 100 cases studies. Also see more details at Gamechangers.pro

11 MOBILIZE...GROWING FURTHER AND FASTER TOGETHER
CHANGE YOUR RELATIONSHIP

Gamechangers recognize that customers have little interest in being loyal to them, but want to connect and do more with other people like them. Brands bring people together with shared values and interests, giving them a platform and even a voice.

- More **collective**...*from customer relationships...to social movements...*They bring people together so that they can share their purpose, actively.

- More **facilitated**...*from incentivizing purchases...to enabling connections...*They curate, enable and support communities to achieve more together.

- More **collaborative**...*from transactional loyalty...to mutual partners...*They work together over time, achieving more together and sharing success.

11.1 RELATIONSHIPS ... LOYALTY TO EACH OTHER, NOT TO BRANDS

Brands are obsessed about building relationships – from loyalty cards to membership clubs, relationship marketing and net promoter scores. The reality is that **customers trust other customers** far more than they trust any brand, and are much more interested in connecting with other people like themselves. Today, the best brands **facilitate** relationships between people who share common purpose and passion. This enabling role builds a community or, better, a **movement** of advocates.

The millions of dollars invested in the pursuit of customer loyalty is usually futile. Recognizing the huge potential lifetime value of an ongoing customer, brands want people to trust them and stay with them. The rise of big data encourages them to do this even more, to profile customer behaviour, to predict and incentivize what they do, to be their best friend.

But people rarely want this corporate over-familiarity, and increasingly resent the one-sided attempts by brands to gain loyalty. Price promotions, discounts and coupons actually drive more **promiscuous** behaviour, the opposite of what brands intend. They make choices more rational, and less emotional. They commoditize rather than enhance brands.

Customers trust, and are most influenced by, their friends and others who share their ambitions and passions. Look at the way in which **Tripadvisor** and Amazon's reviews have replaced holiday and product brochures. People want authenticity, to hear about the good and the bad aspects of a brand. A brochure is biased. It also makes it hard to compare, to understand the inevitable trade-offs involved with every choice.

Brands can build much better relationships, even loyalty, by focusing their efforts on **connecting people** with others like them. This rarely happens. Look at how many people wander around a similar store, particularly a specialist store, in pursuit of great wines, or new mountaineering gear, but never speak. Imagine how many more people this is likely to be online. People are social by nature, they enjoy sharing their passions, learning from each other, and doing more together. It's time for brands to connect people.

11.2 NETWORKS ... EXPONENTIAL VALUE OF CONNECTEDNESS

John Gaure's play *Six Degrees of Separation* popularized our social connectedness. Robert Metcalfe, co-founder of 3Com coined a law that the **value of a network** is proportional to the square of its users. Facebook has more members than any nation's population except India and China, although QQ is catching up.

Most brands are still waking up to the opportunity of connecting their customers, physically or digitally. Social

131

networks are rapidly evolving from communication to distribution channels, whilst physical channels also have the opportunitity to become more social, as meeting places. Whilst it's easy to secure Tweets and Likes, the real opportunity of networks lies in collaboration and participation.

Whilst consumers connect through networks, businesses also embrace networks to serve them. Semiconductor designer **ARM** is a great proponent of **'ecosystems'**, bringing together networks of business, suppliers and collaborators, affinity brands and customers, in order to share ideas, capabilities and impact. Underpinned by digital infrastructures such as Alibaba, and dispersed manufacturing like 3D printing, any business can connect with any other irrelevant of size and geography, to do more.

Networks thrive on **reach and richness**.

'Reach' is achieved through the huge dispersed **interconnectedness** of a network, physical or digital, meaning that communications can reach further with more relevance, than the old mass-market broadcasts, and distribution is no longer dependent on linear supply and distribution models.

'Richness' is achieved through **collaboration**, between companies who work together to enhance offerings, to customers who get involved and do more. The multiplying effect of a network's connections is exponential, whilst its richness further enhances a brand's experience.

11.3 SOCIAL … PEOPLE MAKE NETWORKS WORK

Sara Rosso loves Nutella.

So much that in 2007 she took it upon herself to create **World Nutella Day** to celebrate the addictive hazelnut spread.

More than 40,000 fans liked the event's Facebook page. But brand owner, Ferrero Rocher, wasn't so pleased, their lawyers issuing a cease and desist letter. Sara blogged about the letter, attracting huge media coverage, and fans soon joined in with disbelief that the brand would want to stop their day.

Eventually Ferrero backed down and 5 February is now a fan-driven Nutella festival, with the brand learning to love their celebration too.

Companies have quickly learned that **social media** works. Eighteen months before Ford relaunched its Fiesta model in the USA, it gave 100 social mavens (people seen as most influential) a free car in return for reporting on various driving experiences. Their videos generated 6.5 million views on YouTube, 50,000 requests for information about the vehicle, and helped sell over 10,000 cars in the first week after launch. Almost every brand is now actively managing its social pages and feeds for real-time engagement with people, whether it be spreading endorsements or quickly addressing complaints.

Social media works most effectively when its momentum comes from within, from the interaction between users, rather than driven from outside, for example by a company. This internal momentum is built through:

- **Identity**: participants are transparent and human, which drives more attention and trust, curiosity and connection.

- **Conversations**: chat which is convenient and unlimited, a platform to express ourselves, diverse opinions driving debate.

- **Sharing**: fuelling and provoking conversations through sharing of content, photos and video, news and experiences.

- **Groups**: building tribal groups of known and new connections, with shared interests and objectives.

- **Presence**: all of this instantly, anywhere and anytime, making it accessible, topical and addictive.

Social media also comes with a bewildering array of new language, some of it relevant, some of it not. Everyone should know their 'social graph', which is a visual representation of the many different connections they have across networks. **'Social Search'** combines traditional web search with social influences to better target advertising. 'Socializing content' is about turning content into a form that is easy to talk about and pass on. **'Geo targeting'** is all about engaging people in a specific time and place, to add relevance or influence choices.

11.4 ADVOCACY ... BUILDING A GROUNDSWELL OF INFLUENCE

Who is the best spokesperson for your brand? A paid celebrity who has instant reach and reputation, and whose endorsement is followed religiously by fans; or real customers who are genuine advocates, but have less impact individually? Of course, there is space for both, but the issue is where your brand is anchored, and whose story is the more important.

Most brands prefer the celebrity kudos. Their impact can be rapid, often acquiring values from their own brand, and like big ads they are reassuring symbols that bolster the owner's ego. George Clooney for Nespresso, Kobe Bryant for Nike. But a paid endorsement can easily turn sour. The moment the contract finishes, or the celebrity commits a faux pas, or the fans are numerous but just not the kind of customers you want to attract.

Building a brand through a **groundswell** of real customers, each with their own stories of positive experiences and recommendations to their friends, is the alternative. It takes longer, is less controllable, and acquires scale through cumulative impact. But it is much more genuine, believable and trusted, much cheaper and more enduring. Creating a tribe of advocates gives you the platform to do so much more. To collaborate, to build a community, and extend into adjacent categories where you can do more for the same audience.

Jonah Berger is big on viruses. In his book *Contagious: Why Things Catch On*, the Wharton professor explored the world of **social epidemics** – how ideas, products and behaviours become popular. In fact it was another writer, Malcolm Gladwell, and his book *The Tipping Point*, that sparked Berger's research.

Whilst Gladwell is focused on the **messengers** – finding the really influential people, the early adopters, who can accelerate the spread of ideas like wildfire – Berger is more about the **messages** – the ability of ideas to be packaged in relevant, distinctive and addictive stories that everybody wants to retell.

'Contagious ideas are like forest fires. They cannot happen without hundreds, if not thousands, of regular Joes and Janes passing the message along' argues Berger. Like in the forest, contagions need the right conditions – dry wood, densely packed, hot sun and strong winds. Berger identifies the factors for 'virality' ...

- **Currency**: we share things that make us look good – they give us bragging rights and social acceptance.

- **Triggers**: easy to remember, top of mind, and easy to retell, particularly if it has emotion – funny, interesting, shocking.

- **Emotion**: we engage with it, more human and intuitive, something people care about and therefore share.

- **Practical**: people can use this new idea in some way, be it a new app to download, book to read, or joke to tell.

- **Stories**: from childhood we all love and tell stories; information travels faster when it is given context, when it has meaning.

Berger's research suggests that around 40% of all consumer purchases are now predominantly driven by the recommendation of others. Whilst messages take creativity, the medium is free compared to the cost of ads, billboards and mailings. McKinsey quantifies word of mouth marketing to be a $5.6bn industry by 2015.

11.5 COMMUNITIES ... TOGETHER WITH A SHARED PASSION

Community building, however, is a delicate art. In society communities evolve over time, finding their own values, rituals and structures. These cannot be imposed. When Coke tried to create a youth community called 'Coke, My Music', young people rejected it as too commercial and manipulative. When Pampers provided an online platform for new Mums to share their experiences and advice, Mums loved it, and Pampers for making it happen. A community has to be people-, not brand-, centric. And the more focused, niche if you like, the more relevant it can be. If a brand has defined its purpose well, about what customers want to be able to do, then there should be a good fit. The trick is to provide the right tools for the community to build itself.

In 1983, Harley-Davidson faced extinction; 30 years later, they have one of the world's most valuable brands. Not because of the bikes, but because of the brand community, a group of fanatical consumers with common attitudes and passions. Facing bankruptcy, the brand completely redefined itself around its community strategy – create demand, produce product, and provide support. In addition, a new separate organization was developed reporting directly to the president, the Harley Owners Group (HOG) membership club. This was

no marketing initiative, HOG sat at the heart of a new business model.

A community-based brand exists to serve its members. Rather than just sharing an identity, people typically join communities to connect, to support each other, to develop themselves, and contribute to the great good. They can sometimes be defined by a common adversary – 'Are you a Mac, or a PC man?' – and are defined more by attitudes and relationships than by products. Starbucks is primarily about the 'third place', as well as good coffee. There are essentially three types of **community** models:

- **Pools**: defined by shared values and experiences, like Apple users or marathon runners.

- **Webs**: built on one to one connections, like Patients Like Me or social network users.

- **Hubs**: inspired by a central theme, like Manchester United or the Rolling Stones.

Communities are built by their members, not by a brand that seeks to assert structure and control. Like a village community, they gradually form their own organizing structures, with roles and responsibilities, sustained through rituals and mutual rights. Whilst digital and social media have certainly facilitated communities, they are neither essential nor core to its success.

Part of a brand's challenge is to understand what kind of community it would like to nurture and support. Susan Fournier gives examples of the many different forms a community can take. They can range from a tribe (shared rituals and traditions) to a fort (place of safety), a sewing circle (social interests) to a tour group (new experiences), a patio (more intimate and meaningful) or a bar (more public and shallow), best friends (regular and natural) or a summer camp (irregular but structured).

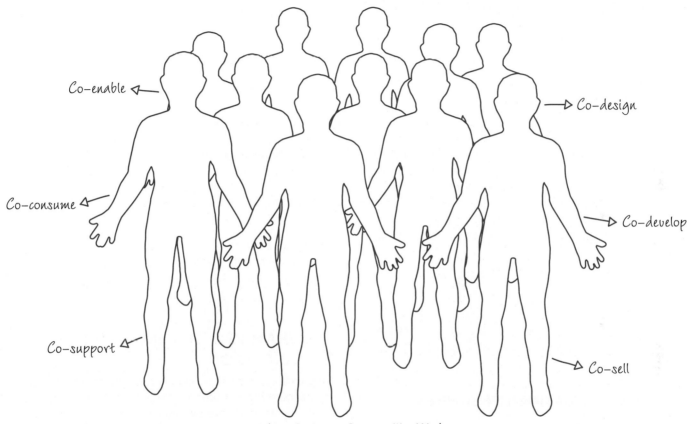

Co-enable

Co-consume

Co-support

Co-design

Co-develop

Co-sell

Making Customer Communities Work

Within a community, people gravitate to different roles, out of need and preference. For example, there will be the mentor who teaches others, the storyteller who articulates purpose, the historian who codifies rituals, the hero who becomes a role model, the decision maker who brings structure, and the host who cares for members. Brands can support communities by creating platforms for these roles.

11.6 COLLABORATING ... DOING MORE TOGETHER WITH CUSTOMERS

Collaboration takes many forms – from crowd-sourcing to open innovation, bringing together the ideas and resources of customers, colleagues, experts and other companies to achieve more, faster and better together.

Lego Factory is a co-creation facility, physical and online, where consumers work with others, and the building-block designers, to build future products. **Ducati's Tech Café** is where bikers hang out and design the next generation of superbikes. IBM's Innovation Centres are where clients run facilitated innovation programmes, and Samsung has a Virtual Product Launch Center where you can find the coolest newest devices.

Whilst tapping into the resources of passionate customers is cheap and often delivers better results, customers will increasingly become aware of their value. Incentives and discounts are increasingly expected in return, and the innovative co-creators will rethink business models in order to share the longer-term rewards with customers, either through pricing strategies or profit sharing.

On the other hand, collaboration builds deeper engagement. A customer who has invested time and ideas in a brand is more likely to stick with it, to buy the product they have had a role in developing, and to become more than an advocate, maybe even an ambassador for the brand.

11.7 CURATING ... MAKING LIFE SIMPLER TOGETHER

In a world of limitless content, curation can add significant value. Less is more, simplicity beats complexity. Whilst brands can themselves act as curators – selecting a small range of products or services which are most relevant to a particular customer – communities can be the most effective, and trusted, curators.

Curation is about collecting and ordering things. The simplest form of curation is achieved through customer rankings. Search for books on **Amazon** or music on iTunes

and top of the list will be the items given the highest customer rankings. Of course, the process can also be automated, Google rankings based on the most frequent searches and active links, **Mashable** fusing together news based on keywords.

Curation also helps a brand to establish itself in a bigger context. Whilst Pepsi has long sponsored music and entertainment events, it was always seen as the drink sponsor. With **Pepsi Pulse**, it is finally becoming an entertainment brand, bringing together the best news in music and entertainment, and by engaging customers as guest authors, adding comments and ranking, it becomes more trusted and authentic too.

At the same time brands want themselves to be curated by others, their latest innovations being featured in a list of must-haves, or their service ranked by the most influential online sites or influential individuals. This comes back to their ability to influence people with relevant, topical and contagious content.

11.8 SHARING ... SHARING IS FUN, PROFITABLE AND GOOD

Airbnb offers travellers an alternative to another night in a sterile, grey hotel room that could be anywhere on Earth. And it gives millions of homeowners the opportunity to monetize their spare rooms. The result is an interesting, quirky place to stay, and a whole new market. The site, which lets people rent their homes or rooms to travellers, has booked more than 10 million nights in 192 countries since its start in 1998. It is one of the best examples of 'collaborative consumption' in doing so, how a new business model can create and shape a new market.

Sharing is human – fun, sociable, and good for the world – and a new way to make money. On **Zilok**, the peer-to-peer rental site, you can rent out the drill you bought and never use. At

Taskrabbit you can find a person with any skill you need. At Zopa you can borrow or lend money from other people at much better rates than a bank, whilst at Zidisha it comes with expert help too. If you want to go somewhere, Buzzcar will help you share a ride. If you're not using your driveway, then hire it out for the day at Parkatmyhouse.

There are three main types of **collaborative consumption**:

* **Renting**: where you never need to buy something and instead just pay a small fee to use it for a limited time.

* **Sharing**: where people choose to share time, space, skills or money, in ways that can benefit both people.

* **Reusing**: where products no longer wanted are sold on to others, often as a positive aspect to the brand experience.

From Velib, the bike sharing scheme which started in Paris and can now be found in most cities, to BookCrossing, where people leave books they've read for others to pick up, collaboration is typically cheap, convenient and interesting. Marks and Spencer launched 'shwopping' as a way of exchanging old clothes as part-payment for new clothes, collecting 3.8 million items in one year and raising over £2m for charity Oxfam.

Big companies have sought to embrace the collaboration market too. Avis recognized the disruptive impact of **Zipcar**, the original car club, and snapped it up, whilst Ikea launched an online site for reselling unwanted furniture, supporting their vision of regularly updated homestyles. Microsoft acquired **LiquidSpace**, enabling mobile workers to find workspace and meeting rooms on demand and rent it by the hour, embedding it into its Office 2013 software. **Patagonia** set up Common Threads to resell old climbing gear, at the same time demonstrating its durability.

Collaboration becomes a particularly useful business model for utilizing under-used assets such as spare time, empty seats or rarely used products. Rachel Botsman in her book *What's Mine is Yours* says 'People are looking around and saying 'Hey, I can rent out my car. I can share my skills. I don't need to own a designer dress, I can rent one. There is a big shift underway from the "me" of hyper-consumption to the "we" culture of collaborative consumption.'

11.9 MOVEMENTS ... MARKETS WITH A MISSION

The best brands go even further. When people really care about something, they start to promote their passion – be it spiritual enlightenment, the joy of running, belief in a better society, or a protest against something. Participants become activists, crusading to achieve something more. Dove achieved this, creating a 'campaign' not by the brand but by the millions of real women who believed in real beauty. Challenger brands are naturally good at this, built around the desire to change something, to make it better. Positive Luxury, an online lifestyle brand community, mobilizes its participants to demand more from brands, in particular that they are more sustainable in their impact, and then curates those that do.

In his book, *Uprising*, Scott Goodson explores the concept of movement marketing. Whilst some brands – like Toms' One for One and even **Raspberry Pi** – have engaged huge audiences in their social-related initiatives, it is charities who have been more effective at building their brands around a shared cause, rather than just doing good.

'**Movements**' are communities with an **active purpose**, not just to share something, but to come together to achieve more. It might be a protesting or political movement like Greenpeace or Occupy, or it might be a collaborative goal, like ParkRun provides free local runs or Fairtrade. Movements tend to require more organization than passive communities, and therefore provide more scope for brands to play a valuable role.

The movement builds the brand by identifying and aligning with an idea that is rising culturally. It articulates the idea more clearly, acting as a catalyst to bring people together and get involved. The movement requires organization, a platform through which people can join and connect, have more influence and a stronger voice together, rally and bring about change.

Movements challenge the conventional marketing model because they are more about the group than the individual. Instead of selling, they promote sharing. Instead of the brand's purpose, they promote the group's purpose. However this is entirely in line with the power shift to customers, and collective potential of social media. One of my clients, **Philosophy** skincare brand, has a deeply engaged audience motivated by the brand's positive outlook on life, and a loyalty to each other, as much as to the brand itself. Rather than just satisfying their own needs, consumers are much more motivated to support each other, to give through gifting rather than buying, and to promote more positive attitudes and lifestyles.

CHANGE YOUR GAME

FUTURE LAB					CREATIVE LAB
	Vision Canvas	Growth Canvas	Insights Canvas	Innovation Canvas	
	Strategy Canvas	Disruption Canvas	Co-creation Canvas	Business Canvas	
BRAND LAB	Brand Canvas	Proposition Canvas	Leadership Canvas	Culture Canvas	PERFORMANCE LAB
	Engagement Canvas	Relationship Canvas	Sustainability Canvas	Performance Canvas	

Practically apply the concepts in this chapter to your business with the relevant tools in the Gamechanger Labs:

* **Relationship** canvas
* **Brand** canvas
* **Engagement** canvas

Practical examples can be found in the 100 cases studies. Also see more details at Gamechangers.pro

12 IMPACT...DELIVERING MORE POSITIVE RESULTS

CHANGE YOUR RESULTS

Gamechangers recognize that success is about creating value that is shared between customers and other stakeholders, and by getting the right balance they can create a far more profitable and sustainable business and make a positive impact on the world.

- More **responsible**...*from business blinkers...to sustainable futures*...They embrace social and environmental issues as a core business driver.

- More **holistic**...*from linear production...to circular regeneration*...They move from make and dispose, to create and reuse in a closed loop.

- More **positive**...*from impact reduction...to innovative growth*...They embrace sustainability to drive creativity, to create more value for business and beyond.

12.1 POSITIVE VALUE ... BUSINESS THAT ADDS TO THE WORLD

Gamechangers typically have a 'millennial' mindset. Whilst they are ambitious and entrepreneurial, they are as much motivated by making the world a **better place** as by securing personal wealth. They see success as a **triple-play**: me, my world, the world. They seek to create a positive **impact** for customers, for investors and employees, and for the wider world, socially and environmentally.

Most people get confused. They see **value creation** as a trade-off between creating more value for customers and shareholders. Of course, through innovation it's possible to do both. They see **sustainability** as the need to have less impact, to reduce. Through innovation, it's possible to create better solutions that are also good. And they feel the **responsibility** is on them, but actually they can be the enabler, helping everyone to live better lives, to create a more positive impact in their own, and in our shared, world.

Business clearly has a **purpose beyond profit**, to add value to the world in which it exists, to make life better in some way. If not it would be a commoditized money machine with no advantage over any other business, and therefore no profit. Purpose galvanizes the organization to do more, it gives all stakeholders – employees, investors, partners and customers – a reason to support it, to contribute, and a direction to follow.

'Value' is the contribution which the business has the potential to make over time. In the same way as, personally, everything we own – tangible and intangible – has a value to us. This is most easily measured financially, because it is tangible and has defined metrics, but can be intangible too. From customers successfully achieving their goal, to the smile on their faces; from a fair deal for suppliers, to the improvement of society, value comes in many forms.

However, achieving the purpose, creating that more holistic view of value, usually requires investment, which ultimately requires making money. Creating a surplus, or a profit, therefore matters in any kind of organization – profit or non-profit – if is to achieve its goals and do better. The only argument therefore, is how fairly – and effectively – this profit is distributed. To employees who do great work, to investors who provide resources, to customers who engage, and to business improvement.

Whilst stock market performance still grabs the headlines, many boardrooms are more interested in the future of their business, beyond past performance, eg brand reputation, customer advocacy, new innovations, and broader social impacts.

'Positive value' is therefore about the potential of the organization to achieve more. It should be measured financially and non-financially. However, the measures of success are not always obvious. More revenue or share does not always deliver more profit. And more profit does not always deliver long-term value. Most importantly it is about finding a balance which enables the business to grow over time, profitably and sustainably.

12.2 CUSTOMER VALUE ... ACHIEVING MORE FOR CUSTOMERS

A better starting point is to consider the value to the customer (not to be confused with the financial value of the customer!). Customers choose brands that offer good 'value', which means those which have the potential to do most for them. Again this might be measured financially by the customer – helping them to generate more income, or save money – and non-financially – helping them to live better, the measures of which are far more subjective and personal.

Whilst 'value for money' might mean the lowest price when all products or services are perceived to be the same, a brand has far more potential to create far more positive value, both rationally and emotionally. 'Enabling' brands are all about increasing this potential, giving customers the opportunity to achieve significantly more. The DIY tools, and support and education, that enable you to create a beautiful home. The great service that enhances your enjoyment of an event. The software tools that help you to work more successfully.

So what is the measure of customer value? Customer satisfaction has long been used, however it is increasingly recognized as 'basic hygiene' in that 5 out of 5 is for many the minimal standard. Customer recommendation has largely replaced it, using 'would you recommend it to a friend?' as a measure of positive impact. **Net promoter score** (NPS) is most popular in this regard, producing a trackable metric based on the sum of 'promoters' (who score 9–10/10) less 'detractors' (who score 1–6/10). 'Output' metrics, such as NPS, are useful to track performance, but 'input' metrics are also needed to understand how to improve the outputs. This is best achieved through customer research, understanding the relative importance of the many different hard and soft factors that go into a customer's experience of a brand. These range from the utility of the product itself, the service and support, through the more emotional impacts of the brand such as fairness, happiness and accomplishment. Each of these factors can be quantified and correlated to the relative investments – activities, resources and finance – required to achieve them. This creates a far more intelligent and actionable 'dashboard' for brands and business than balanced scorecards and other devices.

12.3 ECONOMIC VALUE ... CAPTURING THE FUTURE POTENTIAL

Economic value is measured by the sum of likely **future profits**. If somebody buys a company, or shares in it, the price is based on the **future potential**. This is therefore a measure of a company's ability to survive and thrive in a fast changing world, to make sense of change and seize the best opportunities, to innovate and grow, and to do so in way that is sustainable **for all** of its stakeholders and the world in which it lives.

The **economic value** of a company – measured most simply by the price of its shares on a stock market, or the price which an owner is prepared to buy or sell for – therefore also captures all of the non-financial factors that could enhance or disrupt its success. Internally, this can be calculated through discounted cashflow analysis, built on a projection of future profits – based on chosen strategy, market change, future innovation and commercial performance – which are then discounted based on the likelihood of them actually happening.

Similarly the economic value of a **brand** can be considered the **'uplift'** in these future profits due to the effective use of the brand to increase sales and pricing, to improve attractiveness and loyalty, and certainty of new innovations or entry into new markets. Whilst knowing your brand's value has limited use, it is useful in understanding potential royalty rates for licensing and franchising and for tax reasons.

In most cases, economic value is most useful in order to understand the impact of different choices, an overall measure that captures all the trade-offs involved in strategic options for the business, for evaluating a new business model, for selecting the best innovations, or entering new markets.

More practical is to understand the business **value drivers**, which investments and actions have most 'positive impact' on the business. Value driver analysis is typically done by working backwards from overall value – driven by sales, growth, costs, risks and time – to understand what drives each of these, and in what proportion, and then what drives each of those factors. The model is based on estimates of a changing market, but for entrepreneurs and agile enterprises it provides a navigation tool into the unknown.

12.4 SUSTAINING VALUE … SUSTAINED AND SUSTAINABLE

The real challenge for any business is not just to perform, but to sustain that performance over time. Being able to sustain profitable growth year after year is the holy grail of most businesses – whilst hedge funds might seek to make 'a quick buck', most investors – particularly family and institutional owners – look to the longer-term. Amazon's Jeff Bezos is a great example of a CEO advocating 'long, slow returns' that allow

him to invest initial profits in the business, enabling it to grow to something more substantial – and far more valuable – for Amazon, growing by $171bn over 20 years.

Looking at the TSR (total shareholder return, a combination of share price growth and dividends, over a five-year period) shows quite a different ranking of the world's leading companies, compared to the usual market giants:

Sustaining value has two dimensions – **'sustained'** performance through fast-changing markets, requiring innovation and agility – and **'sustainable'** performance, meaning that the business is in balance as an overall system, with the world around it. The former aspect of being able to change – to be a 'gamechanger' – has been explored, whilst the latter aspect of sustainability – of an organization's social and environmental responsibility – has also become important in recent years. This is not just a business fad, but a response to the genuine crisis in the world's growing population and limited resources. It is also an opportunity to reach out to new markets, to engage customers in emotional issues, to improve efficiency, and a catalyst to **innovate better**.

12.5 CREATIVE GOOD … INNOVATING TO MAKE LIFE BETTER

'The 21st century is a time of scarcity in terms of natural resources' says Santiago Garland, Nike's director of sustainable innovation. 'The 20th century was all about abundance and business externalities were not too important as far as wealth was created. Now, wealth creation must be considered more holistically.'

Business people, he believes, have changed in outlook and want to work with more purpose. 'People don't want to work until they are 60 or 70 and focus only on wealth to retire and

Company	Location	Sector	TSR	Market Value
1. Pharmacyclics	USA	Biopharma	166.3%	$7.8bn
2. GungHo Entertainment	Japan	Gaming	138.5%	$8.3bn
3. Galaxy Entertainment	Hong Kong	Casinos	130.9%	$37.9bn
4. Jazz Pharmaceuticals	Ireland	Biopharma	130.9%	$7.3bn
5. Avis Budget	USA	Travel	125.1%	$4.3bn
6. Great Wall Motors	China	Auto	109.0%	$16.8bn
7. Hexpol	Sweden	Chemicals	101.3%	$2.6bn
8. Sirius XM Radio	USA	Media	96.9%	$21.4bn
9. Plastic Omnium	France	Auto parts	95.6%	$4.1bn
10. Brilliance China	Hong Kong	Automotive	94.6%	$8.2bn
(Selected other companies)				
Tencent	China	Media	58.7%	$117.6bn
Amazon	USA	Retail	50.7%	$182.5bn
Apple	USA	Technology	46.7%	$500.7bn
Volkswagen	Germany	Auto	43.7%	$130.8bn

Sources: S&P, Thomson Reuters, Bloomberg, BCG
TSR = 5 year total shareholder return (shares and dividends), 2009–2013
Market values as at 31 December 2013.

Global Rankings by Total Shareholder Return

drop some coins into a charity to feel they are doing good. Talented professionals today want to integrate their values into their professions and contribute to becoming part of the solution to some of the issues they see everyday in the newspapers. They want to bring the whole of themselves to work and in doing that, they unleash the power of their imagination that is connected to heart affections, to values, to their own search for meaning.'

Nike has turned full circle over recent years – once demonized for the work practices in some of its Asian factories, at a time when few other companies had explored global supply chains and standards had not been written – it is now a world leader in sustainability. In 2010 Nike linked up with NASA and aid charities to form LAUNCH, a sustainable **ideas incubator** to search for innovations that gave opportunities to suppliers in new markets and also searched for better materials and practices. Within the first two years it helped bring clean water to 4.5 million Kenyans, affordable renewable energy to India, as well as new fabrics that are better for the environment, better for customers, and provide jobs in low income countries.

Brands have the power to engage people in important issues, to change their behaviours, and to embrace better practices inside and out. In the same way that Tesla doesn't see sustainability as a compromize, but as a way to do better – in its case combining a zero carbon electric engine with a sleak sportscar design that outperforms a Ferrari – similarly, Nike's Flyknit shoe technology – where the entire shoe upper is knit with a single thread – not only reduces waste, but also significantly improves fit and lightness.

'Where Naomi Klein's iconic book *No Logo* fails' argues Gowland is that 'brands are becoming the biggest lever to transforming the business agenda in a profitable way'.

We are living in the end of an abundance era. And while we go from 6 to 9 billion people – all aspiring to live better – these social, economic and environmental challenges continue to grow. The questions of the role of business in society and the concept of economic growth as we traditionally understand them need to be revised.

The evidence is readily articulated:

'**Health epidemics** and infectious diseases are also on the rise. The world's biggest killers are AIDS, TB and malaria. A child dies every 30 seconds from malaria and pregnant women are particularly vulnerable. More than 12 million children in sub-Saharan Africa have been orphaned by AIDS – set to rise to 43 million by 2020.'

'People living in poverty are disproportionably vulnerable to disease. 15 million children die from malnutrition each year. That's one person every 3.6 seconds. The gap between **rich and poor** continues to grow. As everyone knows, 20% of the world has 80% of the wealth and that wealth is concentrated in the developed parts of the world. Half the world's assets are held by 2% of the population. Or, to put it another way, half the world's population own 1% of its assets.'

'1 billion people lack access to safe **drinking water** and 2.5 billion people – half the developing world – lack access to basic sanitation. Unclean water is a primary cause of diarrhoea – the world's second biggest killer of children. Climate change is now a reality and a growing threat. This century is witnessing the end to abundance. Scarcity is the rule. Driven by growing populations and rising affluence are putting food, energy and water resources under stress.'

12.6 CIRCULAR ECONOMY ... NET POSITIVE BUSINESS MODEL

The 'circular' economy is a closed loop, in that it gives back everything which it takes. This is different from most business models which are primarily 'linear' in that they result in waste, and thereby the depletion of resources.

In other words, by nature or design, 'circular' business models are restorative. They can be biological, in that they are created and regenerated naturally in the environment

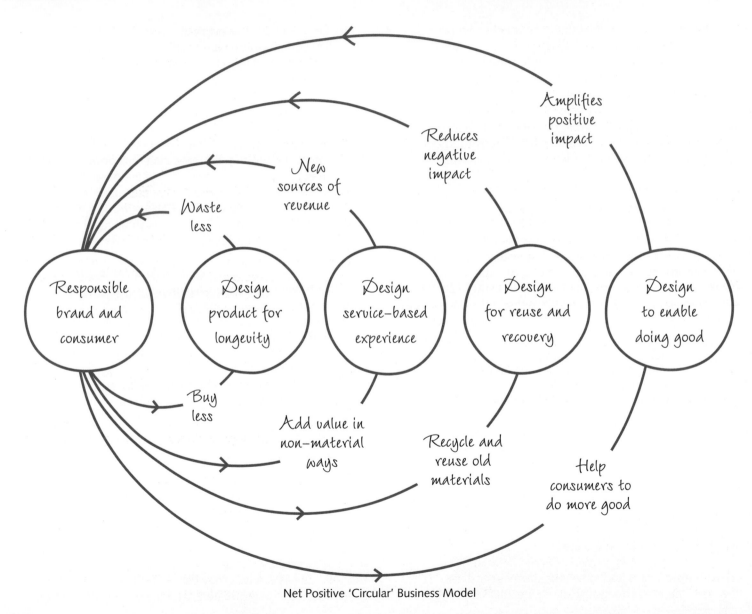

Net Positive 'Circular' Business Model

(such as water or crops) or technological, where artificial components (metals, plastics) that are added can be reused.

The concept emerged from Ken Boulding's circular flow model in *Economics of coming Spaceship Earth*, and was also a feature of China's 11th five year plan starting in 2006. Most recently it has been championed by the Ellen MacArthur Foundation, a charity that has promoted the economy benefits as well as environmental importance of the model.

From **Aussie Farmers** to Le Pain Quotidien, **Method** to Natura, Graal Bio to Tesla we can see the 'circular' principles embraced by companies who are changing the game, in their impact, but also in how they deliver a better customer experience. There are three core principles:

- **No waste**: biological components are non-toxic and can be composted, technical components can be used again or repurposed.
- **Diversity**: achieved through being modular, versatile and adaptive; from the easy to change parts of a Smart car, to the multi-functional use of Blessus's clothing.
- **Renewable energy**: the system is powered in a zero-emissions way. In the case of Graal Bio this is turning unwanted urban waste into useful clean energy.

Developing a circular business model is a design challenge, based around the most effective reuse of assets. Products are developed in a way that meets customer expectations without waste, sourced from materials in regenerative loops and with a revenue model that encourages this. It also requires customer collaboration.

The best circular models, however, are creative – they create a **'net positive'** result rather than a zero sum. Through the positive effect of business, creation and consumption, they add value to the world, for example by doing social good that is an amplication of the effort and resources to achieve it.

12.7 CIRCULAR STRATEGIES ... MOVING FROM LINEAR TO CIRCULAR

There are many practical ways to embrace a circular model, for example any one, or combination of. the following shifts:

- **From product to service**: leasing products rather than selling them (like Amazon's streaming music), offering eduction and advice (like IBM's shift to consulting), doing rather than making (like Persil's home cleaning service).
- **From one life to many lives**: reusing the same materials again, by recovering and reconditioning products after use (like Tata Assured, selling reconditioned second hand cars, or Vertu phones upgraded inside the same case).
- **From product to parts**: salvaging components from one product to be reused in the same or different products (as BMW does with its spare parts service, which come at an 80% discount, and 24 month warranty).
- **From recycling to innovation**: turning an old product into something different (like Starbucks turning thousands of tons of waste coffee grounds into bioplastics and medicines using a series of chemical processes).
- **From individual to sharing**: creating platforms and business models that enable products to be shared, and getting more use out of assets (from renting out spare rooms with Airbnb to passing on kids clothes with ThredUP).

The circular model, like any other business model, is one of the best ways to change the game, particular if has the potential to engage people more deeply, and offer more value, whilst also doing good.

12.8 TOGETHER ... ENABLING PEOPLE TO DO MORE GOOD

Whilst companies seek to do more to address social and environmental issues, the bigger opportunity is for them to enable every one of their **customers** to do more good too. Rather than just one organization making a difference, they unleash the potential for millions of customers to make a difference. This can be a potent force. It is also a far more engaging proposition to customers, who often feel inadequate when facing big challenges in our world, but could feel empowered by a brand's enablement.

When I was asked to help a leading mobile phone brand to develop it's global sustainability strategy, they were initially tempted to focus on the usual token gestures – recycling in offices, build a children's playground – but then realized they had a potential force of over a billion people. If, through their services, they could enable these people to do more, perhaps even in a way that enhanced the basic service too, then it would be incredibly powerful. The connectivity of that huge network, for example to collaborate in creating their own local initiatives, could have an even great **magnifying** effect.

A cause related movement is perhaps the most potent force in society today. Whilst many non-profit organizations champion such causes, brands could help them enormously. **Brands** bring heightened awareness and interest, relevance and reach. Desigual and Nike, Starbucks and Toms are examples. They have existing infrastructures which can be mobilized, and they can combine personal and social benefits – improving my own life, whilst improving life for others at the same time.

12.9 LEGACY ... WHAT YOUR BRAND LEAVES BEHIND

What will you leave when you are gone? What will you, your brand, your business do that has lasting significance, not just in your business or market, but for society as a whole? How will you make the world a **better place**?

For some gamechanging brands, their legacy will be remarkable – from Apple's generational shift in technology, to Aravind's transformational eye care in India – whilst for others, they will take small steps along society's path of progress.

We are **temporary guardians** of our brands and businesses, moving them forwards, creating positive impact, then handing them on to future generations. Large corporations, like GE or Tata, have already passed through many hands, but Jeff Immelt and Ratan Tata through their 'Ecomagination' and frugal innovation have both made their marks on corporate history, and made a positive difference to people's lives.

Entrepreneurs have more chance of going down in history. Steve Jobs and Elon Musk, Jack Ma and Anne Wocicji will be the likely Thomas Edison and Henry Ford, Charles Babbage and Marie Curie of our age, remembered for moving society forwards, enabling new possibilities, changing the game.

The world is making rapid progress on many issues which can be further accelerated and sustained by business. **Hans Rosling**, the Swedish academic who became an unlikely star of TED Talks, points to five major steps forward:

- Fast **population growth** is coming to an end. In the last 50 years fertility rates have fallen dramatically from 5 to 2.5 babies per woman, thanks to better education and healthcare. In the last decade, numbers of children aged 0–14 has levelled off at around 2 billion, and will eventually fall.

- The majority of differences between **'developed' and 'developing'** world have gone. Instead of the polarization as rich or poor, healthy or malnourished, powerful or weak, most nations now lie in the middle. Half the world's economy, and most of the economic growth, lies outside Western Europe and North America.

- People are much healthier. Fifty years ago, average life expectancy was 60 years, now it is 70. Child mortality has fallen by 75%. The health gap has closed faster than anything else. Vietnam, for example, has the same health as the USA had in 1980 but so far only the same income per person as the USA had in 1880.

- **Girls are better educated**. They now receive schooling in equal numbers to boys even in the poorest countries,

although around 10% are still restrained by cultural taboos. Gender inequality, however, still remains in areas such as marital and civil rights.

- The **end of extreme poverty**. This has halved, to around 1 billion, since 1980. Having sufficient income (around $1.25/day) for everyday food has a dramatic impact on fertility and also on health and education, which over the next decade is a realistic possibility for everyone, even in a population that is still growing.

The most significant legacies are those that go beyond technical innovation and really do improve society, for many not just a few, and change lives not just increase prosperity. Whilst positive impact can be measured in many ways, it is quite reasonable to seek to 'change the world'.

CHANGE YOUR GAME

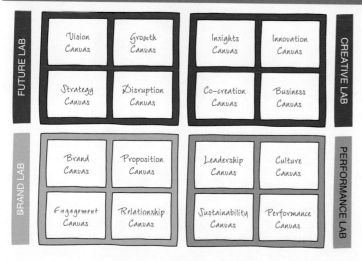

Practically apply the concepts in this chapter to your business with the relevant tools in the Gamechanger Labs:

- **Sustainability** canvas

- **Business** canvas

- **Performance** canvas

Practical examples can be found in the 100 cases studies. Also see more details at Gamechangers.pro

13 AMPLIFY... TRANSFORMING YOUR BUSINESS POTENTIAL
CHANGE YOUR POTENTIAL

Gamechangers do not have to be the biggest companies to be the best. Leaders amplify the potential of others, brands amplify the value of innovations, networks amplify the reach and richness, and customers amplify their own potential by achieving more.

- More **empowering**... *from hierarchical managers... to network leaders...* They bring the organization together to embrace diverse talents and achieve more together.

- More **entrepreneurial**... *from stability and performance... to agility and potential...* Leaders create energy and drive change, increasing the capacity of the business to grow.

- More **enterprising**... *from incremental improvement... to transformational impact...* Leaders enable the organization to achieve more radical, innovative and disruptive impact inside and out.

13.1 AMPLIFYING ... THE CAPACITY TO ACHIEVE MORE

So what have we learnt? ... 'Gamechangers' make sense of a fast-changing world, thinking bigger and different, finding their space, redefining the rules, engaging people on their terms, and creating the future in their own vision. They can be big or small, start-ups or well established.

But success requires more. More than an idea. More than action.

Success requires you to **amplify** – from initial idea to scalable impact, from early adopter to mainstream customer, from positive buzz to profitable growth. Amplifying is about increasing your capacity to succeed, and therefore about changing your potential, personally and organizationally. It doesn't mean you have to be big. Scale and share are not always the route to profitability. But it does mean you have to create a sustainable presence, one that can stand on its own feet and make a difference to the world.

Reflecting on those who have successfully changed their game, a number of common transforming themes emerge.

Good is not enough. **Change the world** ... Google's moonshot factory is not about creating a better search engine, but understanding where a data-fuelled world can go next. From Glass to Space Elevators, intelligent cars and cures, Google doesn't just want to be better than Bing or Yahoo, but to make life dramatically better.

Creating the future. **Living in real-time** ... Whilst disruptive innovations can reframe markets and sustain growth for years to come, they are often slow burners. Business needs to work in double time – creating the future and delivering today. This is particularly the case as consumers have shorter attention spans than ever, and want instant relevance. Social and mobile-enabled marketing resonates with individuals with more topicality and value.

Ideas are fun. **Innovation is commercial** ... Great ideas can captivate your mind, but they only last if they make money. Whilst many digital start-ups struggle to make money, claiming that advertising will eventually come, other companies like Airbnb or Supercell define propositions worth paying for, and a business model that is self-sufficient. New business models, like rental and subscription, can enhance the customer's experience, as well as profitability.

Ideas come from anywhere. **Talent is everywhere** ... iHub is the Silicon Valley of Kenya. With 12,000 members it has launched over 160 companies across Africa's fast growing markets. The best web designers are in Hyderabad, the best fashion designers in Buenos Aires, the best green tech in Shanghai, the best food in Beirut. Open your eyes to a world that is connected yet with pockets of distinctive expertize.

Make the sale. **Enable people to do more** … The pursuit of sales transactions used to dominate business culture and performance. The customer experience ended in payment. But then we realized customers were partners, to be nurtured over time. To do more for, to support and enable them use products to achieve success, and to build retention and referral over time.

Brands are not about business. **Brands are about people** … Brands used to describe companies and products, now they describe customers and their aspirations. Coke is not about refreshment, but happiness. Nike is not about shoes, but about success. Similarly, in a world where customers trust their peers much more than any company, relationships are built more successfully between customers rather than with them.

Collaboration is not a fad. **People want to make and share** … Crowd-sourcing taps into your fan base, people who want to build your brand, and do more together. Threadless fans keep coming back for more. Indeed they are the brand. Collaboration is also about using products and services together, better utilizing assets and reducing waste, and having fun too.

Business used to be bad. **Business is a force for good** … Capitalism used to seem to be at odds with caring. Missions used to worship the pursuit of money. Now they are about making life better. A more inspiring purpose is more engaging and rewarding, and unlocks the power of brands to encourage and enable people to do good. Dual business models like Narayana Hospitals or Toms demonstrate that a company can do both.

Green was superficial. **Sustainability is core** … Whilst early CSR initiatives did little more than relieve corporate guilt, today's businesses embrace sustainability as a catalyst to innovate, to create a better world. Ideally a circular one, which not only reduces the negatives, but enhances the positive benefits to society: 100% of Nike materials are sustainable, Tesla's engines accelerate faster than a Lamborghini.

China used to be cheap. **China is about luxury** … Whilst Apple feels like it has plateaued after Steve Jobs, Xiaomi is innovating for the next generation under rockstar Lei Jun. Whilst most of the world buys Haier washing machines, the Chinese buy the premium version, called Haizan. There was a time with China was admired for its art and culture, education and science. Those days are returning.

Moonshots are not just stardust. **They are the next frontier** … Thinking bigger can seem exciting yet irrelevant. Some companies play with their incubators, then return to today. Yet big ideas, step changes, disruptions, move us forward. In markets where change is the base, incrementalism is the norm. Businesses need something more to inspire people and create new platforms for growth.

13.2 AMPLIFIERS … HOW A BUSINESS ACHIEVES MORE

Brands, more than businesses themselves, define and shape today's world because they can amplify in ways which nature, or traditional institutions, cannot. In a capitalist, consumerist and connected world, it is brands that have created the aspirations and infrastructures to magnify ideas. Whilst some people see this negatively, as superficial and manipulative, it can be incredibly positive.

What are the 'amplifiers' of business?

- **Ideas** ... contagious ideas can spread like wildfire, they require no substrate, jumping boundaries and contexts, facilitated by imaginative contexts and applications. Concepts are fusions of multiple ideas, applied to real problems; stories are narratives that embed and explain ideas over time, often in far more memorable and meaningful ways.

- **Networks** ... their value lies in their connections, which increase exponentially with every additional node. Networks are about partnerships, and enabling partners to win too, often riding on another network to get further, faster. Compare the old linear structures of supply and demand chains, with the reach and flexibility of partner ecosystems and distribution networks.

- **Brands** ... purposeful aspirations that are shared by people, bringing them together with a common code, captured in popular shorthand like names and logos. Brands turn dreams into desires, individuals into communities, enabling them to achieve more. They shape attitudes and behaviours, and therefore when linked to useful actions, or products that enable such actions, can be a hugely powerful force.

- **Business models** ... ideas (or intellectual property) and network-based commercial models allow an organization to amplify financially, whether it is a virally-addictive computer game with a 'freemium' pricing model, a collaboration that encourages greater use of existing assets, or a licensing and franchising model that rapidly replicates a business through partners.

- **Movements** ... customers who come together with a common purpose, often facilitated emotionally and maybe practically by a brand, have the power to achieve much more. With a strong voice, influence and affluence, they can shape markets and economics, politics and society. They fight for their cause, not as ambient consumers, but as empowered and organized activists.

Of course each of these **'amplifiers'** can work against a business too, a reputation, for example, can be built over years but destroyed in minutes. Whilst a business has no control over the contagious nature of markets, they do have the ability to influence, which they must learn to do.

13.3 LEADERSHIP ... INSPIRING AND ENABLING PEOPLE

Leaders are potentially the most effective amplifiers.

Nike has a Manager Manifesto defining how it wants its managers to behave. It's simple ... 'Lead. Coach. Drive. Inspire.'

Leadership is no longer about command and control. Such hierarchical 'top down' management structures emerged out of the industrial age, with the mushrooming of huge workforces, the pursuit of efficiency and consistency as the foundations of competitive advantage. This '2C' leadership style evolved from military practices in the industrial age. It respected rank and conformity, believed in status and privilege, acceptant of orders and grateful for a job.

We don't live in that world. Not only have social attitudes transformed – an equality of young and old, men and women, rich and poor, expert and fresh thinking – but business has different objectives too. Leadership is not about retaining the status quo, but about creating change. It is about unlocking the ideas and talents of everyone within and beyond the business, to seize the best opportunities, to drive innovation.

This calls for a **new leadership model** – from 2C to 4C leaders.

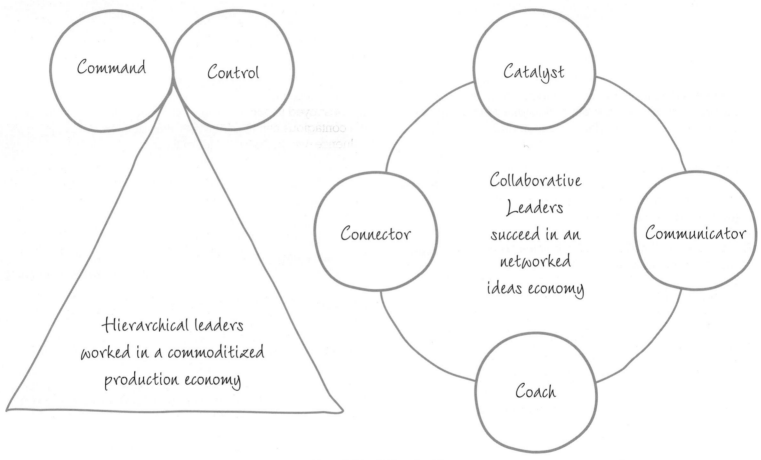

From 2C to 4C Leadership

The '4C' leader is a:

1. **Catalyst** – the leader stimulates and stretches the organization. This might be though asking questions … 'What do customer's really want? What would our competitors do?' … They add energy and urgency, focusing people on specific insights, challenges or goals.

2. **Communicator** – the leader articulates vision and direction, describing a better future, and what matters most in getting

there. At an interpersonal level, communication starts with listening, building trust and engagement through conversation.

3. **Connector** – the leader connects ideas, people, activities and partners. These might be obvious, or unusual, creating new fusions, encouraging learning and innovation. The leader looks for connections to make, then facilitates their combination.

4. **Coach** – the leader is more of a supporter than commander, working with individuals and teams to help them to think, act and deliver better. It is less about instructing and evaluating, more about advising and encouraging during the tasks, not just waiting for the end result.

The **4C leader** is much more active, sleeves rolled up, participating not watching. They are the hub of the network – encouraging and enabling teams to work better together. This is not a leader who sits in a corner office, holds meetings and reads reports. This is a leader who is at the heart of the team, with white board by their side. It requires more flexibility of time, more informal interaction, and more involvement. At the same time, the leader knows their distinctive role, bringing together a team of experts to achieve more together.

There are many definitions of leadership. Creating the inspiring vision, being the guiding conscience, and encouraging followership. The best definition I know is **'to amplify the potential of others'**.

This requires confidence and humility.

Interestingly these are more common traits of entrepreneurial leaders than the hierarchical managers of big business. Entrepreneurs have a natural determination and drive, a purpose supported by passion to make their ideas happen.

They quickly recognize that they are unlikely to achieve their dreams alone, and readily take on help. They know what they are good at, and readily accept their weaknesses. In this way they surround themselves by others who are better in their different ways. They can be also be a nightmare to work with, the rough edge to their determination to succeed.

Compare this to the traditional 'company manager' who rises through the organization through merit, but is always looking over their shoulder wary of corporate politics, or a new rising star. There is a vulnerability to their position. They constantly have to prove themselves, or prove to themselves. Surrounding themselves with others better than them can seem intimidating, or self-defeating. Of course this does not have to be the case. The more enlightened managers recognize that they can achieve more by bringing together a diversity of great talent, and by nurturing it.

Amplifying the potential of others is therefore about connections. The potential is multiplied because of the different talents that come together, but also by the support and opportunity provided by the leader. The superior impact is both individual and collective.

What does all this mean for business leaders? How can they adapt to survive and thrive in a volatile yet vibrant world?

- **Think big and think small**: Leaders need to see the world in multiple ways – to manage the turbulence of fast-changing, unpredictable markets, whilst also seeing the big trends. This requires short and long-term thinking, analytics and intuition, microscope and telecope.

- **Making complexity simple**: We know markets are incredibly complex, as are the analysis and thinking which go into making the right choices. But once a strategy is chosen, a decision made, leaders must communicate them without ambiguity, black and white, with confidence and conviction.

- **Having a map and compass**: In the past change was driven inside out, out of the need to evolve. Today, the forces of change are largely external. Less predictable, less controllable. Strategy needs to be clear and directional, but leaders mustn't be afraid to change and adapt as the journey unfolds.

- **Staying calm amidst chaos**: The calm reassurance of a captain as your plane heads through turbulence makes all the difference to passengers, and the crew who need to be at their best. Today's leaders have to make more choices than ever, requiring huge physical and emotional stamina.

- **Nice guy, tough guy**: Leaders need to be human and accessible, always listening and open to new ideas. But they also need to be decisive, and in particular in making change happen. Human nature is to resist change, at least initially, requiring leaders to push ahead, as well as take people with them.

13.4 CREATIVES ... INNOVATIVE PEOPLE ARE DIFFERENT

When I first met Richard Branson I was underwhelmed. Here was a very normal guy, if anything a little quiet and shy, who is regarded as one of the great entrepreneurs of our time. From space rocket to pantomine queen we see him as the dare devil who will do anything for PR. In reality he is easily embarrassed, stumbles over his words. But once you get to know him, that normality, even humbleness, is actually a great part of what makes him who he is.

Creative people can often seem paradoxical. They appear to embrace contradictory extremes, but looking more closely these 'yin and yang' behaviours are what set them apart from managers who prefer the status quo. They are thinkers and doers, energy givers and takers, selfless and selfish. Here are the traits I have observed:

- **Extroverted and introverted**: full of energy and enthusiasm, yet can also be quiet and reclusive.

- **Smart but innocent**: a broad scope of knowledge and expertize, yet can also seem naïve and unrealistic.

- **Playful yet disciplined**: focused and determined, but at the same time, childlike and even carefree.

- **Imaginative but grounded**: the first to dream, but also the first to point out the limitations of an idea.

- **Humble yet confident**: shy and self-deprecating, but with an inner confidence, and recognition that they are part of their brand.

- **Conform and disrupt**: absorbing the current world before producing ways to challenge and change it.

- **Passionate but critical**: driven by a sense of purpose, whilst also being their most demanding critic.

- **Process and result**: enjoy the process as much as the result; creativity and impact often matter much more than money and recognition.

When Bill Gates and Steve Jobs were interviewed together in 2007, one of the things they immediately agreed on was the role of passion. Whether an entrepreneur in his start-up garage, or an entrepreneurial CEO of a huge corporation, passion to make things, to do better, to change, is what they both saw as the most important factor in their success.

13.5 MINDFUL ... HARNESSING THE ENTREPRENEURIAL MIND

In 1940 Alvin Toffler said 'We need to learn to think in new ways to cope, let alone thrive in this world of chaotic complexity and ever changing rules.'

'**Mindfulness**' is a theme of Buddhist tradition, and means being present to what is going on around you, rather than the just being focused on your own little world. Meditation, quieting the mind, is probably the best-known way to do this. 'Presencing' (or 'becoming one with one's deepest source of future potential' according to Otto Scharmer) and 'action inquiry' (doing the task, and evaluating how you are doing it at the same time, as developed by Bill Torbert) are approaches used by the likes of Microsoft and Eli Lilly.

Mindfulness is about conditioning people to **think better** – more focus, clarity, creativity and compassion. It is about having a heightened level of attention on what matters, learning not to be distracted by relatively trivial things, embracing ideas from more diverse sources, and doing it in a way that has compassion for people and communities.

System thinking becomes essential. Issues like improving sustainability are much more complex than transactional challenges like launching a new product. System challenges are a 'spaghetti' of causes and effects, with every aspect having implications for many others. In an interconnected world, leaders need to think about how to think, not just think. I worked with **Mastercard** to create an incredibly useful model for decision making – finding new opportunities, testing new ideas, optimizing current performance. Similarly, innovators like Novo Nordisk developed multi-million dollar dynamic system models to simulate cause and effects.

As consumers become more intelligent and empowered, as business becomes more collaborative and complex, and as success is driven by thinking rather than just doing, the business brain matters more.

First let's take a simplified understanding of **the brain**. There are four characteristics that matter most:

- **Analytical**. This part seeks data and turns it into patterns, out of which come logical interpretations.
- **Expressive**. This part likes stories and visualization, it is about engagement and inspiration.
- **Curious**. This part likes to explore and investigate, it seeks discovery and sense making.
- **Sensual**. This part is about aesthetics and feelings, it is how we appreciate beauty, design and humanity.

Winning in a changing world requires '**ambidextrous' minds** that can switch back and forth between the two strategies, using the different parts of the brain. In simple terms, we use the left (logic and structure) and right (intuition and emotion) sides of our frontal cortex to achieve this. The interesting question is whether entrepreneur's brains are wired differently.

Research by IE Business School shows that managers prefer the left side, whilst **entrepreneurs use both**. When faced with a new problem or opportunity, entrepreneurs tend to use 'think bigger' techniques to evaluate a problem more simply and quickly, intuitive as much as logical, but then begin to focus in more deeply, once they have embraced the problem. Non-entrepreneurs, or typical corporate managers, tend to spend more time considering an opportunity, being slower and more cautious. This may, of course, be because of how they have been conditioned to behave.

Entrepreneurs are likely to enjoy riding speedboats more than supertankers, to build on our early analogy. Their way of thinking is more likely to embrace new opportunities faster. Whilst you could argue the rigour of the corporate manager results in less risk, it is more likely that he will struggle to embrace new rules and paradigms within his existing structures, and therefore there is a far greater risk that he will reject many of the best new opportunities. The implication for strategy and innovation is to keep evaluation broad and simple, then get into the detail once you have a focus, once you have found the space in which you want to be special.

13.6 COGNITION ... CHANGE YOUR BRAIN TO CHANGE YOUR GAME

Topfler also famously said 'The future belongs to adaptive learners and ambiguity surfers'.

Dr Tara Swart is the world's leading expert in neuroplasticity. 'The reality is that our brains don't decline, they just become more malleable. They are shaped by how we use them, but we can equally proactively shape them to help us be better.'

Kaleidoscope thinking, pattern recognition and scenario planning, reframing ideas and brands in different contexts, innovating through creative fusions, and being able to resonate with different audiences, are examples of the way gamechangers need to think differently. Swart argues that 'the ability to **learn, unlearn and relearn** demands that we constantly re-shape our brains'.

The brain grows until people are around 25 years old, rather than around 18 as we used to think. From 25 to 65 it has plasticity, before starting to decline in old age.

Swart says: 'The brain works in three dimensions – horizontal (left and right), vertical (body and brain), and across (gender and culture). The agile mind can work on both sides of each of these dimensions.'

Innovators adopt a 'growth' rather than 'fixed' mindset:

Fixed Mindset	Growth Mindset
Seeks perfection	Seeks opportunities
Fear of mistakes	Fear of missing out
Failure is painful	Failure is adventure
Innovation is incremental	Innovation is transformational
Most managers	Gamechangers

Making the shift requires a more agile mind. The emerging science of 'neuroplasticity' explains how this can be achieved.

Swart says 'Innovators are constantly learning, and therefore constantly **sculpting** their own brains'. They do this through explicit learning (left brain) such as reading and formal education, and by implicit learning (right brain) through real experiences, successes and failures.

Changing your brain means understanding which aspects to stimulate and how to achieve this. The starting point is keeping your brain fit. This is both a physical and mental challenge. Physically it's about more glucose, more water, more exercise to deliver more oxygen and more sleep. 'Don't drink alcohol or use digital media within one hour of going to sleep' warns Swart in all seriousness. Mentally it's about staying curious, having diverse interests and learning. Learning a new language is one of the best ways.

A healthy brain is more active, more connected. The bundles of neurofibres help us to make sense of the bigger picture, and think in bigger, faster ways. Women have a natural advantage in this, born with four times more connective tissue than men. As a business leader we face a barrage of knowledge, be it endless spreadsheets of data, or infinite sources of information. The challenge is not about how much we can process, but how we synthesize and apply it to our worlds, how well we make the connections.

Organizational ways to encourage this more agile mindset in business include rapid prototyping (fail fast and often), disruptive innovation, design thinking, and resource limiting. 'Cognitive stimulation is the key. Trying new and different things because learning keeps your brain active. Fluidity matters. Neurones that fire together, wire together.' Or most simply, use it or lose it.

13.7 SPEEDBOATS ... WINNING AS A SMALL BUSINESS

The new world favours the 'speedboats', the smaller companies who are **fast and agile**, more focused on global niches than large heterogeneous markets. They are able to seize new opportunities quickly, to jettison redundant capabilities and find new ones through partners.

Air Asia to Airbnb, 23andMe to Shang Xai ... like judo players, they understand their relative strengths and weaknesses, a smaller player using his speed and agility to topple a much larger and stronger opponent.

Speedboats win by staying small and focused, riding the waves of change. They don't play by the old economics of scale, where large volumes and market shares were required to cover huge capital investments. They jump across profit pools, creating brands of high perceived value, through relevance that focuses on what matters and eliminates what doesn't.

The winning characteristics of **speedboats** are:

- **Focus**: a highly selective approach to markets – geographies and segments, categories and solutions – they know who they are for, and what they are not. Guided by a clear sense of purpose, they know where they want to go, and how they will get there.

- **Fast**: they have the speed and agility to move markets, to seize opportunities, and form new partnerships quickly. They are not hindered by infrastructure or inertia, they are light and flexible, always ready and waiting for what's next.

- **Fearless**: they thrive on change, on uncertainty and ambiguity. They are not afraid to go where others haven't, or to break the rules where others are. They have little respect for convention or competition. They are much more interested in customers and the future.

Newness typically emerges in the margins not the mainstreams, and therefore speedboats have the ability to explore these more precarious waters, looking for new insights and deviant behaviours.

However, it is easy to get caught up in the excitement of newness, particularly if your pockets are lined with the cash of investors.

1999 was the year when the infantile internet bubble burst. I remember working in Silicon Valley in the months earlier, as meteoric IPOs delivered massive wealth creation, at least on paper, and red Corvettes cruised the Interstates heading to beach parties. People worshipped at HP's founder's 'garage' and even Microsoft was loved. I read a book called *The Monk and The Riddle* by Randy Komisar, which talked about leadership with purpose, to create a better life of more than money. But few people bothered.

Whilst many investors emerged with their fingers burnt, and many start-up kids went back to college to study accountancy, or some other grounded subject, there were a number of companies who rode the storm, and emerged stronger and better.

Amazon's Jeff Bezos became almost repetitive in his letters to shareholders saying 'We must **stick to our vision** no matter what, but fine-tune it with data'. He insisted that Amazon would always build value for shareholders over the long term, but to do this he would 'extend and solidify our current market leadership position' and 'focus relentlessly on our customers'. That persistence has delivered $185 billion market value. The team tracked data on shoppers, how they used the site, what mattered most to them, constantly evolving to improve their experience.

Netflix thrived by focusing on what matters to people in good times and bad. As Reed Hastings said in *Fortune* magazine 'When there's an ache, you want to be like aspirin, not vitamins. Aspirin solves a very particular problem someone has, whereas vitamins are a general "nice to have" market.' People will always want to watch movies. The trick is to keep changing. In the DVD rental market Netflix moved from charging per item, to monthly subscriptions, and then as broadband networks improved, it was the first to offer streamed content.

Priceline was one of my favourite business models of the late 1990s. It asked you to name your own price for a hotel room, and then searched for a supplier to match it. Whilst its success was modest, it learnt more about the online travel market than anyone else. After the dotcom bust, Priceline snapped up booking sites like Agoda and Booking.com, quickly becoming the market leader in Europe and especially in Asia, and now the world's fastest growing travel market. That perseverance and agility makes Priceline a bigger success than even Amazon or Netflix.

The implications are important. For start-ups, it means that the holy grail is not simply to be big, nor will success come instantly. Most start-ups **pivot** a number of times before they find out what really works. For larger companies, it means that growth might come from smaller brands, or venture businesses.

13.8 SUPERTANKERS ... WINNING AS A LARGE BUSINESS

At the same time, markets are still dominated by the supertankers. Huge multi-billion dollar organizations, from Adidas to AT&T, Volkswagen to WalMart, who continue on their steady course. They win through their scale – familiar and convenient brands, well-established business models and channel structures – and by taking often smaller margins in huge markets.

The temptation is to reach out to everyone – either through a diverse portfolio of brands and products, or less successfully, by trying to be all things to everyone. As organic growth plateaus they go on acquisition sprees, sucking up the smaller companies, hoping that their entrepreneurial magic will rub off on the larger company. As we know from Ben and Jerry's in Unilever to Body Shop at L'Oreal, this rarely happens. Speedboats become inseperable from their supertankers.

However there is a future for large companies if they learn to play in the new world and to change their game. Whilst Apple seems to be slowing, Amazon is speeding up. Jeff Bezos has been playing a long-term customer-centric game, developing a multitude of businesses and services that support each other whilst also reaching out to new categories and markets. From Air to Audible, Fire and Fresh, his concepts are more like speedboats with a shared plan.

The winning characteristics of **supertankers** are:

- **Flat**: avoiding the complex hierarchies that slow most organizations, so business units can work more easily alongside each other, creating horizontal rather than vertical flows. Leaders empowering operational managers to adapt to locality and the needs of individuals.

- **Flexible**: prioritizing innovation and change ahead of efficiency and stability, defining and measuring success on outcomes, being ready to use old assets in new ways, and to let go of declining brands and markets. And culturally, having an attitude that loves creativity and newness.

- **Further**: unlocking the advantages of scale – well established brands, global networks of distributors, huge communities of customers, access to capital and to take new ideas further and faster, whilst also adapting the old models by learning from and respecting smaller players.

One of the most popular traits in large companies is the desire to rediscover their entrepreneurial spirit. GE wants its managers to recreate the spirit of Thomas Edison. They seek to recreate these 'intrapreneurs' with idea incubators and entrepreneurial boot camps.

Coke's Venturing & Emerging Brands (VEB) team, set up in 2007, seeks 'to identify and build the company's next generation of billion-dollar brands'. It is a combination of venture capitalist thinking, brand incubator process, driven by foresight and imagination. The team focuses on unmet consumer needs, then develops new concepts to address them. Innovations range from NOS energy and FUZE juice drinks, Honest Tea and Zico coconut water, Core Power protein drinks and Illy Issimo ready to drink coffee.

VEB is a combination of art and science, research and serendipity. It starts with an insight of what consumers are looking for, now and in the future. It collaborates with all different types of people, from social influencers to wellness experts, entrepreneurs and early-adopter consumers, distributors and retailers. Most importantly, the team values being 'out there' rather than reading research and reports based on existing mental models.

Whilst it is certainly easier for speedboats to be 'gamechangers', supertankers have many advantages too – brand and reputation, heritage and presence, outlets and partners, systems and processes, and of course people.

13.9 GAMECHANGER ... BOLD, BRAVE AND BRILLIANT

You're ready to change the game ...

Big or small, young or old, whatever your background, and wherever you are, there is **nothing stopping you**, except your imagination.

- Be curious in the world, constantly seeking to make sense of change.

- Live in the present, don't wait for the future to happen.

- Don't accept the future as a given, set about **creating** it in your own vision.

- Embrace technology, but remember that the world is human.

- Keep thinking about how you are **making life better** for people.

- Recognize that there are many paths to success, so find one that suits you.

- All you need is a **good idea**, there are partners for everything else.

- The best way to learn is to try. Never stop learning.

- Don't be afraid. We are all equal in the future.

And remember Steve Jobs, 'your time is limited, don't waste it living somebody else's life'.

Be bold. Be brave. Be brilliant.

CHANGE YOUR GAME

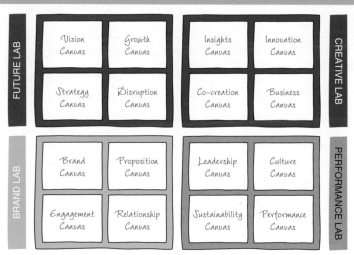

Practically apply the concepts in this chapter to your business with the relevant tools in the Gamechanger Labs:

- **Leadership** canvas

- **Culture** canvas

- **Performance** canvas

Practical examples can be found in the 100 cases studies. Also see more details at Gamechangers.pro

PART 3
THE GAMECHANGERS

Next generation brands are shaking up every market. Alibaba to Zidisha, Ashmei to Zilok... Big and small, East and West... retail to banking, fashion to healthcare...fusing and adapting the 21st century toolkit in their own vision...Which brands are changing your world? What's their new game, and how are they winning?

WHO ARE THE GAMECHANGERS?

Ideas are good, but the future is created by **applying** them in the real world. In today's markets the future is rarely created by the large, slow and complex corporations, and more often by the fast and **free-thinking** smaller companies who see and **seize change** first.

Newness is created in the **margins** not the mainstream.

I asked 100 game-changing **entrepreneurs**, thinkers and business **leaders** about what inspired them, who they would nominate as 'gamechangers'. Familiar innovators like Amazon, Apple and Nike were popular choices, but they also talked about many other local and emerging brands – showing that every one of us could be a gamechanger:

'Natura, the eco-friendly Brazilian cosmetic company who has changed their entire view on what cosmetics of the future is all about – focusing on ordinary woman.'
Martin Lindstrom, author of *Buyology*, Copenhagen, Denmark

*'To point out one we would maybe say **Nike**. The company moved away from "plain jane" product (although very good ones!) to an extended halo of services that together with brilliant advertising is really making a difference for users. They recognized that it is not only about the product but also about user experience, sense of belonging to a community, personal overcoming, etc. Just brilliant! Just do it.'*
Paulo Miguel Pereira da Silva, CEO of Renova, Torres Novas, Portugal

*'A purpose driven inspirational leader prepared to fail fast, learn fast and fix fast. Ideas that create loyalty beyond reason and are dripping with mystery, sensuality and intimacy. Whilst I would say **Lovemarks** (Robert's own concept of enhancing a brand with more purpose and passion) is a gamechanger in the advertising business, but I would also nominate **Manchester City FC** for its community roots that go beyond football.'*
Kevin Roberts, Worldwide CEO of Saatchi and Saatchi, Auckland New Zealand

*'I choose **Ebay**, for revolutionizing the concept of trust in strangers and building a practical system powered by the new concept of trust ... **Wikipedia**, for showing the world the heights that can be reached by a community of virtual volunteers ... and **Amazon**, for pioneering the integration of customer reviews and independent sellers to better serve customer needs.'*
Julia Kurnia, founder of Zidisha, Nairobi, Kenya

*'I'm big on disruptors – those companies who change the basic paradigm of a core industry or transform consumer behaviour. The obvious examples would **Apple** and iTunes who transformed the way we consume music, or **Amazon's** disruption of the book distribution model. If you are at the helm of creating a "digital product" that becomes mass adopted and in doing so kills the traditional physical distribution layer, then I think you have a much more deliberate role in changing the game than networks or other products generally. If you eliminate the need for a physical product in a physical store, then that's massive.*

*In finance, I've been particularly impressed with **Square**. Not only did Dorsey found Twitter, but he then went on to use his newfound momentum to attack an area of real friction in the small business space. There are roughly 30 million small businesses in North America today that don't have the ability to take a credit card payment. He made it as simple as filling out an online form, downloading an app and plugging a Square "dongle" or device into your smartphone – and now*

you can accept credit cards. That's why they built a business with 2 million new merchants in just three years. Their ability to take the friction out of an old, outdated, protected process and make it easier for small business owners and consumers alike, is the real innovation of Square.'
Brett King, author of *Bank 2.0*, and founder of Moven, New York, USA

*'I would choose **Apple**. I have used their products since 1991 because they made sense. They were the tool of choice for designers because they worked. Simple. They looked no different to PCs and were known as the underdog due to their poor compatibility with PCs. How times have changed. Apple solved their performance and quality, but it's only when they adopted some style that the brand really became mainstream.'*
Stuart Brooks, founder and CEO of Ashmei, London, UK

*'**Apple** is an iconic brand for many industries, but we admire their mobile products because they have forever changed the way healthcare professionals access information. The iPad Mini, launched in late 2012, comes in at the perfect size for a lab coat pocket. More clinicians are adopting this device due to the lightweight portability, easy readability and medium screen for basic data entry. Plus, applications clinicians need at the point of care, like Epocrates, run beautifully on the platform.'*
Rob Cosinuke, CMO of AthenaHealth, Boston, USA

*'**Fair Trade** is a great game-changing business. It is more an NGO, it developed a standard for fair treatment of suppliers, co-workers and contributors within the supply chain and became a business model. [Our organic food brand] ISIS is not only inspired by FairTrade, but created and implemented the Economy of Love, a business model where everyone in*

the supply chain is getting a fair part of the added value, enough to develop himself, satisfy his own family needs and community.'
Helmy Abouleish, MD of SEKEM, Cairo, Egypt

'We look at who is best in class rather than best in our sector for inspiration. To us, those companies that have consistently and continuously innovated and are strongly focused on value creation are role models. We strive to emulate them, leveraging the talent and vision of our own business.'
Sarah Lockie, Senior VP of DP World, Dubai, UAE

*'I would choose **Abercrombie** for selling you a simple t-shirt but with a smell, music, atmosphere, sells you a whole feeling. **Emirates**, who were laughed at in the beginning but knew which markets to give attention and created an image of exquisite comfort. **Amazon** for changing customers' buying habits.'*
Aline Kamakian, Chef and Founder of Mayrig Restaurant, Beirut, Lebanon

*'I greatly admire **Nike** who since various child labour scandals in the 80s and 90s have implemented stringent social and environmental policies throughout their business model. This is a company that is not simply appeasing demand for retribution but striving to better themselves in all aspects of the company for the present and for the future. In the "Clean Air-Cool Planet" environmental survey, Nike ranked among the top three companies and is leading the way with inspiring and pioneering programs such as the Nike Reuse-A-Shoe program which benefits both the environment and the community by collecting old athletic shoes of any type in order to process and recycle them. The material that is produced is then used to help create sports surfaces such as basketball courts, running tracks, and playgrounds.'*
Diana Verde Nieto, founder of Positive Luxury, Beunes Aires, Argentina

169

'Gamechangers are brands that question the accepted wisdom of the market, and change the rules, for example how to be low cost and great quality. They do what is right for the brand, right for the customer, and what is socially responsible.

*My examples would include **GiffGaff** because they tapped into a completely unexplored segment and threw away their risk models. **Metro Bank** because they have managed to bring a human face to banking with a different experience. **Burberry** because as a 156 year old company it is leading the way in integrating online and offline retail. **Lush** because they innovate everything from cosmetics to campaigns, ethics to experience. And **Sugru**, the self-setting rubber that can be moulded in your hand.'*

Shaun Smith, co-author of *See Feel Think Do*, London UK

'GAMECHANGERS' BY SECTOR AND REGION

Large and small, start-ups and corporates, across every sector of business, and from every corner of the planet, they each offer ideas and inspiration for us to apply. Whilst the concepts and tools are quite common, it is the distinctive ways in which they **combine and apply** them, and the impact they have on specific markets, that is quite spectacular. They use their imagination and insight to find innovative ways to combine new business models with sustainable practices, social media with new value propositions, fast-growing markets with a new approach to leadership.

How do each of these brands **'change the game'**? How do they create markets in their own vision, combine and apply the concepts and tools in relevant and distinctive ways, to deliver success?

We explore the brands by sector, highlighting their 'gamechanging' approaches, because this is where they have most impact, shaking up our worlds. For each sector, we consider three in more detail, including the **'pivot points'** of significant change, and some of the many other innovators more briefly. What is interesting is how differently each brand chooses to innovate, producing a mosaic of possible futures to explore individually, and also the potential of combining them into new **market models**.

Futurestore

- Amazon ●
- Fab ●
- Positive Luxury ●
- Aussie Farmers Direct ●
- Ekocycle ●
- Etsy ●
- Rackuten Ichiba ●
- Inditex ●
- Trader Joe's ●
- Le Pain Quotidien ●

Futurebank

- Moven ●
- Umpqua ●
- Zidisha ●
- Square ●
- La Caixa ●
- Commonwealth Bank ●
- Fidor ●
- Itau Unibanco ●
- First National Bank ●
- M-Pesa ●

Futurehealth

- 23andMe ●
- Epocrates ●
- Narayana Hrudayalaya ●
- Aravind Eyecare ●
- Genentech ●
- Organova ●
- Intuitive Surgical ●
- PatientsLikeMe ●
- Scanadu ●
- Second Sight ●

Futuregadget

- Renova ●
- Method ●
- Nike ●
- Apple ●
- Godrej ●
- Lego ●
- Natura Cosmetics ●
- Oculus Rift ●
- Pebble ●
- Philosophy ●

Futuremedia

- Coursera ●
- Spotify ●
- Netflix ●
- Al Jazeera ●
- Future ●
- Pledge ●
- Ushahidi ●
- Red Bull ●
- Supercell ●
- Pixar ●

Futurefashion

- Toms ●
- Ashmei ●
- Threadless ●
- Gilan ●
- Desigual ●
- Editd ●
- Kering ●
- Rapha ●
- Patagonia ●
- Shang Xai ●

Futuretravel

- Zipcars ●
- Airbnb ●
- Virgin Galactic ●
- Aeromobil ●
- Air Asia ●
- Emirates ●
- Kulula ●
- Pipistrel ●
- Red Bus ●
- Starwood ●

Futurefood

- Juan Valdez Cafe ●
- Zespri ●
- Mayrig ●
- Yeni Raki ●
- Aerolife ●
- Beauty'in ●
- Graze ●
- LA Organic ●
- Moa Beer ●
- Nespresso ●

Futuretech

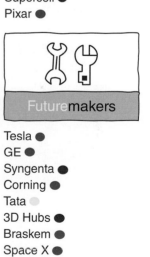

- Samsung ●
- ARM ●
- Raspberry Pi ●
- Alibaba ●
- Bharti Airtel ●
- GiffGaff ●
- Google <X> ●
- Huawei ●
- Tencent ●
- Xiaomi ●

Futuremakers

- Tesla ●
- GE ●
- Syngenta ●
- Corning ●
- Tata ●
- 3D Hubs ●
- Braskem ●
- Space X ●
- Dyson ●
- Local Motors ●

■ North American   ■ South American   ■ European   ■ African/Arab   ■ Asian/Oceania

The 100 Gamechangers

14 FUTURESTORE

CHANGING THE GAME OF RETAIL

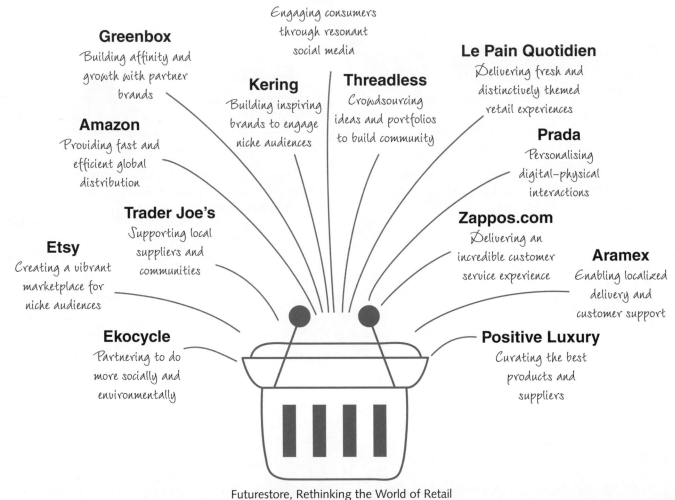

Fab
Engaging consumers
through resonant
social media

Greenbox
Building affinity and
growth with partner
brands

Le Pain Quotidien
Delivering fresh and
distinctively themed
retail experiences

Kering
Building inspiring
brands to engage
niche audiences

Threadless
Crowdsourcing
ideas and portfolios
to build community

Amazon
Providing fast and
efficient global
distribution

Prada
Personalising
digital–physical
interactions

Trader Joe's
Supporting local
suppliers and
communities

Zappos.com
Delivering an
incredible customer
service experience

Etsy
Creating a vibrant
marketplace for
niche audiences

Aramex
Enabling localized
delivery and
customer support

Ekocycle
Partnering to do
more socially and
environmentally

Positive Luxury
Curating the best
products and
suppliers

Futurestore, Rethinking the World of Retail

From Amazon to Etsy, ZaoZao and Zappos … through branded boutiques and online marketplaces, digital walls and mobile marketing, big data and personalized promotions … what is the future of retailing, in general, and for your business?

Walking around the **Burberry flagship store** on London's Regent Street, with its beautifully arranged clothes, its magic mirrors that superimpose your image in the clothes of your fantasy and place of your choice, and the VVIP room on the top floor, it is a world of imagination, where emotions not rational desire prevails. It is the work of designer Christopher Bailey who has overseen the rejuvenation of the brand from its 'chav' ubiquity to its super premium status. The $100,000 limited edition white alligator skin jacket, not to everyone's taste, perhaps demonstrates this stretch. It is a brand that is truly global, more Asian than European if measured by its custom, and more digital then physical, based on the focus of its innovations. Burberry showcases the future of retail – as a niche focused, premium branded, hybrid experience.

SMART SHOPPERS, SMART STORES

Online retail has grown rapidly over the last decade, from a marginal bolt-on, to major revenue stream in a **multi-channel** model. In the USA, it has grown by around 18% per year, and now accounts for 8% of all sales. But digital is more that this, it is not just another way but a fundamental capability that can enhance every channel. Search on your phone, buy

online, pick up in store. Go to the store, use your phone to buy, delivered to your home. Retail innovation is about **hybrids**, combining physical and digital activities and options in a more experiential and valuable way.

Retail purpose, formats and incentives all change – whilst loyalty cards originally drove behaviour through points, people soon became wise that the rewards were trivial compared to special offers in store. Whilst stores have enhanced their **shopper experiences**, markets have fragmented with more space for discounters. In Turkey, for example, BIM has taken around 40% of the food market with low price, small outlets across cities. At the same time, online players have morphed into credible alternatives, where Amazon sells wines and eBay replaces physical outlet stores. More emotionally, technologies such as Synqera from Russia can 'mind-read' a shopper's emotions, judging how to best engage them as they shop and how to make them smile.

DIGITAL HYBRIDS, DATA AND MOBILE

Mobile is already a huge factor: at upmarket fashion retailer Gilt, 50% of shoppers and 30% of sales are by mobile. It is the glue that brings together online and offline, creating more personal experiences, from individual promotions geo-targeted, to in-store research and navigation, price checks and comparisons, as well as fast and safe payment. As newspapers are replaced by digital news, TV is on demand,

and online retailers never close their doors, the way retailers engage and serve consumers changes. We expect 24-hour access, we don't tolerate stock outs, compare prices instantly, shop beyond our borders, and demand delivery in 24 hours.

Big data, the huge quantities of transactional data, mashed with other sources of personal and behavioural data through complex algorithms, means that marketing is highly personalized. Around 35% of all Amazon purchases and 75% of Netflix movie choices are based on **recommendations**. Of course these suggestions compete with the much more trusted recommmendations of friends and peers on social media, often valued around 10 times more highly than anything from a brand. A brand therefore needs to think laterally about how to influence **communities**, and give them the abilities and incentives to influence each other. Consumers also become much less tolerant of failures, unavailable products or poor service, they expect free and easy returns, and they immediately tweet their feelings, particularly the negative ones, to thousands of people like them.

GAMECHANGERS

Together, our gamechangers show how the variety of innovations builds a future vision of retail. The demand side is led by the engaging, personal experiences – driven by the passion of Zappos, the collaboration of Threadless. On the supply side, this is about the efficiency and speed of Amazon, the reach and richness of Aramex or Etsy, and the transparency of Positive Luxury. In between is the ability to match niche segments with lifestyle store experiences, and whilst the Abercrombie brand portfolio is not without challenges, it knows how to connect.

Amazon ... putting the Zappos into selling everything

Amazon, from Dash to drones, Kindles to Zappos, uses technology to disrupt and redefine a range of adjacent industries, and then do it again, whilst adding new business models that create a convenient and personalized customer experience.

Jeff Bezos laughs with a distinctive cackle. He is still the hands-on CEO, strategist and innovator, keeps a relatively low profile, but his innovations have become bolder. His Kindle Fire, significantly better than his early e-book reader, is now challenging the iPad, whilst his repurposing of books into short-read 'singles' is challenging the whole book trade. The development of self-publishing has helped Kindle to 'own' exclusive content, whilst acquisitions such as Audible (audio books, 2008), LoveFilm (videos on demand, 2011), Goodreads (reader community, 2013) and Twitch (gaming, 2014) has extended the content beyond books, and interactions beyond purchases.

Zappos, famed for its customer service in selling shoes online, became part of Amazon in 2009. This heralded the way for many more types of everyday products. In 2010 more acquisitions such as Quidsi and BeautyBar added personal care, pet supplies, toys, and groceries.

Whilst Amazon has acquired around 50 businesses as it has grown and diversified, it keeps the businesses small and distinctive, whilst connecting them through the retail platform. Zappos, for example, which started by selling shoes, has built a much-admired culture of happiness. In his book, *Delivering Happiness*, founder Tony Hsieh explains the moment when he realized women don't buy shoes, they buy happiness, an insight that transformed his business.

The $75 billion business is truly international, with versions in everything from Chinese and Japanese, to Spanish and Brazilian Portuguese. Whilst the profits from its devices and content sales have been much slower than Apple's, Amazon has always played a longer-term game, shaping the market first, then letting the rewards follow.

Bezos likes to point out the shift in power from companies to consumers, yet Amazon becomes more powerful every day. The Kindle Fire now rivals the iPad, Amazon Prime's annual membership that gives free next-day shipping was a masterstroke, whilst the same-day grocery delivery service, Amazon Fresh, is set to transform behaviours and expectations further. And we wait to see whether the former investment banker's vision of 30-minute delivery by mini-drones will come true.

Pivot points for Amazon in 'changing the game' of retail have been:

EXPLORE   Making sense of changing markets, finding the best growth opportunities

DISRUPT   Shaping the markets in your own vision, rewriting the rules of play

DESIGN   Creating business models that are consumer-centric and scalable

ENABLE   Delivering a more personal, sticky and contagious customer experience

Amazon is just at the beginning of its journey, says Bezos; commenting in his recently acquired *Washington Post* he said 'In a sense it's still day one. There's still so much you can do with technology to improve the customer experience. And the rate of change continues to accelerate'.

Fab ... from fabulously gay to simply fab

Fab is an online curator of beautiful products. From initially targeting a niche demographic, they found that by relaunching more openly, and with a strong use of social media, they attracted a more attitudinal audience.

'Fab is the place to discover the most exciting things for your life' say founders Jason Goldberg and Bradford Shellhammer.

Back in 2011, entrepreneur and designer were frustrated by the lack of progress of their social network Fabulis.com, which was trying to be the Facebook, Tripadvisor and Groupon all-in-one for the gay community. It wasn't working, stuck at 150,000 users, so they decided to shut down and start again.

They recognized they needed to learn from their experience, but also refocus with an almost clean slate. They reduced their team to its core, and put up a 'Coming Soon' notice to hopefully retain the curiosity of previous users. Three months later came their 'pivot' moment, relaunching as Fab.com, a flash sales site for designer clothing, accessories and homewares. Within six months they had two million users, 100 employees, and $50 million in venture funding. By the end of 2012 they had doubled their funding, and attracted 10 million users, buying 5.4 products every minute. The bold branding and clean, colourful, ever-changing page design plays to its audience.

Fab's exponential growth demonstrates how social media can drive retail, with a mobile-centred experience. Community is sustained by an ever-changing Inspiration Wall, and Live Feed where users share their desires and purchase, linking to Twitter and a user's Facebook Timeline. The next step is physical, with flash stores opening in cities where virtual communities are most vibrant.

Pivot points for Fab in 'changing the game' of retail have been:

EXPLORE   Targeting a niche audience, not defined by gender but by attitude

DISRUPT   Staying agile to learn as you grow, not afraid to change direction

RESONATE   Using social media to connect with, and connect, your consumers

AMPLIFY   Unlocking the power of contagious networks to drive growth

Positive Luxury ... the butterfly mark of better brands

Curation is a key role for retailer, editing and guiding in a world of infinite choice. Making sustainability positive, being better rather than less bad, being authentic and natural, softer or brighter.

Positive Luxury's mission is to curate and champion an exclusive collection of stylish, responsible brands, or as founder Diana Verde Nieto puts it 'creating the ultimate destination for people looking to live a more positive life'.

> 'Our vision is for a world where people and the environment prosper together – where companies and brands are part of the solution. We believe that the best way to promote positive living is to make it attractive, enjoyable and profitable for people, businesses and communities.'

What that means in practice is that people need inspiration and information about what is fashionable and innovative, but also the social and environmental impacts of the brands and companies too. This is particularly the case for luxury brands that were slower to embrace ethical practices.

Consumers want good stuff, and they want to do good too.

Positive Luxury's butterfly 'trust mark' is a simple way of labelling the products and brands that have you can rely on. Living, and shopping, should be a positive experience, argues Verde Nieto, not about wading through claims and counter claims. 'We make it easy to live more positively.'

She chose the logo because of its beauty and fragility – the Large Blue was wiped out in the UK in the 1970s, thanks to new farming techniques and over-eager butterfly collectors. In 1983, conservationists started importing the species from Sweden, which with the help of 23 organizations became the most successful insect reintroduction programme in the world.

'We believe we can all play a part in reversing environmental damage, and that making more informed choices about the brands we choose to buy can help us each to create our own blue butterfly story. In other words you get to look good and live well without changing your habits – you just have to know where to shop. And we're doing that bit for you.' All you have to do is look for the butterfly mark.

Pivot points for Positive Luxury in 'changing the game' of retail have been:

THINK   Making sense of consumers, making sustainability desirable

INSPIRE   Creating a brand trusted and desired by businesses and consumers

DESIGN   Building a business models with multiple revenue streams

IMPACT   Helping people live a better life, and brands to build a better world

Aussie Farmers Direct ... fast and fresh, field to fork

Aussies love the outdoors, fresh and natural. So the farmers jumped on the milk floats and brought together the best of local, authentic produce from across the nation, ready to deliver direct to the door. The business model is lean and networked, taps current trends and builds community.

Graeme Beevers from Mildura in Victoria grows the tastiest Aussie oranges, John Bruce produces highly sought-after Aussie beef from Cape Grim in Tasmania, whilst Michelle Wilkinson is a superstar in the mushroom world, knowing just when to pick her cups. Authentic, curated and delivering direct to your home, Aussie Farmers Direct have transformed the definition of fresh food down under. By bringing back the much loved 'milko', or local milkman, a network of franchisees deliver a huge selection of the best 100% Australian owned, grown and produced products every morning.

CEO Braeden Lord says 'We started with an underlying philosophy around supporting the Australian farmer, and making a stronger connection between the farm and the urban household and the front doorstep by cutting out the middlemen and looking at the most expedient and efficient way to take great quality Australian produce and deliver it to people's front doorsteps.'

Since 2006, the network has grown from three people and one milk float, to a company with 250 franchisees who provide almost 250,000 households across Australia with fresh fruit, vegetables, milk, eggs, bread, meat, seafood and more. It's also the largest supplier of organic food. Yet there is still much potential, having so far only gained around 4% market share. The network is also investing in suppliers; for example, buying a dairy plant in 2011 that had been mothballed for 12 years in a small rural community.

AFD is about personalization and community, a preferred choice for many farmers tired of the buying power of large supermarkets. Quality and sustainability come before price, recognizing that its target consumers will pay a little more for such things. It is also about advanced technologies. Most orders come through its smartphone apps, allowing easy ordering and fast delivery.

Ekocycle ... Will.i.am and Coke declare war on waste

Ekocycle is part of Coke's ambition to 'live positively' ... and Will.i.am's desire to inspire a new generation by making old stuff cool. Through partnerships and creative design, brands can be enriched and do good.

Black Eyed Peas lead singer, writer and producer, designer and innovator, **Will.i.am** (known as William Adams to his mother, the kid who grew up in the tough neighbourhood of East LA, and was encouraged to find music rather than a life of crime) created Ekocycle with The Coca-Cola Company.

Will has a hate of waste, and Coke wanted a new platform to make a bigger difference to the world. Instead of just reducing or recycling, Ekocycle ('ekoc' is Coke backwards, you note) set out to create new things from old materials, to encourage any brand or individual to get involved, and start making and selling their art, clothing, gadgets or whatever. To inspire and enable young people be sustainable and, of course, cool.

Coca-Cola pledged $1 million start-up investment, and the first products in 2012 included special edition, made from waste, headphones from Beats by Dr. Dre, one of Will's own ventures. The headphones, priced at around $350 are primarily made out of three types of recycled plastic bottles. In 2014, Ekocycle launched the Cube 3D printer, encouraging people to turn their waste plastic bottles into wonderful creations, or as Will put it, into things which are 'beautiful and better'.

Ekocycle is as much about inspiration and education as simply making money. Demonstrating that sustainability isn't about less but more, not just about reducing consumption and emissions which can feel a little tiring at times, but about creativity and innovation, finding new materials that actually work better, design that is novel, and products that are more individual.

Etsy ... digital craft market for the world's artists

Etsy has given local markets a global reach, bringing together like-minded buyers and sellers as a passionate movement. The business model makes it fair and accessible to the smallest trader.

Etsy has brought the world of local artisans and handmade crafts, vintage collectors and bored websurfers to the wider online world. Everything you might find in a local market, independent stores or Turkish Bazaar, is now accessible on Etsy. Handmade jewellery is the top seller, followed by wedding goods with oil paintings not far behind. Whilst most goods initially came from North America (in particular from Oregon and Utah, sold to consumers in Alaska and Massachucetts), Chinese and Indian goods are rising fastest.

'Etsy is the marketplace we make together.

Our mission is to reimagine commerce in ways that build a more fulfilling and lasting world.

We are a mindful, transparent, and humane business.

We plan and build for the long term.

We value craftsmanship in all we make.

We believe fun should be part of everything we do.

We keep it real, always.'

Etsy was founded in 2005 by Rob Kalin – a keen painter, carpenter, and photographer – finding no viable marketplace to exhibit and sell his creations online and other sites like eBay full of overstocked electronics and fake goods. The business charges $0.20 per listing and takes a 3.5% cut of the sales price. In 2012 membership doubled to 22 million, with 14 million people making 1000 million purchases, resulting in revenues of close to $1 billion for the online marketplace.

Etsy Labs are an educational and physical showcase for small artist communities in Brooklyn and Berlin. They include free events and workshops that focus on teaching people how to make things. From screenprinting and knitting, to photography and bike repair. In an online world, they help to build creative communities physically too, and also have pop-up labs in major cities.

The business model is built around a community of participants, brought together by a love of great products rather than cheap prices. Blogs and forums, apps for every platform, links to Facebook and Twitter, keep the market active 24 × 7. Reputations are crucial to both sellers and buyers, with both able to rate and review the other. The Etsy brand defines a marketplace, a community that is local and global, a movement of people with shared values, and as Kalin himself says, 'about we more than me'.

Members love Esty so much that they themselves created a niche social media site to support their community. etsylove. ning.com has over 11,400 members who love the brand and being connected to each other, driving more purchases, more livelihoods and more art.

Rackuten Ichiba ... crabs and kimonos with 'omotenashi'

As markets become more fragmented into specialist niches, the economics of local stores gives way to online platforms. With careful focus, small businesses can become global and profitable, without the costs of becoming big.

Rakuten Ichiba is one of the world's largest online shopping malls. Founded in Tokyo in 1997, it has built a $5 billion global presence through acquisitions of complementary businesses such as Buy.com in USA, Ikeda in Brazil, Tradoria in Germany and Play.com in the UK.

Whereas other marketplaces may compete directly with sellers, Rakuten empowers merchants to deliver 'Omotenashi', a Japanese attitude to customer service and hospitality, intended to help sellers create lasting relationships with buyers. An example is when the host anticipates the needs of the guest in advance and offers a personal service that guests don't expect. This is particularly important in Japanese culture where guests who make their requests directly are considered unsophisticated

Rakuten is like a mainstream, Japanese version of Etsy. It's an online mall in the sense that it creates a platform where 30,000 independent retailers set up their virtual shops selling over 1 million different products. Like Amazon, it builds up rich data-driven profiles of consumers, to anticipate needs and match them with relevant retailers. It has central warehouses from where the retailer's goods a centrally collated and then distributed to consumers. Like eBay it has an auction facility. This business model is sometimes referred to as a 'B2B2B2C' model, just like a physical shopping, where retailers are charged a site lease fee, but also commissions on sales.

Tatsuya Abe is Japan's crab-meat king. His Yamato seafood company based in Shiogama offers the best-quality seafood, in particular the local favourite Alaskan and Russian taraba crab. However his wealthy consumers are niche and dispersed, making the investment in stores unrealistic. Instead he set up a virtual store on Rakuten Ichiba and was able to deliver his premium crab meat overnight. From initial monthly sales of ¥130,000 (around $1500) he has grown his business, through online brand building, to ¥40 million ($45,0000) per month.

The company's intent is 'to create the number-one internet services company in the world' through continuous innovation, building on the 77 million consumers, who are attracted by online shopping and banking, to investments and travel, entertainment tickets and golf-course reservations.

CEO Hiroshi Mikitani sees two big challenges for Japanese to become a global business – adopting English as the practical language of the world, and getting over Japan's sense of national superiority, which he believes is increasingly isolating many Japanese businesses. At the same time, Mikitani has made it his mission to give economic hope to small traders across Japan, saying there are so many merchants who could have gone bankrupt without his business, including the entire kimono industry.

Inditex ... fast fashion from La Coruña to Zara

Inditex group has built on the global success of Zara and its fast fashion, to develop a range of retail brands that carefully target adjacent market segments with distinctive and relevant fashions. As markets and trends evolve the portfolio gives the group strength and agility.

Amancio Ortega likes to say 'fashion is like selling fish'. Fresh fish, like a freshly cut jacket in the latest colour sells quickly at a high price. An old catch has to be discounted or thrown away. 'Selling fish' has made Inditex one of the world's largest clothing retailers. From the first Zara store in the Spanish fishing port of La Coruña, opened in 1975, Ortego has added almost a hundred companies designing, making, and distributing the latest fashions. It has made him the richest man in Spain, and third in the world; with 6200 stores worldwide, and brands ranging from Bershka to Pull and Bear, Mango and Zara.

Zara achieves speed and efficiency through an integrated system of design, production, logistics and distribution which also keeps stock minimal, and the store range evolves almost weekly. Employees also convey a continuous flow of shopper information,

what they try and buy, and why they don't. The 200 person creative team each has direct links to a store around the world to ensure insights are captured directly and quickly, and the brand anticipates and responds to the latest trends.

Whilst competitors make clothes in distant low-cost markets, Inditex values the speed and proximity of Spain, Portugal and Morocco. New designs arrive every three days in stores, often in the same week as similar designs appear in magazines or fashion shows. They sell out quickly, usually at full price, and consumers come back weekly to see what's new.

However Inditex's centralized structure, now controlled from The Cube head office in Arteixo, a small fishing town in northwest Spain, is both a strength in Europe and a weakness in other parts of the world. Whilst a $324m Fifth Avenue flagship store has been successful in New York, Zara with its tight slim-fit has struggled in other parts of USA. China is now the second largest market with over 150 stores. Fast, yet standardized, fashions work less well around the world.

Trader Joe's ... quirky, healthy neighbourhood stores

Trader Joe's curates to simplify and humanize. With less it can do more, bringing its personality to life through discovery, humour and storytelling while at the same time caring about community, environment and good value.

Trader Joe's calls itself a neighbourhood store, yet boasts 350 locations and $8 billion in annual profits. Unlike most stores sprawling with 50,000 or more items, curation is key here, with less than 4000 different products on the shelves. Careful selection helps the chain generate $1750 per square foot, twice as much as Whole Foods.

Joe Coulombe was the original Trader Joe, and having started out as Pronto Market convenience stores in 1958, moved to his own name two decades later. Joe did things differently, and his stores reflected his love of Hawaiian beach culture with walls decked with cedar planks and staff dressed in cool Hawaiian shirts. Most importantly, he started putting innovative, hard-to-find, great-tasting foods in the 'Trader Joe's' name.

Value mattered to Joe. And the premium, exotic specialities he brought together were complemented by his low-priced own-label ranges which combined quality and quirkiness. In 1979 Joe sold his brand to Theo Albrecht, better known for his low priced Aldi food stores in Europe. Aldi and Joe both believed in keeping things simple. No discounts, points cards, or members' clubs. With a limited range the store drives a better supply deal in return for bigger volumes, and quickly drops unpopular items.

Storytelling is everywhere at Trader Joe's, from the hand-written signage and rustic displays, to the free coffee and sampling, the radio ads and chatty check-out dudes. Whilst most stores focus on automation and speed, this store is real and human, worth coming just to chill out. Even if you never get to visit a store, sign up to the Fearless Flyer online. With off-beat stories and cartoon humour, unusual recipes and showcased products, it's an intriguing read.

Le Pain Quotidien ... rustic breads and communal tables

Le Pain stands out in a cookie-cutter world of standard formats as authentic and sustainable, human and communal. Whilst the world becomes anglicized, it's great to see a little French on our streets, albeit Belgian.

Le Pain was founded in Brussels in 1990 by Alain Coumont, and is now famed around the world for its organic breads, coffee bowls and long wooden communal tables. As a young chef, Coumont was unhappy with the quality of local bread, so he began making his own sourdough loaves. He furnished his cafés with pieces from antique stores and flea markets. The bakery became a restaurant, most famous for its tartines (traditional, open-faced sandwiches).

'Whenever we can, we source organic ingredients. This way, we not only do what is good for the Earth, but we also ensure our ingredients are of the highest quality. It's about finding the very best, in a way that is good for all of us' says the Belgian entrepreneur, writing on his own website.

This philosophy influences every part of the way Le Pain works, from the food served to the design of the stores, to the materials used to build it. Speaking at a recent MCT summit in Istanbul, he proudly told me how they use reclaimed wood and recycled gypsum, energy-efficient lamps, and environmentally friendly cleaning supplies.

Of course, the rustic look could easily be seen as just another cosmetic branding device 'To us, organic is not a marketing gag as it is for other businesses who only offer environment-friendly coffee and basically greenwash the rest. Our ingredients are expensive, and we invest a lot of time and effort in locating the right suppliers. Organic is a tough business.'

The 'communal table' is the centre piece of each bakery-café-restaurant (it's difficult to say which it really is). 'Without this table we would not be where we are today,' says Coumont. Believing that food is only as good as the people who share it, he adds 'a big table is like a good movie; the setting is not the only criteria – the actors are also important'.

Whilst Starbucks has modernized and multiplied the Italian coffee experience, and McDonalds has tried to bring some humanity and goodness to its plastic formats, Le Pain is the real thing. Authenticity, a sense of goodness, a natural and human experience, pervades each of the 200 locations in 20 countries. Each serving big Belgian bowls of hot coffee without any handles.

15 FUTUREBANK
CHANGING THE GAME OF FINANCE

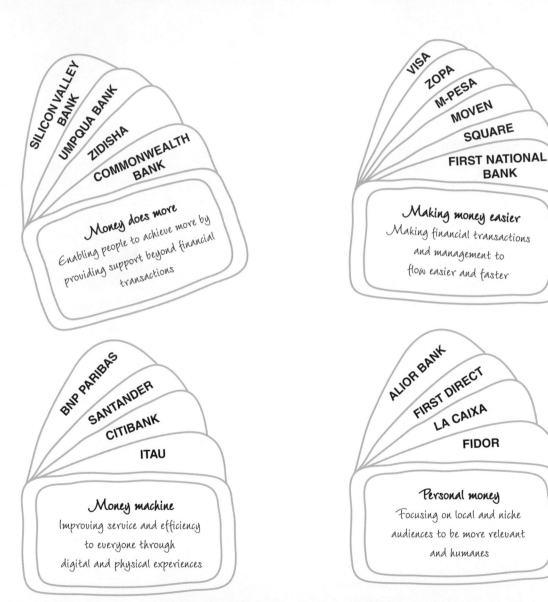

SILICON VALLEY BANK
UMPQUA BANK
ZIDISHA
COMMONWEALTH BANK

Money does more
Enabling people to achieve more by providing support beyond financial transactions

VISA
ZOPA
M-PESA
MOVEN
SQUARE
FIRST NATIONAL BANK

Making money easier
Making financial transactions and management to flow easier and faster

BNP PARIBAS
SANTANDER
CITIBANK
ITAU

Money machine
Improving service and efficiency to everyone through digital and physical experiences

ALIOR BANK
FIRST DIRECT
LA CAIXA
FIDOR

Personal money
Focusing on local and niche audiences to be more relevant and humanes

Futurebank, Rethinking the World of Finance

From Alior Sync's social banking for Polish Gen Y, and Spain's La Caixa loved by the people of Catalonia … to Moven's money management concept launching in New York, and Zidisha enabling peer-to-peer lending for African entrepreneurs … the future of banking goes **beyond money**, to being about what people do with their money.

LIFE FLOWS BETTER

In the past, every local community had its own bank, with a queue of people and bars between you and your money. In fact you were lucky to even get there, given that they only opened when everyone was at work. Even today, most banks still seem antiquated. They work hard to hide the best deals from customers, and simple processes, like an international payment, can take a week. Whilst it was the greed and incompetence of corporate banking that drove the world to financial crisis, most customers see the whole banking system as opaque, bureaucratic and not to be trusted.

The next generation of banks does things differently.

They have no time for these out-dated practices. They design their services **around the customer**, less interested in outwitting innocent account holders with complex schemes and random charges, instead focused on (as a Visa ad campaign said) helping your money to **flow smoother**, and life to **flow better**. They focus on adding value to people's lives, where money is an enabler, applying and embedding finance into richer lifestyle experiences, be it for managing your home, shopping, travelling or entertainment.

ESCAPE THE BRANCH

The best ideas often emerge from low tech environments. When Safaricom started operating a system of text-based promises to pay, M-Pesa emerged as a digital currency for Africa. Eventually the major players like Visa followed suite with V.Pay. More generally, the **smartphone** is seen as the future of branches, creating everything you need to manage your money, anytime anywhere. Brett King, author of Bank 3.0 recently put his theories on the line, launching his own solution, Moven, entirely virtual.

In the real world, the full service trend goes **beyond a smile**, pioneered by Umpqua Bank where Ray Davis created a fusion of Gap, Starbucks and Ritz Carlton hotels in the form of a boutique bank. When Richard Branson promised to make money fun, he created lounges and started serving cocktails. Somewhere in between these worlds are the kiosk formats, favoured by the likes of Citibank and Bank of America, providing convenience on each street corner, supported by video-based advisors.

MONEY ENABLES MORE

Banks that stand out tend to focus on specific audiences, rather trying to be all things to all people. Alior Sync creating a social media enabled, gaming embedded, digital bank just for 20–30 year olds, Bank of Inner Mongolia chose targeting China's wealthy mining region, Bank Nizwa of Oman chose to focus on creating the state's first Islamic bank. Silicon Valley Bank is specifically designed for entrepreneurs, and Indonesia-based Bank BTPN focuses on micro loans, and in particular its hugely profitable pension loans service.

Once you are focused on a specific audience, it is much easier to **do more** for them, understanding their specific needs, and then linking to other partners who can offer a more complete experience. Finding a vacation to match your preferences and budget, or the best deal on your new car, is what customers do. This also opens up a wide variety of new channels and affinity brands through which to enable more.

Consider, for example, you buy a new suitcase to go on vacation. Selling travel contents insurance, maybe as an annual subscription, is an obvious way to reach consumers 'in context'. Or imagine you are hunting for a new house. It shouldn't be hard to take out your smartphone, take a photo of a property you see for sale. With visual recognition, the house can be found on the database of estate agents and details pulled up. Connecting to your financial profile, funds available and credit scores enables an instant assessment of whether it is affordable for you. Rather than the bank becoming the major obstacle to such transactions, it becomes the enabler.

The question, however, is whether banks themselves will provide these human-centred, integrated and enabling interfaces, or whether other brands will embed financial processes within their richer, more inspiring lifestyle experiences.

GAMECHANGERS

From physical to digital, money and time, lifestyle and growth, we explore some of the businesses who are shaking up the world of financial services in different ways.

FUTUREBANK
Moven

Moven … Bank 3.0 that promises to be different

Moven is a digital financial manager designed around the mobile consumer, making banking and life easier, and through a range of easy and fun analytics, embracing games and social media, even makes you a rockstar!

Brett King was excited, only days away from the launch of his new 'bank'. He'd written three books about what he should do. Now he was doing it. 'While industries like media and retail undergo seismic shifts, the banking world hasn't really changed in hundreds of years.' Moven seeks to change that.

At the core, Moven is trying to evolve the basic day-to-day bank account. In the 1960s a bank account was personified by an account book. In the 70s and 80s it was your cheque book. Today it's a debit card. 'Undoubtedly the bank account of tomorrow will be based on your smartphone' says King.

Actually Moven isn't a bank. It's a digital solution designed around the customer, helping you to shop, buy, live and manage your money better. Whilst most banks are simply trying to shrink their websites down to the size of the phone screen, and perhaps allow you to put your debit card details into a 'mobile wallet', Moven is rethinking the banking concept.

Opening a Moven account includes a significant behavioural shift for consumers. Personal payments can be made by email, text or Facebook. Store payments are encouraged by contactless technology. Plastic cards are available for those without the confidence to go completely digital.

However the real difference is how it helps you. As you pay, you can see your balance before and after a transaction, with real-time feedback that helps you understand the impact of simple spending decisions.

'Think of buying a coffee at Starbucks in the morning. You buy a $6 coffee and a Bagel for $4. If I ask you how much you spent at Starbucks each month, you might guess $100, maybe $120 dollars – so when you find out via our smart receipt that you've already spent $230 at Starbucks this month, you might be surprised.

Day by day as you interact with Moven, we get to know more about your typical spending habits and start to gently coach you to save more each month. When you do start improving your overall financial health, we give you great deals on savings and investments that help you lock away the savings improvements you've made.'

The new funky and friendly tools include MoneyPulse which will analyse spending behaviour and provides visual cues (green, yellow and red indicators) and MoneyPath which charts a customer's spending over time. There is also CRED which is a simplified scoring system to assess risk and financial potential, and Financial Personality which defines your attitude and behaviours … artist or breadwinner, professor or rockstar!

Pivot points for Moven in 'changing the game' of money management include:

EXPLORE   Creating a better experience from the consumer's point of view

DESIGN   Being an interface, escaping the limitations of being a bank

RESONATE   Making it easy, even fun, to understand and manage everyday payments

AMPLIFY   Using Brett King's fame as a banking thought leader to build the brand

Umpqua ... the world's greatest bank, where you fall in love

Umpqua reimagined the banking experience around customers, inspired by parallels such as Gap and Starbucks. A passionate focus on people and service has created a digitally-enabled physical experience like no other.

'Fall in love at Umpqua Bank ... We want our customers to be really really happy' is not the proposition you'd expect from a serious bank, particularly in tough economic times. But this bank is different. Is there any other bank in the world where you would consider buying a branded t-shirt or baseball cap?

In 1994 new CEO Ray Davis woke up the sleepy little bank, taking everyone on a visit to Gap and Starbucks, to discover what it means to deliver a great customer experience. They returned, turning branches into "stores", even meeting places, with relaxing sofas and magazines, coffee and cookies. Cashiers became a concierge desk, long queues were replaced by 'relax, sip, surf' and staff that come to you.

Umpqua has won more admired company and best places to work awards than anyone else, and also managed to stay ahead of competitors, in a time of severe turbulence and an industry generally considered not to work.

In his book *Leading for Growth* Davis describes the challenge as to 'find the revolution before it finds you'. The bank now has over 200 stores, stretching from Seattle to San Jose, assets of $11 billion, and a strategy to build as a lifestyle brand – about people's lives rather than their money.

You might notice large colour coded wall displays of the latest financial services – 'your green account', 'in your prime', 'the business suite' (themed to the audience, not just standard products promoted on their % APRs). You might be inspired by the successful local restaurant owner, whose story is described this week on the Hero Wall.

Bright, colourful, modern (the Gap influence), products are cleverly packaged on shelves, and there are book clubs, movie nights, neighbourhood meetings, 'business therapy' gatherings, even 'stitch and bitch' sessions.

Freshly brewed coffee, Umpqua Blend (which it also sells in bags), is always ready waiting, whilst every transaction occurs with a piece of gold-wrapped chocolate served on a silver platter.

Umpqua's Innovation Lab, an experimental store on Portland's Waterfront, goes further. It includes the largest Nintendo Wii bowling alley you have ever seen. People, usually office workers in their lunch break, come along wearing their bowling shirts, ready to play.

Davis argues that banking doesn't just need a paradigm shift, but the whole industry needs to be rethought, reinvented and rebuilt. Whilst most banks feel they have little to say, except who has the cheapest interest rates, Umpqua plays a different game.

Pivot points for Umpqua in 'changing the game' of retail banking include:

DESIGN   Reimagining the customer experience, learning from other types of brands

INSPIRE   Creating a lifestyle brand that is human, collaborative, fun and inspiring

RESONATE   Packaging, marketing and selling products around people's aspirations

MOBILIZE   Creating a contagious brand, building community and a place to hang out

This is a bank that wears its passion with pride. Above the doors it says 'Thanks for being part of the world's great bank'.

Zidisha ... peer-to-peer microfinance in developing markets

Zidisha is a non-profit organization that matches African entrepreneurs with peer-to-peer loans from around the world, keeping interest rates low by cutting out intermediaries and using simple technology.

Zidisha is the world's first direct peer-to-peer lending service for disadvantaged individuals in developing countries. Founded by Julia Kurnia, it stands out for reducing the cost of microfinance by eliminating local intermediary organizations. Started initially in Senegal, the business connects entrepreneurs in the world's most impoverished regions with the chance to improve their family's incomes through fairly priced business loans.

Kurnia describes her insight:

'Entrepreneurs in low-income countries often face a dilemma: their business activities don't earn enough to support their families, whilst they also lack the investment capital needed to make the businesses grow. Restrictive political and economic conditions and geographic remoteness make it expensive for local banks to lend to small business owners. Many of these borrowers turn to microfinance institutions, but individual business expansion loans usually require prohibitive collateral and interest requirements due to high administrative costs. So the businesses don't grow, and the families they support remain impoverished.'

Whilst focused on Africa, and other emerging markets, Zidisha is actually a USA-based non-profit organization where Kurnia previously worked with the US African Development Department. It lets ordinary web users make microloans to individuals in the world's poorest countries. The loans allow the individuals to start small businesses to help them escape poverty, and the loan funds are repaid with interest.

'What makes Zidisha unique is that there are no intermediaries. The borrowers themselves post their loan applications and communicate directly with lenders as their business investments grow.'

Linking entrepreneurs directly with the international peer-to-peer lending market gives them the chance to find investment far more easily and affordably than has ever before been feasible in their locations. The global average interest rate for microfinance loans is around 40%. The average rate paid by Zidisha entrepreneurs is around 9% according to Kurnia.

Zidisha uses every type of technology to connect the world, quickly and at low cost. 'In Kenya we use M-Pesa to send loans from our PayPal account directly into the mobile phones of a Masai entrepreneur in the photo, instantly and cheaply.'

Unlike the postings on other microlending platforms, the loan applications and comments posted on Zidisha's loan pages are written by the borrowers themselves. This opens the way for dialogue between lenders and borrowers. It builds genuine interest too, For example, a lender who is a dairy farmer in Wisconsin may discuss cattle rearing with a dairy farmer in a small village on Kenya's Rift Valley Mountain.

Pivot points for Zidisha in 'changing the game' of business loans include:

DISCOVER   Insight from previous African development role spurred her into action

DISRUPT   Redesigning the market model to eliminate intermediaries, and their costs

DESIGN   Simplifying process using basic technologies for developing markets

MOBILIZE   Building a community of real interest, between entrepreneurs and lenders

From Senegal, Zidisha has spread across the entrepreneurial communities of Africa, and is now looking to Asia and South America too.

Square ... making payments easy, anywhere anytime

Square's insight came from the millions of small businesses who lose sales because they cannot accept credit cards. Empowering first the retailer, and the consumer, Square had to fight to change the rules of the market.

In 2009, Jack Dorsey distributed '140 Reasons Why Square Will Fail' to potential investors , partly to demonstrate the challenges he faced, but also to articulate the difference he sought to make with his Square card reader. The thumbnail-sized device seeks to allow anyone, anywhere, to take credit card payments.

Dorsey knows about innovating amidst adversity, having previously developed Twitter when everyone said micro-blogging would never take off. He makes a point of not having a finance background, believing it would limit his imagination, and doesn't recruit anyone who does. However complex the challenge, he believes that any new innovation should be so easy and intuitive to use that people wonder why it never existed before.

Square launched its card reader in 2010, basically a white dongle that plugs into the earphone socket of an iPhone or iPod, Android or Blackberry phone turning it into a credit card reader and processor. Within a year, a million small retailers were using Square to process $5 billion in transactions, numbers that almost tripled in year two. The business valuation grew rapidly too, worth around $3 billion, compared to the $341m invested by VCs including $25m from Starbucks. The dongle is free to buy from Square.com, and once activated connects to Square

Register, a point-of-sale phone app that behaves like a check-out, allowing customers to pay with cash or swipe a credit or debit card and sign on the screen. In 2011, SquareWallet was launched to consumers, creating a self check-out, which connects to the retailer's account.

The business model is compelling too. Square charges retailers around 2.5% per transaction, or for small retailers a flat fee of $275 per month compared to the much high rates charged for low volume businesses by most card companies. Square is such a no-brainer that it hasn't needed a sales team, spreading by word of mouth between market stall holders, corner shops, tradesmen and start-ups.

The insight that gave birth to Square came from Dorsey's friend Jim McKelvey, an artisan glassblower, who missed out on a $2,000 sale because he was unable to accept payment by credit card. Technology was not the obstacle, but the major credit card companies were. With a small business model that was unviable for small businesses, Square saw a role for itself as an intermediary who could aggregate small traders, and reduce their costs. Over the next six months Dorsey and team had to change the mindset of banks and card companies in order to get his new process accepted. Those companies are now imitating the start-up, including Visa's Samsung-partnered PayWave app, and Bank of America's Mobile Pay on Demand.

With Starbucks as a shop window, entering new markets across Asia, and a huge potential small business market, Square's growth is set to accelerate.

La Caixa ... love and loyalty for the bank of the Catalans

La Caixa is the bank of the Catalonians, proudly small and regional, and inspired by a great brand identity. The bank embraces mobile technologies and local partnerships to do more for people in their daily lives.

In the late 1970s, *Caja de Ahorros y Monte de Piedad de Barcelona* asked Lando's design team to create a brand identity that would be easily identifiable and feel owned by the customer. The Caja was a local bank, and Catalonia is a fiercely independent and proud region of northeastern Spain. They commissioned Catalan artist, Joan Miró, who developed the image of a blue star and two coloured circles, reflecting a child depositing a coin in a piggy-bank. Miró's original tapestry is on display in the foyer of the bank's headquarters in Barcelona.

Through its turbulent history, the bank, now simply known as 'La Caixa', has remained focused on savings and pensions for working class families of Catalonia, and is loved for it. It is the bank of its people, and has no desire to be more global, particularly in a world where people typically don't trust big banks.

Organizationally, the bank is actually CaixaBank which emerged from the wreckage of Spain's banking crisis as a restructured organization, with major stakes in Spain's leading telecoms and oil companies, Telefonica and Repsol. These partnerships have been particularly useful in helping La Caixa to reach out to people in their daily lives. There is also a charitable arm that continues its support of social projects in the region.

La Caixa's mission is about doing more for people – to encourage saving and investment – whilst there is a strong commitment to social issues and maintaining the region's identity. This, for example, includes building PremiaT as an online community of local businesses, promoting them to local customers, but also enabling fast and simple online transactions. The La Caixa payment card therefore becomes a kind of regional passport, securing discounts and loyalty benefits. The online services are also underpinned by community building, sharing the pride and passion for Catalonia.

Commonwealth Bank ... making banking more human

Australia's CommBank demonstrates what it means to be a customer-centric bank. Whether you are searching for a new home, or business growth, the bank partners with others to do more than just manage your money.

Andy Lark says he is changing the way banking happens. He is CMO of Australia's most innovative bank. Leading the way in using mobile and social media, 'CommBank' is using technology to enable its customers to achieve more, as well as making transactions fast and easy. It sees the intimacy of social relationships between its customers as the best way to rebuild trust and transparency, whilst mobile apps seek to help people in their everyday lives, beyond money.

With over 1100 branches, the 48,000 employees work as one collaborative team, supported by Chatter, an internal social network. Externally, the bank uses Facebook as its platform to make each customer's experience more personal and relevant. Apps then enhance this experience in different ways for different situations.

Take buying a new house, for example. CommBank forms relationships with real estate companies to transform the home buying experience. Bank customers get advance notice of new properties. Find the location on the smartphone map. Arrive and see the details with augmented reality. Check the asking price, and how much mortgage payments would be from CommBank. Click to buy, and the bank will bring together all the necessary people and paperwork to make it happen.

Fidor ... interest rates based on Facebook likes

Engaging customers through social media can often seem nice but superficial. Fidor has built its banking platform around the customer, embracing customers socially to dramatically change the banking experience.

Germany's Fidor Bank is famous for its interest rates which go up with every additional 'Like' it receives on Facebook. Every additional 10% in its Likes results in a 0.1% increase in its savings rate. But there is much more to Fidor than just that innovation.

CEO Mathias Kroener loves to innovate, arguing that if he just followed the conventions, there would be no choice and no progress. Fidor is a web-based bank focused on four areas to engage customers – social, mobile, e-commerce and gaming.

Kroener and his co-founders believe that the bank and customers are a community living together, captured in the motto 'banking with friends'. As the website says 'we focus on openness, fairness, and the involvement of our customers ... Banking is fun not

fear: 24/7, online and mobile, "pay and play" in real time, virtual Fidor prepaid MasterCard for free, savings products, peer-2-peer lending, crowdfunding, precious metals, foreign currencies – all in one account with no account management fees.'

Customers and bank staff can chat online, late into the evening, about specific financial issues or about the latest games, improving their homes or travel plans too. This is a far more human, collaborative experience than with most banks, and provides customer insight too. The Facebook interest rates are a great example of customer-driven pricing, and how to embed social capabilities into meaningful and real-time customer participation.

Building on the retail banking success, Fidor is now exploring a white-labelled version of the bank called Fidor TecS, where it can license its business model and technology platform to other banks around the world.

Itau Unibanco ... the bank riding the wave of Latin America

IU seeks to be the commercial and human face of Latin America over the next decade, as it extends across the globe, but staying true to its local responsibilities, helping consumers and businesses to improve themselves.

Brazil's Itau Unibanco has a strategy for global growth, riding on its vibrant economy and vast population. 'We want to be considered the global bank of Latin America by 2020,' says VP Ricardo Marino. Formed through a merger of Banco Itaú and Unibanco in 2008, it is now one of the world's top 20 banks.

With a local presence in Argentina, Chile, Paraguay and Uruguay, Itau sees Colombia, Peru and Mexico, where it already has a credit-card operation, as its next frontiers. However its vision is global, acting as a face of the fast-growing Latin American market, and a catalyst to local entrepreneurs as they grow.

Customer satisfaction and sustainability are core to Itau's responsible growth plans. They recognize that sustainable

performance means creating shared value for employees, customers, shareholders and society, to ensure the longevity of the business. That's a long-term goal, achieved more easily in growth markets where it is less about re-slicing the value cake, than sharing in an ever bigger one.

For the bank, sustainability focuses on a social imperative – giving more people access to credit, investing in good business, and providing insurance where others might not, in order to support people's lives and businesses. Underpinning this is education, improving the financial literacy of everyday people.

For businesses, Itau's micro-credit business encourages entrepreneurship and local development in socially vulnerable communities. The bank is also a pioneer in supporting art and culture since the creation of the Instituto Itaú Cultural in 1987, and Itaú currently owns one of Brazil's largest private art collections.

First National Bank ... eWallet becomes your financial hub

FNB puts innovation at the heart of its culture. The bank's innovative eWallet, hosted on your phone, acts as a hub for many other creative solutions to make money flow easier and faster.

The Acacia tree in the brand logo represents a bank with roots that run deep in South African society. FNB is the oldest bank in South Africa, originally the Eastern Province Bank founded in 1838, and today, a division of FirstRand Bank Limited.

'FNB lives and breathes innovation' says CEO Michael Jordaan in an interview with The Banker. 'Every employee can be an innovator and can change the way we work' based on what he calls bottom-up strategies, delivered by a bottom-up organization hierarchy.

These innovations include FNB Africa's 'Bank in a bag' making joining a very tangible experience, online personal banking, a rewards program, digital apps and links to other retail loyalty programs. At the heart of these initiatives is a mobile 'eWallet' from which customers can make cardless payments and cash withdrawals using SMS confirmations, Pay2Cell and Facebook Vouchers.

The eWallet service allows customers to send money to anyone in South Africa with a valid mobile phone number. Funds can be transferred instantly, and the recipient receives a text message indicating that funds have been sent to their mobile phone.

The recipient is then able to withdraw cash at FNB ATMs, buy pre-paid airtime or electricity, send money to another phone, purchase and/or get cash at selected retailers, as well as make one-off payments.

To encourage and sustain this innovation drive, FNB has an annual innovations award, encouraging staff to creatively deliver solutions aligned to the company's strategy, and contribute towards growth targets. Over 1000 initiatives contend for the award each year.

'It's incredible to be part of an organization where its people continuously come up with innovative ideas that are very often implemented. As a leader I encourage people to think out of the box and come up with an innovative set of ideas or solutions that will ultimately benefit our customers, so that our business evolves with new mindsets and visions of the future,' says Jordaan.

M-Pesa ... Safaricom creates a new currency for Africa

M-Pesa became the mobile currency of Africa, embracing phones to do more than connect people, and improvising for the lack of infrastructure in fast growing markets.

M-Pesa (M for mobile, *pesa* is Swahili for money) is a mobile-phone based money transfer system that grew out of 'I owe you' text messages promising future payments in a region where banking is still primitive and credit cards are rare. Developed by Kenya's mobile operator, Safaricom, and also licensed to Vodacom, it offers a fast and easy payment method across Africa.

Such has been its simple but successful development, with over 3 billion M-Pesa accounts registered (that's almost half the world's population?!), that it has become the most admired mobile payments system in the developing world, allowing users with an identity card to deposit, withdraw and transfer money easily with a phone.

Having seen how markets without fixed-line telephones leapfrogged directly to mobile devices, what is interesting here is how consumers embrace the added value services of their phones much more quickly and actively than in developed markets.

Launched in 2007 as part of a Kenyan high school technology project, M-Pesa initially focused on providing loans to local entrepreneurs from the Safaricom stores. However, people quickly started paying back the loans immediately, or getting others to, in the form of payments and transfers. It has rapidly been adopted for all kinds of transactions, from paying bills to accessing real bank accounts.

The service now allows users to deposit money into an account stored on their mobile phones, to send balances using SMS to other users (individuals or businesses), and to redeem deposits for regular money at the nearest bank, post office, or Safaricom store. Users are charged a small fee for sending and withdrawing money.

Safaricom recently launched a second financial brand, M-Shwari in partnership with Commercial Bank of Africa, allowing M-Pesa customers to save and borrow money through their mobile phone, earning interest on the money saved. It includes an emergency loan facility at affordable interest rates, unusual for Africa. From a new payment currency, the business has become a licensed bank.

Making life smooth and easy ... or 'Lainisha maisha na M-Shwari', as they say in Swahili.

16 FUTUREHEALTH

CHANGING THE GAME OF HEALTHCARE

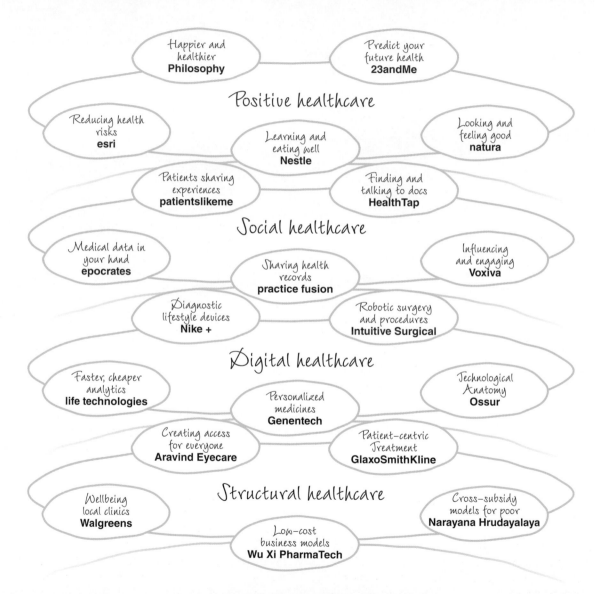

Positive healthcare

- Happier and healthier **Philosophy**
- Predict your future health **23andMe**
- Reducing health risks **esri**
- Learning and eating well **Nestle**
- Looking and feeling good **natura**

Social healthcare

- Patients sharing experiences **patientslikeme**
- Finding and talking to docs **HealthTap**
- Medical data in your hand **epocrates**
- Sharing health records **practice fusion**
- Influencing and engaging **Voxiva**

Digital healthcare

- Diagnostic lifestyle devices **Nike +**
- Robotic surgery and procedures **Intuitive Surgical**
- Faster, cheaper analytics **life technologies**
- Personalized medicines **Genentech**
- Technological Anatomy **Ossur**

Structural healthcare

- Creating access for everyone **Aravind Eyecare**
- Patient-centric Treatment **GlaxoSmithKline**
- Wellbeing local clinics **Walgreens**
- Cross-subsidy models for poor **Narayana Hrudayalaya**
- Low-cost business models **Wu Xi PharmaTech**

Futurebank, Rethinking the World of Healthcare

Aravind to Epocrates, Intuitive Surgical to 23andMe … through **positive** wellness and **personalized** pharma, robotics and **genetics**, digital applications and **patient-centric** business models … the future of health is about specialization and innovation, patient-centric solutions that are faster and more efficient.

PERSONAL, PREDICTIVE AND POSITIVE

For just $99 we can see our life before us, with a DNA profile from **23andMe**, and as a result we go to **PatientsLikeMe** to find out how others have responded. We eat the best foods from GSK, and check our daily fitness with **Nike+**, maybe with a little help from **Avumio**'s diagnostic apps and online advice from Dr Koop.

If we need help, we turn to **ZocDoc** where a local nurse with **Epocrates** at his fingertips prescribes a standard drug from Wuxi, or a custom prescription from **Genentech**. A night in W Hotel's clinic, or a surgical trip to Antalya is unlikely. Instead we spray on our L'Oreal skin protection, sip on our super-vitamin Zespri kiwi juice, and smile.

The future of healthcare is **personal**, **predictive** and **proactive**, using advanced diagnostics so that people can themselves understand their likely conditions, and take better actions now to reduce risks or avoid illnesses. In this sense it is about

positive wellbeing, rather than caring or curing. However when misfortune does strike, then care is about **patients** and **personalization**, putting people at the heart of the medical process, supported by physicians and pharmaceuticals which are right for individuals.

Today we live in hope that we will stay healthy. Improved diets and active lifestyles intuitively reduce our concerns, but when something does go wrong we put our faith in a system that is largely designed around medical science and operational efficiencies. We wait in line for a hospital bed, for a standard procedure, for a generic drug. And once we get the all clear, we disappear until the next problem. When was the last time when you talked to a doctor whilst feeling good, and staying fit?

The future is different. It sees a **convergence** of sectors, enabled by an integration of **technologies**, the personalization of science, and **business models** that are more human and commercial.

We recognize that prevention is better, and cheaper, than cure: cholesterol-reducing margarines, UV protection built into cosmetics, anti-statins to every over 50 in order to reduce the risk of heart disease, regular scans for people with family histories, blood pressure monitored daily by your smart watch, fitness parks designed for middle aged retirees, compression socks for long-haul flights. Drug companies make functional foods, sports companies create wellbeing devices, hospitals offer fitness programmes, medical centres offer beauty treatments, cosmetics brands help you look good and live better.

From biotechnology to pharmaceuticals, governments to surgeons, sports clinics to supermarket pharmacies, cosmetics to functional foods, mobile technologies and online communities, many different **partners** and services will **come together** to keep us alive and well.

DIGITAL AND MOBILE, CATALYSTS OF CHANGE

Big data for fast and remote diagnostics, wearable sensors for body management, sit alongside more innovative solutions like 3D organ printing and robotic surgery. Advances in technology are allowing for the provision of affordable, decentralized healthcare for the masses and are lowering the barriers to entry in less developed markets.

Of all the advances, **mobile technology** is the catalyst for change. The phone and tablet enable distribution of a broad range of medical and support services in hospitals, and particularly in countries with little or no healthcare infrastructure and areas in which there are few trained healthcare professionals. These technologies also allow trained professionals to perform quality control remotely.

Amongst the many significant developments is a shift towards **one-on-one**, in-field diagnostics and monitoring. Services that were once only available at a doctor's surgery or hospital are now available through low-tech, affordable solutions. Remote systems (often as simple as doctors using Skype) allow for fast, easy and cheap diagnosis that can improve many more lives.

GAMECHANGERS

Gamechangers in the healthcare business are shaping their own competitive spaces, but are also seeing the bigger picture, forming new partnerships and solutions, that transform the patient experience into positive and personal wellbeing. We explore some of the companies who are 'changing the game'.

23andMe ... the $99 DNA profile that could change your life

23andMe can transform our attitudes to health, diet and mortality ... but also entire industries, drugs driven by future needs, healthcare refocused on prevention, insurance premiums to reflecting new risks.

Anne Wojcicki wants to change the face of health care. 23andMe is her personal genetics testing company based in Mountain View, California and part funded by her husband, Google's co-founder Sergey Brin.

By simply taking and mailing a saliva example from your home, and receiving analysis and interpretation within a week, 23andMe enables people to learn about their inherited health traits and genetic links to certain diseases. With around $120m investment, 23andMe can now offer 244 reports on health and personal traits, as well as genealogy and ancestry information that people can share socially **all for $99**.

For a price equivalent to a new pair of running shoes, the self-testing package is now accessible to millions of consumers, curious to understand the secrets locked in their DNA, and what it might mean for them. Imagine how it can change people's lifestyles – prompting new diets and fitness regimes – as well as transforming insurance policies and healthcare planning.

It also enables 23andMe to create the world's largest private database of genetic information, to explore and distribute this rich knowledge bank (around 90% of patients are happy for their aggregated data to be used). The results can be used in research conducted by Wojcicki's team, plus pharmaceutical and healthcare partners, to drive innovation and focus investment.

Pharma companies believe that genetic data could be instrumental in creating better, more targeted treatments for diseases.

Genentech is working with 23andMe to learn if genetic factors influence a person's response to the cancer drug Avastin, whilst Amgen recently bought DeCode, a company that explores the link between genes and diseases, for $415 million.

At the time of launch, in 2006, the business didn't seem like a gamechanger of the drug industry, let alone the patient experience. The process was expensive, $999 for a much more limited analysis, and was dubbed 'spit parties' by the press as wealthy Silicon Valley types shared saliva with their cocktails. The price has fallen dramatically since, making it affordable to most people. At the same time this has rung alarm bells with regulators, an inevitable challenge if you want to break rules and all part of the journey.

Pivot points for 23andMe in 'changing the game' of genetic profiling were:

DISRUPT   Making a high-tech specialism relevant to everyday consumers

RESONATE   Communicating propositions around wellness, and even ancestory

MOBLIZE   Engaging pharma companies in using the collated data for depth research

AMPLIFY   Reducing the price to $99 to make it more accessible and build community

Wojcicki recently told *Fortune* magazine 'We've always had a vision to introduce a new type of healthcare model that is focused on prevention and consumer-driven research,' she says. 'If you have lots of individuals thinking of prevention, who know information that could have a meaningful impact on their lives, it changes the model for drug research and healthcare.'

Epocrates ... the doctor's brain in the palm of his hand

Instant access to technical and patient knowledge transforms the speed at which doctors can offer diagnosis and treatment. This results in improved decisions, delivering faster treatments, at lower costs.

The world of medicine is changing incredibly fast, new diseases and drugs, new services and expectations, it's not easy to stay updated, to complement experience with the very latest knowledge and techniques.

This is where Epocrates comes in ... as simple as an app on the doctor's phone or tablet.

Epocrates develops mobile solutions for healthcare, giving professionals instant access to the world's most comprehensive knowledge source of symptoms, diagnostics and responses, as well as managing their own time and business.

Rob Cosinuke, Chief Marketing Officer of AthenaHealth which recently acquired Epocrates, described why he believes Epocrates is a 'gamechanger' saying 'You can't change the game unless you know your audience. You can create a tool, but if you don't fundamentally understand the people you are building it for, it will fail despite good intentions.'

He goes further in describing that for Epocrates, this means three things:

1. **Be invaluable** ... 'We want to help clinicians save time, money and increase patient satisfaction – this means making an intuitive product that helps answer questions, instead of making more. Epocrates has over 300,000 US physicians and over 1 million members worldwide using its products.'

2. **Think like a doctor** ... 'Our amazing design and development team is complemented by a group of in-house physicians, nurses, pharmacist and other healthcare professionals that work together to deliver our products. Our focus is on helping healthcare professionals be more efficient.'

3. **Solve a problem** ... 'When Epocrates was first developed, we saw a need for physicians to instantly access information at the point of care. As technology changed we ditched paper and moved to the tablet. To be ahead of the curve, solutions should be developed with long-term goals in mind, not just short-term fixes.'

Cosinuke admits that he is inspired by Apple, and how their innovations have enabled his business to do more for his customers.his inspiration. 'Apple has forever changed the way healthcare professionals access information. The iPad Mini, for example, comes in at the perfect size for a lab coat pocket. More clinicians are adopting this device due to the lightweight portability, easy readability and medium screen for basic data entry, and is perfect for apps like Epocrates'.

Pivot points for Epocrates in 'changing the game' of healthcare information were:

DISCOVER   Focus obsessively on getting the right information to the point of care

DESIGN   Connect relevant information, i.e. about patients, treatments, medicine

MOBILIZE   Develop partnerships with complementary services to the same audience

RESONATE   Ride on the back of new devices that make your content better and sexier

AthenaHealth acquired Epocrates for $293 million in 2013, making it the leading mobile knowledge platform for doctors, partly attracted by the high brand recognition of Epocrates of over 90% of US physicians.

Narayana Hrudayalaya … low-cost hospitals with a heart

Narayana operates a dual business model, one funding the other. Whilst knowledge and equipment are not compromized, the growth in medical tourism subsidizes low-cost heart surgery for the poor.

Narayana Hrudayalaya is a leading network of hospitals based in the Indian city of Bengalura. Founded in 2000 by a 40-year-old Indian heart surgeon, Dr Devi Shetty, it has performed a record-breaking15,000 surgeries on patients from 25 countries, with the relentless pursuit of extending access for more people to more services, at low cost.

Narayana is perhaps most famous for its heart hospital on the outskirts of Bangalore, one of the largest in the world, and with a particular focus on children, where the average open-heart surgery costs less than $2000, a third or less what it costs elsewhere in India and a fraction of what it costs in Western countries.

By thinking differently about its role, scale and partner benefits, the hospital can achieve huge economies of scale. The company negotiates for better prices and buys directly from manufacturers, cutting out distributors. Starting with cardiac care, an equipment-intensive specialty, made it easier for the hospital group to expand into other areas that require the same infrastructure.

Shetty recognized that most Indian hospitals are exclusively for the wealthy. 'My hospital is for poor people, but we also treat some rich people. So we're mentally geared for people who are shabbily dressed and have trouble paying. We don't look at them as outsiders. We look at them as customers.'

He has grown the Bangalore hospital into what he calls a 'health city', a series of huge medical centres specializing in eye, accident, and cancer care spread across 35 acres. There are also hospitals in 14 other Indian cities.

The 'telemedicine' practice, where each surgeon has Skype on his laptop, reaches across the developing world, including 50 partner locations in Africa, offering support at no charge. His latest initiative, dispersing 5000 dialysis machines, will make the company the country's largest kidney-care provider.

Beyond low costs, Narayana Hrudayalaya finds creative ways to make its economics work. The company started a micro-insurance business that enables 3 million farmers to have coverage for as little as 22 cents a month in premiums. Free patients are effectively subsidized by premium patients, including foreigners for whom a $7000 heart operation, access to an experienced specialist, and a deluxe private room seems like a bargain.

Every day surgeons receive a profit and loss statement of the previous day that describes their operations and the various levels of reimbursement. The data allows them to manage the mix of payment levels.

Pivot points for Dr Shetty in 'changing the game' of low-cost healthcare were:

THINK   Have an inspiring vision as to how you can make the world a better place

EXPLORE   Build a reputation in one area first, to refine the model and grow reputation

DESIGN   Explore new business models, including subsidies between segments

AMPLIFY   Embrace new technologies as emerging markets change quickly

In 2012 Dr Shetty received the Padma Bhushan, one of India's top three public honours. *The Wall Street Journal* called him 'the Henry Ford of heart surgery'.

Aravind Eyecare … a vision to cure blindness in India

Aravind wins by offering basic healthcare in emerging markets with a low-cost business model that substitutes expert doctors for 'good enough' advice, supported through mobile technologies.

Aravind started with the vision of one man, Dr. Venkatasamy, often known as 'Dr V.' In 1976 he founded the eyecare business, as a semi-retirement project, inspired by a local philosopher, Sri Aurobindo, who believed in the 'transience of humankind', the need for a collective and radical transformation of 'consciousness of the human spirit'.

A typical patient pays $1 for an eye test, and treatment for common conditions such as glaucoma and uveitis. Fast and simple, Aravind Eyecare is helping millions of Indians to overcome blindness.

Aravind's hospital gleams white and clean, treating over 1200 patients every day, and hundreds of thousands more through Skype-enabled remote diagnosis and procedures, assisted by local nurses. Since 1976, the network of eye hospitals has seen 32 million patients, and performed more than 4 million eye surgeries, often free.

Dr. V originally set out to bring sight to the 12 million people in India suffering from preventable blindness. But he struggled to find a bank willing to lend him money, told he was too old, and that a business model that offers a free service would never work. By mortgaging all his family's jewellery, he was able to create a 12-bed hospital in Madurai, one of India's oldest cities. It operated as a not-for-profit trust, with patients who could choose whether to pay or not, and securing income from supporting activities such as the manufacture of low-cost optical lenses for eyeware brands around the world.

Venkatasamy's vision spread wider, using a franchise model to extend his model across Africa and Asia. Today Aravind Eyecare is the largest provider of eye surgery in the world, with seven major hospitals, over 50 vision care centres, whilst also working with eye hospitals in over 30 countries. It treats over **3 million patients** each year, reflecting around 7% of the total worldwide.

Genentech ... drugs gets personal, pharma gets focused

Focus enables niche specialization leading to relevant innovation and profitability. Whilst most pharma companies try to do everything amidst declining margins, Genentech plays a premium game.

Whilst many pharma companies have attacked cancer with a bombardment of drugs, broad and intense, Genentech takes a much more personalized, targeted approach.

Founded in 1976 by a biochemist, Herbert Boyer, and venture capitalist Robert Swanson, Genentech is seen as the original biotech company. In the early days, Boyer demonstrated how enzymes could be used as tools to cut and recombine DNA fragments, and with others was able to create the first synthetic human insulin.

Today, Genentech has more than 12,300 researchers working in the fields of molecular biology and protein chemistry, bioinformatics and physiology. It is now part of the Swiss company Roche, having been acquired in 2009 for $46.8 billion, and over time has secured more than **10,500 patents**, and brought 35 new types of medicine to market.

Regularly voted as one of the best companies to work for, Genentech inspires its employees with its **human mission** – 'life'– through tear-jerking stories of how patients who had lost hope found a future, and families who would give anything to find a cure, found Genentech.

In 2012, Zelboraf became the first drug to target and shut down a gene mutation associated with about half of melanoma cases. As pharma increasingly divides into generics and specifics, Genentech expect annual sales to hit $732 million by 2015.

Organova ... 3D printing of body parts to order

Organova is embracing the latest technologies to transform surgery, from the 3D printing of muscle tissues to complete organs for transplant, saving lives and raising huge ethical issues too.

New muscle tissue, replacement arteries, livers and kidneys, even a heart transplant ... Organova's 3D printers are ready to play with nature, made to order in a lab. As millions of people sit waiting around the world for organ transplants, an alternative is rapidly emerging. Print the perfect replace now, ready in a few hours, rather than waiting years for a suitable match.

Co-founder and CEO of the San Diego-based innovator, Keith Murphy told Inc Magazine that 'Surgeons are very limited by what they have available today. If you can give them tissue to order, you can multiply, exponentially, the types of surgery that we can even envision doing. By uniquely using a patient's own cells, surgeons can do even more remarkable things.'

Working in partnership with the University of Missouri, Organova leads the way in bio-printing, or tissue engineering. The NovoGen MMX Bioprinter uses human cells and shapes them into real tissue, unlike other players who make the organs out of synthetic materials and then bond them to existing cells. The printer ejects a liquid filled with thousands of human cells, guided by lasers. The process repeats, creating hundreds of layers of cells, held together with a gel. The cells begin to grow, meshing themselves together, as they would in the body, and grow into actual tissue.

Organova partners with commercial businesses like Pfizer, and academic institutions, including Harvard Medical School, to bring together the best research and expertize, and to test the emerging tissue samples. Hundreds of patents have been filed, and sample kidneys and livers already produced.

Intuitive Surgical ... the heart surgeon with the joystick

Intuitive Surgical harnesses robotic technologies to enhance human capability. Better surgery, faster and more precise, is the main benefit, whilst also reducing the time and cost of operations.

You lie on the hospital bed, wheeled along corridors towards a date with your heart surgeon. As the doors of the operating theatre swing open, you are met by bright lights and gadgetry. Sedated, your eye scans the room for the cheery surgeon in his green gown, maybe putting on his mask and reassuring you that everything will be fine.

Instead you see a gleaming $2.5 million, multi-limbed machine. This is da Vinci, your robotic surgeon, now operating with more **precision, speed and efficiency** than is humanly possible in over 2500 hospitals around the world. Relax. As the anaesthetic now kicks in, you are in safe hands, of sorts.

In fact the surgeon is (currently) still part of the procedure, sitting with a computer interface that shows a 3D image of your body's interior, using a joystick instead of his forceps and scalpel.

The $50,000 endoscopic camera helps the surgeon navigate through the body, as if playing a computer game. An array of diagnostic and operating tools are available, either with **manual or intuitive** controls. Surgeons quickly learn to finesse the new

instruments, although it could be argued that a game-playing teenager might be even better at handling the controls.

Intuitive Surgical develops and builds the robotic da Vinci systems from its base in Sunnyvale, California. It brings together expert experience as diverse as NASA's ability to operate the space station from Earth, and more traditional hands-on surgeons. Innovations in components, and the software that supports it, are developing fast. A new fluorescent imaging system is able to quickly identify cancer, whilst a new portable da Vinci system can be placed on a table and operated with the help of a Microsoft Kinect gaming set.

The benefits are huge – the procedure is better, because the surgeon combines his own skill and judgement with the precise movements and instruments of the machine – but also faster and cheaper, with many operations possible by accessing the body through a small belly-button insertion which enables much faster procedures and patient recovery.

Having originally been developed under contract to the US Army for battlefield surgery, da Vinci is becoming available, and mostly preferred, by surgeons worldwide. With investments of almost £3 billion, Intuitive is now generating annual revenues over $0.5 billion and growing.

PatientsLikeMe … bringing people together to get better

Online communities can seem trivial in their content. Unless the topic is about life and death. Connecting with others with similar conditions, helps patients to find the best treatment, and to form networks of mutual support.

In 1998, 29 year old Stephen Heywood was diagnosed with Gehrig's disease, also known as ALS, or amyotrophic lateral sclerosis. As his condition deteriorated, Stephen's family made desperate attempts to find expert and alternative care, any way to relieve his symptoms. Eventually they turned to the internet in search of others with the same condition, who they hoped might have some answers or at least might feel better for being able to share their experience. They reflected that millions of people around the world struck down with life-changing, chronic diseases could benefit from connecting with others like them. To share the inevitable questions: Am I the only one? How do you cope? Is there anything I can do?

PatientsLikeMe was founded in 2004 by Stephen's brothers, Jamie and Ben Heywood, and friend Jeff Cole, to bring such people – patients – together. The site helps patients to document their own case histories, whilst also sharing and comparing with others, either one-to-one or anonymously.

Members suffering from over 1500 conditions have now used the site, everything from ALS to more common problems like depression and psoriasis. Using a health profile, members monitor their health between doctor or hospital visits, document the severity of their symptoms, identify triggers, note how they are responding to new treatments and track side-effects. They learn from the aggregated data of others with the same disease and see, often for the first time, just how they are really doing. They also get and give support from and to others that will help them live better day to day.

With over 100,000 members, PatientsLikeMe's communities have proved most popular. Since the first ALS discussion board in 2006, there are now also communities for everything from HIV and multiple sclerosis, to chronic fatigue syndrome and mood disorders. Over time, the company has expanded its scope and opened its doors to any patient with any condition.

Scanadu ... Dr Spock's 'tricorder' comes to life

Wearable technology devices that bring together multiple sensors and information to monitor your wellbeing, alert you to any potential illness and improve your fitness.

Walter De Brouwer spent nearly a year in hospital watching his 5 year old son slowly recover from severe brain injury caused by a 40 foot fall. The daily routine inspired him to create a simple mobile device that could assess the same vital signs that nurses checked each morning. Inspired by the 'tricorder' device used by space travellers in Star Trek, he launched Scanadu.

In 2012 he launched his first prototype, the Scanadu Scout, which could clip on to a person's clothing to remotely measure body temperature, heart rate, blood oxygen, respiratory rate and blood pressure. He set a target price of $199, and declared on Indiegogo that he was 'ready to revolutionize healthcare'. With $14 million investment from Zappo's Tony Hsieh, and $1.6 million crowd-funded pre-sales, the company was ready for clinical trials.

The Scout, developed with IDEO and designer Yves Behar, is lightweight and gives a full body check in 10 seconds, combining an array of sensors with intelligent algorithms. It enables the user to keep a check on their wellbeing, to anticipate the onset of illness from colds to heart attacks before they happen, and monitor their improving fitness levels. Connecting the aggregate data of many users enables benchmark levels to be identified, as well creating new revenue streams from personalized medicine developers.

Second Sight ... recreating vision for the blind

Second Sight really does change lives, using advanced biotechnology to simulate vision artificially, then connecting to the brain to make it real.

Second Sight's retinal implants, discretely lodged in designer glass frames, can give sight to the blind. No exaggeration. Founded in 1998, and after a decade of testing, their implants restore partial eyesight to people with retinitis pigmentosa, a degenerative eye disease that affects around a million people.

The Sylmar, California-based firm initially focused on hearing, developing cochlear implants which artificially stimulate electrodes in the inner ear of deaf patients to create sounds. That proved the inspiration for sight. Despite exhaustive trials, gaining regulatory approval in the USA has been difficult because of the surgical risk to the eye, although a blind person is unlikely to be left worse off.

In Europe, the $100,000 implants are surgically inserted into the patient's eye and a wireless camera mounted on a pair of glasses worn by the patient. The camera records light and transmits it wirelessly to the implant, which then stimulates electrodes within the eye. The brain interprets the resulting patterns as low-resolution black-and-white images, which cofounder Robert Greenberg hopes will soon be in higher resolution colour.

17 FUTUREGADGET

CHANGING THE GAME OF CONSUMER PRODUCTS

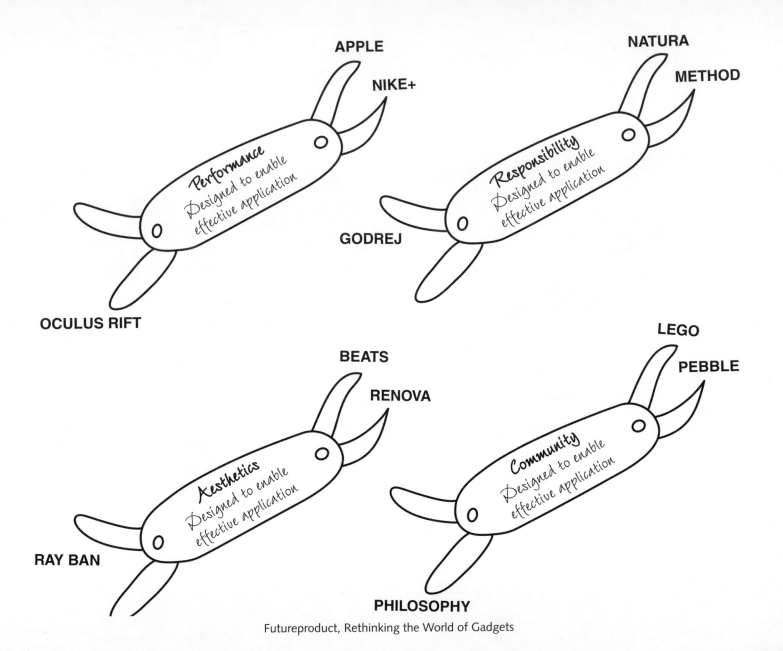

APPLE

NIKE+

Performance
Designed to enable
effective application

OCULUS RIFT

NATURA

METHOD

Responsibility
Designed to enable
effective application

GODREJ

BEATS

RENOVA

Aesthetics
Designed to enable
effective application

RAY BAN

LEGO

PEBBLE

Community
Designed to enable
effective application

PHILOSOPHY

Futureproduct, Rethinking the World of Gadgets

The future of products is about **human-centric** design concepts that **enable** people to achieve more, emotionally and functionally, bringing together the best ideas and technologies through embedded intelligence, intuitive and aesthetic, personalized and enabling experiences, building communities and movements.

DESIGNS FOR A BETTER LIFE

The obsession with which Jonny Ive and his team develop a new Apple product is in stark contrast to the beige plastic boxes that used to package expensive technologies. Similarly in household cleaners, the beautifully styled and colourful containers of Method, stand out from the ugly containers of other cleaning or soap brands. And then there is the toilet paper of Renova … black, red, pink, yellow. 'Why does toilet paper have to be boring?' asks the Portuguese brand's CEO.

'Human-centred design' sounds obvious, yet the majority of product designers and developers are still preoccupied with their product. They are makers, with a love of craft, technology and tinkering, features and style. This matters, but what people do with the products matters much more. HCD was pioneered by IDEO to rethink the design process, to start with the person, then find a better way to solve their problem or seize their ambition.

Products bought off a store shelf and left for the consumer to use are rarely engaging. The experience they have in using it, getting more out of it, is what really matters. The musical genius of Apple was not the iPod, but iTunes. Similarly the App Store brings the iPad to life. Disneyland makes fictional characters become real. Sharing experiences across a user community makes Lego more fun, and difficult to imitate.

Products are rarely enough. The future of products lies in how they are applied, and link with other products and services to help people achieve more.

HUMAN, INTUITIVE AND INTELLIGENT

In the future products will be ever more:

- **Aesthetic** – products are objects of desire as well as functional devices, with beautiful ergonomic designs, materials and colours.

- **Human** – they are more human in what they do, and how they work, but also with personalities of their own, from Alessi 'bird' kettles to Asimo robots.

- **Intuitive** – forget the instruction booklet, products should be so intuitive that you can use them in minutes, with easy navigation and control.

- **Compact** – miniaturization of technology, and particularly of power supplies, drives flat screens, small devices and spray on nano-tech.

- **Intelligent** – your phone has more computing power than a NASA space shuttle, and most electronic toys are smarter than a jumbo jet.

- **Connected** – wireless and online, but also connected to each other, to the cloud, controlled remotely, talking to other devices, sharing experiences.

- **Personalized** – designed uniquely for you, whilst a device might come in a small number of styles, the components will be infinitely customizable.

- **Sustainable** – sourced, produced, packaged and delivered responsibly, enabling reuse or recycling, efficiently using power and other resources.

GAMECHANGERS

Here are some of the most significant 'gamechangers' in the world of products, and how they changed the game, each one with a different story and inspiration to learn from.

FUTUREGADGET
Renova

Renova ... the sexiest toilet paper in the world

Renova is on mission to brighten up your life. Why is toilet paper white? The Portugeuse brand is a hit in Hollywood bathrooms with its black paper. Colour is a bold, but simple, way to change the game.

Renova makes toilet paper. Colourful and sexy, not white and boring. As CEO Paulo Miguel Pereira da Silva says 'We think that Renova is the living proof that no product is too dull or commoditized to be reinvented and no product is too stigmatized to be loved.

People now create emotional relations with our products whereas before it was all rational.'

The Portugeuse brand, founded in 1818 as a paper maker, first came to attention by adding micro droplets of smoothing cream to its toilet paper called Fresh & Clean. However its 2002 ad campaign that introduced sex appeal to toilet paper, with Francius Rousseau's black and white photography, really grabbed attention from Hollywood to Japan. Renova Black Toilet Tissue soon followed, and then other colours. 'With this product and the subsequent range we pushed the borders of what toilet paper was all about in order to establish a new design icon that is loved and talked about.'

Other colours followed. Red is said to be the favourite of Beyonce. As did extensions into napkins, kitchen rolls, wet wipes and writing paper.

Yet bathrooms remained the priority with ads proclaiming 'The Sexiest WC on Earth'. Toilets are one of the most intimate, personal spaces, yet they appear sterile and bland. 'We are not afraid of being different and of following what we believe in. We try to be very careful with the aesthetics of everything we produce as we like aesthetics in simple things.'

Pivot points for Renova in 'changing the game' of toilet paper were:

THINK Audacious to think differently, to break the rules, and be different

DISRUPT Reframing their market space, from tissue paper to 'sexy bathrooms'

DESIGN Embracing functional and aesthetic design, bold and surprising

RESONATE Connecting with consumers through celebrity endorsement and PR

'We seek to bring a shining light into a heavily under-glamorized, over-homogenized and even stigmatized category. Every day we work to make people's day better even if in a very small way. Why not? Why be normal?' says da Silva.

Method ... superheroes who made cleaning products cool

Method is the cleaning products that believe in doing good whilst also being iconic features and beautiful fragrances for your home. With attitude and ambition, they declared war on dirt.

Adam Lowry and Eric Ryan were childhood friends, who became (in their own words) 'brainparents' of one of America's fast growing consumer goods brands. Adam trained as a designer and marketer, whilst Eric studied chemical engineering. Method emerged out of their maddening frustration with cleaning products – poorly designed, environmental pollutants and many just didn't work. They declared war on dirt, and dreamt of a cleaning world which was eco-friendly and non-toxic, stylish and exciting.

They started by mixing soap formulas in beer pitchers labelled 'do not drink'. In 2001 they got (slightly more) serious, and launched the Method brand as 'people against dirty', and declared themselves 'superheroes' for seeking to rid the world of dirt.

Mollie Stone, a Californian grocery store, was their first customer, stocking a range of cleaning sprays. They were good, but didn't stand out. Packaging design was their response, starting with an hourglass-shaped bottle of dish soap, and within a year they were being stocked in Target supermarkets across the nation. By 2003, their designer Karim Rashid started winning awards, particularly for his tear-drop bottle of hand wash.

They articulated their distinctive attitude as 'the Humanifesto' which includes 'we look at the world through bright-green colored glasses', 'to get out and fight dirty, take deep, satisfying breaths all day and sleep easy at night', 'We're entranced by shiny objects like clean dinner plates, floors you could eat off, nobel peace prixes and tasteful public sculptures', and 'above all we believe dirty, in all its slimy, smoggy, toxic, disgusting incarnations, is public enemy number one'.

Within four years, the brand extended to Canada and UK, now also with a concentrated laundry liquid. They focused on their environmental credentials, winning awards from PeTA and ensuring their bottles were 100% biodegradeable. Growth followed rapidly, as did their product range.

A year later, Adam and Eric set up B Corporation, a non-profit network of organizations collectively committed to 'solving the big social and environmental challenges through the power of business'. Alongside Method, they attracted brands as diverse as Ben & Jerry's, Etsy and 750 others to join, sharing best practices and resources, creating a standard certification and a shared platform for promoting a better way to do business.

Pivot points for Method in 'changing the game' of cleaning products were:

EXPLORE   Establishing a market for 'better' cleaning products, cool and caring

DESIGN   Designing better products and packaging, emotional, beautiful for the home

IMPACT   Balancing doing good for the environment with long-term financial success

AMPLIFY   Getting together with the largest competitor to take on the world

In 2012 Method was acquired by Ecover, the Belgian manufacturer of green cleaning products, although continuing to operate as a separate brand. The two brands seek the economies of scale to improve profitability in a market where there is still little scope to charge a premium, and also to reciprocate each other's distribution networks.

Nike ... business designed at the speed of the swoosh

Nike is a design and branding business, with a focus on digital technologies and 'amplifying nature'. It is about function and fashion, but most of all about athletes and achievement.

Look at the tag inside a pair of Nike shoes. It says 'to bring inspiration and innovation to every athlete* in the world' with a footnote explaining the asterix '* if you have a body, you are an athlete'.

Some of the highlights in Nike's running shoe innovation timeline include the early waffle sole design, which provided grip and differentiation. Then there was Nike Air, the patented midsole cushioning approach, and the Nike+ range of technical gadgets to help measure and enhance the run.. Nike Considered is a business process, ensuring that every aspect of sourcing and production is sustainable. Nike Free is about minimalism, taking away the unnecessary cushioning which built up over years, to replicate natural motion. And most recently Nike Flyknit is an entire shoe upper made from one thread, enabling more comfort and lightness.

Mark Parker's CEO office is full of creative stimulus, tech gadgets and electric guitars, fashion items and artistic sculptures. There is even an Andy Warhol and props from Batman. Beyond strategies and spreadsheets, he sees his job to get Nike thinking beyond what they do. He sees a fusion of digital and physical worlds, as demonstrated by Nike+ watches and monitors. The Nike+ Fuelband, for example, is worn through the day measuring the amount of 'fuel' consumed, against target levels and linking to online games, social media and community.

'The last thing we want is to be a big dumb company that feels we can put a swoosh logo on something and people will buy

that', Parker says in an interview with Fast Company magazine. 'Things are accelerating. It's a high-velocity world, we're digitally connected, everything is changing.' Nike's management style doesn't come from a business school textbook, its more intuitive and fast moving, like the culture of sports. Fast and competitive, where records are there to be broken.

Nike's biggest challenge, according to Parker, was to bring focus to what seemed like infinite choices for growth. He saw Nike as idea rich, full of opportunities, but less good at making choices. He addresses this by adding pressure and criteria through which to focus, and then the support and resources to amplify. He sees his role as searching for new ideas, both inside and outside. Years earlier Nike founder Phil Knight had come across Parker as a junior designer, drawing little windows into the soles of Nike shoes, making the air cushions visible. It became a $1 billion idea for Nike.

Pivot points for Nike in 'changing the game' of sportswear were:

THINK   Ideas driven by people and aspirations, not products and capability

INSPIRE   Building a brand that has passion brought to life by incredible athletes

DESIGN   Focusing on concept innovations, like Air and Free, as brand platforms

ENABLE   Creating enabling experiences through events and adjacent products

When Parker arrived 30 years ago, Nike was a niche brand, smaller than Adidas. Today it is 25 times bigger than its rival.

Apple ... designed in California, loved around the world

Apple's story is retold a thousand times. But in a world of relentless innovation and imitation, the brand needs to reassert itself, as more than its products and more than Steve Jobs.

On 21 May 2013 Tim Cook stood before the US Senate. Apple had enjoyed unprecedented success over the last decade, and globally the brand's popularity has soared with international revenues double those from local markets. He was asked whether Apple is still proud to be an American company. He emphatically replied yes, more than ever. Whilst the question was supposed to be about taxation, Cook replied with a bigger passion. Whilst iPhones and iPads are manufactured across the globe, the ideas behind their success – design and innovation – happens within one zipcode, 95014.

At Cupertino, in the heart of California's Silicon Valley where Steve Jobs grew up, then surrounded by orange orchards, and later by tech start-ups, Apple is building a new futuristic campus. Shortly before he died, Steve Jobs made one final public appearance, in front of Cupertino's planning committee. He talked of his love of the place Apple calls home, and the people, 'the brightest, most creative people on the planet' he called his team. He wanted to ensure he secured a great place for them to continue his work.

In the same month, Apple launched a huge marketing programme with the slogan 'Designed by Apple in California'. It's a signature that has been enscribed on the back of every Apple device for decades, but it says more about Apple and the business world now than ever before. It reminds us that we live in an ideas world, that Apple is a creative business, working with the best technical partners across the globe to create great products, with a brand that captures the world's imagination. Whilst most businesses are now a mosaic of nationalities, heritage and iconic images are what inspire us.

The rest of the Apple story has already been told. From the early days of 1976 when Jobs and Steve Wozniak launched Apple 1 at the Homebrew Computer Club, and made his first million that year, to Apple 2 two years later when his wealth had grown to $100m. In 1984 the 'Mac team' flies a pirate flag above their office, and launches the Mac at that year's Superbowl. But soon after, they were gone, refusing to be slaves to conventional management.

Rejoining Apple in 1997, having made $1.5 billion at NeXT and Pixar, Jobs 'thinks different' with his multi-coloured iMacs. iPod and iTunes, iPhone and iPad soon followed. Whilst people loved and hated Jobs, his passion was to make things people loved, to create a better life. This purpose, more than the pursuit of money or innovation, is what has inspired Apple, and inspired consumers, to build a great brand.

Godrej ... frugal innovators of the emerging markets

Godrej's ChotuKool is a simple, affordable innovation for the millions, even billions, of consumers who want to store food and drink, but for whom a fridge is unaffordable and unnecessary.

India's Godrej was founded in 1897 by Ardeshir Godrej, the lawyer who became a locksmith and a relentless innovator of engines to appliances, food and furniture. With his brother Pirojsha, the $4billion Mumbai-based company is now in over 60 countries, typically emerging markets with the same types of consumer needs as fast-developing India.

'ChotuKool' is a great example of frugal innovation – addressing the basic refrigeration needs of rural families in India, and inspired by Clay Christensen's passion that simple solutions can disrupt complex ones. Electricity is rare or unreliable in many rural parts, and most people earn less than $5 a day.

The Godrej team wanted to explore how some form of fridge might transform food purchases and healthy eating. Local 'immersion' research explored how people bought, stored and used food. They concluded it wasn't so much about fridges, more about a simple way to store milk and vegetables for a short time.

Bringing together local people, they co-created potential solutions. 'ChotuKool' meaning little cool in Hindi, looks more like a cool box, fitted with a thermoelectric chip that maintains a cool temperature using a small external battery. With 45 litres of space, the box is simple and efficient to use. At $69, it is far more affordable than a mains appliance and more portable too. The concept resulted in Godrej being named India's most innovative company by the Indian Government.

Lego ... rebuilding the business with 'creative play'

Lego almost died. Under pressure from an avalanche of digital games, the classic toy brand responded by seeking to imitate its challengers, losing sight of what made it special.

In 1947 Ole Kirk Christiansen bought the first plastic-injection moulding machine in Denmark to start manufacturing plastic toy bricks. Within four years he had patented the stud-like bricks that locked together as systems.

For the next 56 years, Lego seemed the perfect company. An iconic brand, the business was still run by the family, grandson Kjeld Kirk now the CEO. However, in 1993 sales slowed dramatically, blamed on everything from low-priced Chinese imitations to kids' new love of computer games. Lego responded with wave after wave of innovation. Jumbo sized for toddlers, pocket sized for girls. Computerized 'Technics' range for the most inventive, and video games for the lazy. But kids were growing up faster.

Licensing of Star Wars and Harry Potter ranges tapped into trends, but were short-lived. It sought out new spaces – fanatical about finding uncontested 'blue oceans' rather than more competitive 'red oceans' – and encouraged diverse creativity. Clothing and jewellery, theme parks and education added to the brand's extensions.

Yet in 2003 Lego almost went bankrupt. The unbridled innovation had lost a sense of direction, trying to be too many things to too many people, forgetting what it was really about – 'playing well' as the brand's origins in the Danish phrase 'leg godt' translate.

The family ceded control to a professional CEO, Jorgen Vig Knudstorp, who brought tighter focus to the portfolio and added discipline to the creativity. He sold the theme parks, moved out of the head office and outsourced production to Czech Republic and Mexico.

However Knudstorp still believed in innovation, it just needed discipline. It wasn't about blazing a trail into every market, but focusing on the best opportunities for profitable growth. Investment focused on the ideas which fitted best with the core brand and delivered a long-term return. By 2006, the world's third largest toy maker started growing again, with profit growth double revenue growth, always a healthy sign.

Natura Cosmeticos ... the beauty of the Amazonians

Natura is one of the most loved brands of Brazil. Its commitment to sustainable practices, and indeed using nature to its advantage, has built the brand across Latin America, and it has leapfrogged to new markets.

Beauty brand Natura, based at Cajamar, near São Paulo, is one of Brazil's most loved and valuable brands, with products ranging from make-up to fragrances, skin care and hair care. Founded in 1969, Natura has over 50 million consumers, reached largely through a direct sales model, incentivizing consumers to sell to their friends and neighbours, like Avon or Oriflame.

Around 40% of Brazil is covered by the Amazon rainforest. From rubber to timber, commercial exploitation of South America's iconic rainforest has usually meant one thing: environmental destruction. Natura wants to change that, and has pledged to buy the majority of its raw ingredients from sustainable sources in the Amazon. It is also investing one billion Reals ($500m) in the region; building an interdisciplinary network of 1000 researchers focused on the Amazon; and involving between 10,000 and 12,000 small producers in its supply chain. Natura has a modest R&D team, but amplifies this with a sophisticated network of 25 universities around the world, exploring everything from the science of ageing to more sustainable packaging.

As a small player in a huge market, Natura sought to be different, turning to the Amazon's biodiversity as a 'technological platform' for research and development. Around 75% of Natura's dry ingredients already come from natural sources. Sourcing from the rainforest is not easy or cheap. 'It makes innovation more difficult' says CEO Alessandro Carlucci in an interview with *The Guardian*, 'So we have to think differently, about how we can have more economic impact with less environmental impact. This challenge drives our innovation.'

The consumer trend towards natural, ethical consumption in Brazil, and across the world, helps Natura, recently recognized as one of the most sustainable companies on the planet. However it is not just in South America, Natura is increasingly sought after in Europe and Asia too.

Oculus Rift ... the 3D headset that goes inside the game

Oculus Rift is the virtual reality headset that signposts a next generation of digital experiences. Crowd-funded it has captured the imagination of gaming fans, and internet entrepreneurs looking for the next big thing.

Pull down the helmet and suddenly you're inside a virtual world that seems incredibly real. You can run around, fight, race and fly, doing things gamers have never done before. What was once the stuff of Hollywood fantasy is now possible. Oculus Rift was made possible through crowd-funding when in 2012 it raised $2.4 million on Kickstarter to fund the development of its virtual reality headsets. Inventor Palmer Luckey was ecstatic when his required amount $250k was raised in 36 hours, such was excitement of VR fans.

In 2013 Marc Andreessen saw the potential of Oculus as the future of gaming – maybe even education, media and travel too – investing $75 million. He only had to wait four months for a return, when Facebook snapped up the business for $2 billion. Zuckerberg sees virtual reality as the next platform after mobile, as games and brands move from collaboration and real-time, to immersive experiences.

Pebble ... kickstarting a new generation of wearable devices

FUTUREGADGET
Pebble

Pebble is a crowd-funded smartwatch that is the vanguard of the wearable tech revolution. Like many start-ups unable to convince investors, it turned directly to consumers instead.

The Pebble is a smartwatch that failed to attract conventional investors, and so turned to Kickstarter, breaking all crowd-funding records to raise $10.3m from 69,000 fans.

Eric Migicovsky's design, developed with the initial support of Y Combinator's business incubator, enables the watch to display messages from a smartphone. The challenge with Kickstarter, of course, is that once the money is pledged, you are contractually obliged to deliver, unlike other investments which can disappear into more R&D.

The Pebble team quickly grew to 30 people with a mission 'to create the world's best smartwatch and ecosystem'. Whilst their first priority was to fulfil orders, they also needed to build a third party app platform, incentivizing developers to find new ways to exploit the wristband. Within 90 days the first Pebbles were being shipped, in red, black and silver, a new status symbol for the crowd-created age.

Philosophy ... inspiring people to believe in more

FUTUREGADGET
Philosophy

Philosophy is a skincare brand with a message to inspire your life. Rather than functional science, consumers engage in emotional wellbeing and being part of a community who believe in better.

Philosophy was founded in 1996 by Cristina Carlino, who brought over 30 years of experience in clinical skincare and beauty, including her previously created brand Biomedic, a medically-based skincare range.

What Cristina believed in more than anything was the combination of function and emotion, science and inspiration. 'What is in our bottles and jars inspires better skin, what is on our bottles and jars inspires better days', the latter a reference to the quirky poetry that adorns every piece of packaging.

The philosophy is based on both advanced science (for example, millions of women get hooked on the hydrating properties of its 'Miracle Worker' cream), and on 'celebrating the beauty of human spirit'. Everyone knows that there is no magical formula to prevent skin ageing, but Philosophy gives you 'Hope' recognizing that beauty is as much a feeling inside as an outer appearance. 'We believe that skincare can give us better skin and inspiration can give us better days' it goes.

But that's the point ... the brand isn't about the product, it's about the consumer ... whilst the product is scientific and functional, it's the inspiration that engages people, that brings like-minded women together and that builds loyalty and advocacy. It's not about how good the manufacturer thinks the product is, it's what the consumer believes. Philosophy as a brand inspires its consumers to believe not just in the product, but that they can be more. And together, as a like-minded community, they can be even more.

18 FUTUREMEDIA
CHANGING THE GAME OF CONTENT AND MEDIA

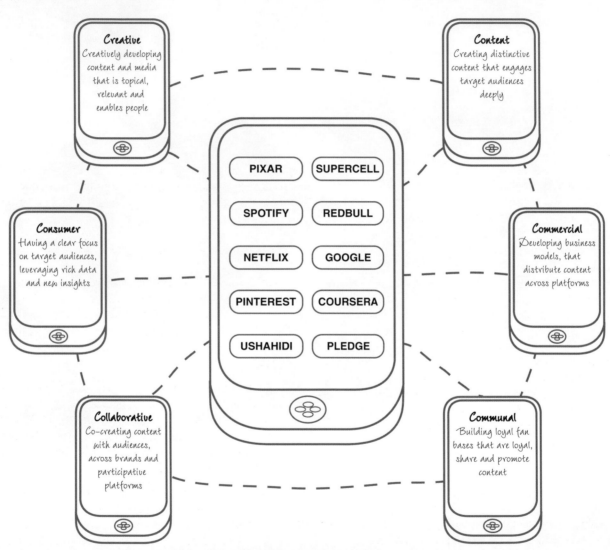

Creative
Creatively developing content and media that is topical, relevant and enables people

Content
Creating distinctive content that engages target audiences deeply

Consumer
Having a clear focus on target audiences, leveraging rich data and new insights

Commercial
Developing business models, that distribute content across platforms

Collaborative
Co-creating content with audiences, across brands and participative platforms

Communal
Building loyal fan bases that are loyal, share and promote content

PIXAR   SUPERCELL
SPOTIFY   REDBULL
NETFLIX   GOOGLE
PINTEREST   COURSERA
USHAHIDI   PLEDGE

Futuremedia, Rethinking the World of Media and Content

When Dietmar Mateschitz declared that Red Bull is a media company much more than a drinks brand, it made people think about what media really is today and how value is created. Here was a manufacturer, through its adventures into extreme sporting events, that realized that its brand stood for much more than adrenelin in a can. From magazines to movies, the attitudes and activities of the brand were captured in many ways.

The phrase **'media'** used to be quite obvious. Printers and broadcasters gathered content and delivered it to you through their books, newspapers, TV and radio channels. Now it is much more complicated. We live in a world surrounded by **multiple screens**. Screens are our windows into a mashed-up world of endless content and channel options. It can seem like overload, but at the same time we are in control of what, when and how we consume it. We search, select and shape the content we want. We increasingly create and share it too. As a result content is about collaboration and media on shared platforms.

Audiences have transformed from passive masses into individual **participants**, demanding and discerning, emotional and addictive. We consume on demand, absorbing information in snack size chunks, preferring images rather than words. We also like to occasionally indulge in an entire box set in one day. Advertisers are left thinking about how to reengage with people who skip their disruptive breaks, but at the same time see a world of **augmented** reality where we can click to buy Brad Pitt's jeans on impulse, or to dive deep into areas of interest beyond our superficial view.

What matters most in the new world of content and media is:

- **Consumption**: forget mass audiences, people consume on their terms, so what matters most is their loyalty and advocacy – building fan bases that emotionally engage, participate and advocate. Netflix harnesses the power of monitoring every behaviour, whilst Pledge Music engages fans before the music is even created.

- **Collaboration**: content is richer and more relevant when it is created together, consumers with consumers, with creators and with other types of partners. This taps into the diverse creativity and passion of many different players, whilst also engaging consumers deeply as demonstrated from Pinterest to Ushihida.

- **Convergence**: as content flows across platforms, richer experiences emerge that enable brands to do more, sports and entertainment to become more immersive as well as convenient. Technologies, from gaming for example, spread across other platforms making interfaces more engaging and human.

- **Commercialization**: the notion that content is free, legitimately or not, challenges every content owner to think more creatively about how they create more perceived value and monetize it. Coursera offers you the content of Harvard free, Spotify offer you everything on iTunes free. New business models are key.

GAMECHANGERS

The future of content and media is perhaps one of the most important and exiting categories in which 'gamechangers' are being most disruptive. Of course, it can seem like technology, but that simply enables content, access and application. Here are some of the businesses shaking up this world:

FUTUREMEDIA
Coursera

Coursera ... the best education available to everyone

Coursera, and other MOOCs, are on the verge of fundamentally disrupting education, knowledge and expertize, across the world. By moving the best university courses online, with a business model that allows universal access, they can be transformational on society, and have opportunities for everyone.

Anyone, anywhere can now study paleobiology with the help of the University of Alberto which has made its 'Dino 101' course available free online, and uses interactive techniques developed for the gaming industry to bring the science of the dinosaurs to life. It is just one of thousands of free study modules available through Coursera which has signed up over 100 of the world's best universities since its launch in 2012. Within a year it had 4.8 million students in 195 countries, giving anyone – old as well as young – the opportunity to study almost anything, free and from their home.

Coursera, founded by two computer science professors, Andrew Ng and Daphne Koller, at Stanford University is leading the MOOC revolution in education. 'Massive open online courses' are transforming who and how the world learns. Inspired by the Khan Academy, Ng started posting his course material on YouTube in 2008. Before long, each video had generated at least 100,000 views compared to his Stanford class, which by contrast had just 400 students a year, paying up to $200k for their degrees. To reach

a comparable audience, he would have had to teach at Stanford for 250 years.

The business model is still evolving. Whilst it is not easy to replicate some aspects of a university experience, Coursera with partners as diverse as Duke and Tokyo, and rivals like edX supported by Harvard and MIT, can transform the lives of billions of people looking to start, advance or change careers. Coursera, as a non-profit, plans to charge $100 for certificates, shared with university partners, but free to those who cannot afford it. Many courses count towards degrees. More significant revenues could involve licensing content to community colleges, and recruitment fees to potential employers.

Pivot points for Coursera in changing the game of education are:

THINK   Imagining a future of lifelong learning available to everyone

DISRUPT   Bringing together the best academic content, free to access

DESIGN   Redesigning course material for self learning, eg using gaming

MOBILIZE   Engaging new audiences, communities schools, and employers.

Spotify ... the freemium business model for music

Spotify grew out of deviant behaviour – imitating the actions of illegal downloaders to find a legal business model which combines free access with the ability to also make money as a business, and for artists and publishers. The brand is contagious, driven by consumer collaboration, and staying topical.

Whilst most people choose Spotify for free access to streamed music, co-founder Daniel Ek is focused on ensuring that the premium services, such as the ability to download and play the music offline for a monthly subscription, significantly exceeds the diversity of royalties it pays to record labels, collecting societies, artists and publishers.

When Ek first invited big music labels, he forgot to mention that they were all invited together, causing panic on arrival at Stockholm airport. Ek apologized for his naivity, whilst telling them he was about to change their world. Sweden was already home to the notorious Pirate Bay file-sharing hub, and Swedes had grown used to not paying for content. He therefore started with his home market, streaming music in a way that was faster, easier and less risky than piracy.

A six-month free trial starts upon account registration, allowing the user to listen to an unlimited amount of music supported by visual and radio-style advertising. After the trial, there is a listening limit of 2.5 hour a week. The 'unlimited' subscription removes advertisements and time limits and a 'premium' subscription introduces extra features such as faster, higher quality, and offline access to music. There is also a close partnership with Facebook, encouraging people to access through the site and then share activity with friends.

Spotify now provides unlimited streaming access to 25 million songs. Around 25% of users pay $10–15 a month for a premium version, a fee that is shared with record companies whose royalties are higher than for many years. Around 70% of music revenues now come from digital streaming, and Spotify is at the forefront of a revolution that is spreading rapidly across the globe.

Growing by a factor of 10 every year, Spotify is generating significant revenues, with 70% going to artists and record labels. Whilst the business is still unprofitable, as it focuses on entering new markets with its free service, its early Nordic markets are now profitable, and the company was valued in 2014 at $10 billion.

Pivot points for Spotfy in changing the game of streaming music were:

EXPLORE   Looking for deviant behavior in the margins of markets

DISRUPT   Making content free but in a way that is commercial

DESIGN   Continually evolving the business model to find a better solution

MOBILIZE   Building a community of advocates, the cool thing to do

Netflix ... changing what and when we watch

Netflix grew out of consumer frustration with the stupid rules of an old model. This provoked one guy into creating a better solution, which has continued to evolve in format and business model as new technologies emerge, and competitors catch up. The next horizon of data-driven content creation is perhaps the most intriguing.

Netflix is transforming the way we find movies and when and how we watch them. Founded in 1997 as a DVD by mail service, it soon migrated online to offer more than 100,000 movies streamed to your screen for a monthly subscription. Reed Hastings, and colleague Marc Randolph, set up the business after making $700 million selling their Pure Software business, and then being fined $40 for the overdue return of his rented copy of Apollo 13. Outraged he vowed to find a better model.

Within two years of launch it had moved from charging per DVD, to a flat subscription. Within a decade it had 25 million subscribers and had delivered a billion DVDs, although most users now preferred online streaming. Netflix found the customer base actually grew faster during the economic downturn than at other times – partly as broadband penetration grew, but mainly because a Netflix subscription had become a household essential.

Whilst the business might appear to be about distribution, the data on subscribers and their viewing behaviours became most significant. Initially this provided a highly accurate way of targeting advertising, but even more profitably in creating original content that specifically matched the preferences of target audiences. Big data started to replace, or enhance, creativity. Netflex invested $100,000 in 'House of Cards' based entirely on data algorithms, seeking to create the perfect TV series to match its target audience and advertisers.

Pivot points for Netflix in changing the game of online movies were:

EXPLORE   Observing the frustrating limitations of existing approaches

DESIGN   Creating and evolving a new business model, on demand then streaming

RESONATE   Using big data analytics to match audiences and content

AMPLIFY   Harnessing network-based models to exponentially grow

Al Jazeera ... Arabic news for the English speaking world

Al Jazeera has challenged the world – locally conservative and globally prejudiced – to listen to a different point of view in news broadcasting. In a region where news is often conditioned or controlled it provides an alternative perspective on the events, issues and motivations of one of society's melting pots.

Al Jazeera presents 'the opinion and the other opinion', seeking to bring a more open approach to news in the Middle East where news was often controlled or sensored. The media channel was launched in 1996, based in Qatar with the support of Sheikh Hamad bin Khalifa to be an impartial platform for news and debate about Arab issues. However it also challenged people on issues from morality and religion to politics and conflicts, sometimes banned by governments or accused of supporting particular groups. Despite the controversies, it developed a large following of people seeking an unsensored view of their world, with a 35 million audience within 5 years, making it the largest broadcaster in the region.

The channel also became popular with global audiences. During the 2003 Gulf War, it provided the only voice from within Iraq, its feeds in demand from every news agency and from viewers seeking stories beyond military press conferences. Its sports coverage became a major driver of growth in recent years, gaining exclusive rights often in partnership with Western media brands. In 2004, former US secretary of state, Hilary Clinton, said that Al Jazeera, with 50 million viewers across the world, 'has become the leader in changing people's minds and attitudes. And like it or hate it, it is really effective.'

Future ... innovative publisher doing more for readers

Magazines seemed like a medium in decline, but Future thought differently. It focuses on niche audiences, combines physical and digital experiences, topical news with in depth analysis, and building communities with a passion for its chosen topics, sustained through dedicated fan packs.

Future is an international media group with leading publications in everything from Technology and Gaming, to Photography and Cycling reaching more than 51 million consumers a month. The business is also a leader in embracing new technologies and business models in an industry which has seen more innovation than most.

Future is a global leader in tablet publishing, shaping much of the design and content of Apple's Newstand magazine store, and creating new ways in which consumers can sample, buy and subscribe. Broadband connections and tablet devices are shaping the way content is created and consumed – fast and interactive, integrated across media. Niche content businesses flourish in this environment – particularly those that are built around news, trusted advice and video. These are typically premium markets, where audiences may be amateur cyclists, Linux programmers in Korea, or digital musicians in Japan. Supporting the business model, with all its additional costs, is the fact that these audiences are still highly attractive to advertisers.

PledgeMusic ... crowd-funded music direct to superfans

From books to music, publishing was crying out for a new model. PledgeMusic offers not only a better way to fund new and existing artists, but to engage people more deeply, and to build enduring communities directly with lovers of music genres and bands.

'Record, release, promote' was the old way of launching music, says British musician and entrepreneur Benji Rogers, before describing his vision to The Music Network. 'We see a better way, a deep engagement between musicians and their fans, where the recording process is part of the promotion.' Launched in 2009, PledgeMusic is a form of crowd-funding that engages and enables 'superfans' to enjoy music that might otherwise never reach the market.

Unlike Kickstarter, for example, it is only about music, which enables it to build strong communities around certain types of

music. It doesn't retain any rights, has minimal costs, and allows 'pledger' refunds if they change their minds. Like Kickstarter, it is international, and encourages artists to offer a diverse range of incentives such as events and additional content that enriches the music experience. Fans are therefore much more involved in projects, building communities around bands and genres, which was never possible with a record label or music store.

At the same time, PledgeMusic is not in competition with more traditional recording and distribution models, and could positively enhance them. Many artists are already signed to labels, working with Pledge to engage fans in pre-sales then offering a richer purchase and listening experience, whilst other artists get signed up through the platform. Both Sony and Universal have formed partnership agreements. As Benji Rogers proclaims in his website: 'We are creating the future of music.'

Ushahidi ... Kenya's crowd-sourced news channel

Born out of the chaos and recriminations of tribal warfare, Ushahidi has emerged as another example of Africa's ability to embrace mobile technologies and collaborative business models.

Ushahidi is a non-profit African media platform that develops free software for collecting information, visualizing and mapping it – 'democratizing information, increasing transparency and sharing stories'.

'Ushahidi' means 'testimony' in Swahili, and was initially developed as a website to map violence in the aftermath of Kenya's 2008 elections. Developed in desperation by young journalists to map the violence and try to find peaceful solutions, 45,000 joined in the cause, creating a new movement to encourage democracy.

Since then the platform has become a crowd-sourced news platform, and is particularly powerful in regions where media is controlled or filtered by governments. The platform has spread rapidly across Africa, sharing local and regional news, but also for niche interests from athletics to business. It has also been adopted by communities across Asia and South America too.

Ushahidi was made possible by a group of Kenyan activists and tech experts who wouldn't stand by idly as a crisis engulfed their country. Ory Okolloh was born to a poor family in rural Kenya, before going to study at Harvard then returning as a journalist. In a recent TED Talk, she says 'For most Africans today, where you live, or where you were born, and the circumstances under which you were born, determine the rest of your life. I would like to see that change, and the change starts with us ... as Africans, we need to take responsibility for our continent!'

Red Bull ... space jumps, air races and now a media house

Red Bull is much more than a drink, it's a brand that reflects an attitude to life and can therefore do more. In fact it has become a media company, with some of the world's most extreme physical events, amplified as digital content. Not as a promotion for its drinks, but as the core business, with drinks on the side.

A snowboarder glides upside down over a forest of trees and sticks his hand out to brush the top of a tall pine. He does it so casually, whilst a high-speed camera catches the treetop moment, just another glimpse of Red Bull action. In fact you might be forgetting that Red Bull is actually a drink. The logo is everywhere at these events, but the brand is more than an energy drink.

'Red Bull gives you wings' says the slogan, emblazoned across the sky by stunt aircraft taking part in the brand's Air Race in front of millions of spectators crowded along the banks of the Danube in Budapest. It's the same message at the Flugtag when homemade aircraft take flight and flop just a quickly, at the Cliff diving from the tall buildings into Boston Harbour, or the Soapbox race when rickety go-karts hurtle down a mountain side. It's all pure adrenalin and fabulous entertainment.

In 1987 Dietrich Mateschitz was in Bangkok selling photocopiers. After a long flight he collapsed into the chair of a hotel bar. 'I know exactly what you need, Sir' proposed the Thai waitress. She quickly returned with a glass of *Krating Daeng* (daeng means red, krating is a guar, or very large bison). Whilst the original ingredients were said to contain bull's testicles, Mateschitz was soon energized, returning to his native Austria with a plan to modify the recipe and launch his new brand.

Having sold 6 billion cans, the world's largest energy drink is often called 'liquid cocaine'. But the focus is not the ingredients, it's the possibilities of the brand – how it makes you feel, not what it is. This is where the high adrenalin sports come in. Red Bull Media House makes the movies of each event, on a budget of around $2 million, but sells the movies for much more. There are a regular NBC reality TV shows featuring its stars, online communities, and Red Bulletin magazine. In fact such content is as important as the product in building the brand, so much so that Mateschitz now calls Red Bull a media company.

Supercell... the best gamemakers in the mobile world

Games are the most contagious form of content, particularly with Gen Y. Supercell recognized that staying small, focusing on less and better content was its pathway to success. Whilst it is yet another product of Helsinki, it proves that geography is irrelevant in a connected world.

Ilkka Paananen sits in a glass room, a tall Helsinki office block vacated by Nokia, saying the best way to make money in gaming is to simply have fun rather than thinking about sales. 'It really is that simple. Just design something great, something that users love,' says the 30-something Finn. He launched the gamemaker in 2010, with two games specifically focused on mobile platforms and with

'freemium' business models, free to access then charging players (once they're hooked) to access increasing levels of peer-rivalling complexity.

The games – Clash of Clans, about fantasy tribal warfare, and Hay Day, about running a farm – were initially placed on Apple's App Store and soon became the most downloaded apps in 121 countries, generating revenues of $2.4 million a day, with 30% going to Apple. Within two years Supercell, with its team of 80 designers, was 51% acquired by Japan's Softbank for $1.5m. However Paananen wants to stay small, keeping the close team together making a few great games, which they love to play.

Pixar... inspiring humanity through the power of storytelling

Pixar creates the world's most loved movies. Creating animations is relatively slow and costly, but with a focus on character building and incredible storytelling the brand has created hit after hit. Its creative process – based around ideas and stories – is a great model for any type of brand building and communication.

Realizing that he could not draw, aspiring animator Ed Catmull decided to change his academic focus to physics and computer science. He joined a small off-shoot of George Lucas' filmmaking empire, Graphics Groups, which actually made visual technology products for healthcare. Combining science and art, Catmull drove the creation of 'PhotoRealistic RenderMan', an image-rendering process used to generate high-quality images. It was a business that intrigued Steve Jobs, who bought the business in 1986.

Whilst the technology was cutting edge, it wasn't a good business, and to stay afloat Catmull started making short animated commercials. John Lasseter, a creative director, soon joined to help. Out of financial necessity emerged one of the most imaginative movies of all time, *Toy Story*. It was the beginning of a long sequence of award-winning success. Both *Finding Nemo* and *Toy Story 3* are among the 50 highest-grossing films of all time, and all of Pixar's films are among the 50 highest-grossing animated films,

with *Toy Story 3* being the all-time highest, grossing over $1 billion worldwide.

The Walt Disney Company bought Pixar in 2006 for $7.4 billion, but retained its independence, allowing the creativity and technological inventiveness (perhaps best articulated in *Wall-E*) to flourish without the distractions of a big business. Pixar's movies and licensed characters continue to be loved by children – and adults – across the world. Steve Jobs loved the brand so much, that even when he didn't own it anymore, he still used his Pixar email address rather than Apple's address, 'because it's much cooler'.

Pixar's 'Braintrust' meets once every few months, putting its smartest, most passionate people together in a room for the day to think bigger ideas, solve the most difficult problems, and do what individuals can't or daren't. In his book, *Creativity, Inc*, Catmull says 'a hallmark of a healthy creative culture is that its people feel free to share ideas, opinions, and criticisms'. Pixar finds that decision making is better when it draws on the collective knowledge and candid opinions of the Braintrust group, finding that straight talking encourages collaboration and more daring creativity.

19 FUTUREFASHION
CHANGING THE GAME OF FASHION

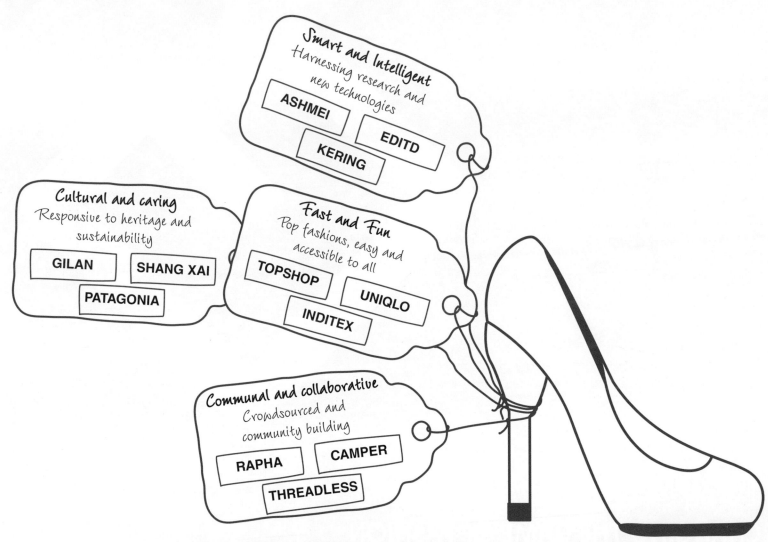

Smart and Intelligent
Harnessing research and new technologies
ASHMEI
EDITD
KERING

Cultural and caring
Responsive to heritage and sustainability
GILAN
SHANG XAI
PATAGONIA

Fast and Fun
Pop fashions, easy and accessible to all
TOPSHOP
UNIQLO
INDITEX

Communal and collaborative
Crowdsourced and community building
RAPHA
CAMPER
THREADLESS

Futurefashion, Rethinking the World of Clothing Design

The future of fashion is being transformed by technology. Just consider the potential of **big data** that pinpoints trends, to **3D printing** that creates new structural designs, and wearable tech that enhances the functionality of clothing. Runways are turned into **multimedia**, participative experiences whilst shopping malls, both physical and digital, are intelligent and personalized. Fashion brands are about more than products, they are about the audience. Enabling people to achieve more, functionally or emotionally, and bringing people together in communities with shared interests or shared expression.

SMART AND LUXURY, LOCAL AND GLOBAL

The global market for clothing, accessories and luxury goods is worth almost $3 trillion and continues to grow even in difficult times, largely driven by youthful aspiration and a relentless thirst for luxury goods in emerging markets. A connected world becomes a melting pot of cultural influences, at the same time polarizing into more fragmented niches.

Trends are more diverse and eclectic, fashion more extreme and transient. **Advanced materials** and manufacturing processes enhance both function and form, whilst the social and environmental impact of sourcing and manufacturing matter more. The **cross-pollination** of ideas sparks new trends – from new interpretations of ancient designs into modern pieces, like Gilan jewellery and Shanghai Tang clothing, to the leopard-skin print of Puma running shoes or urban minimalism of Gyakasou by Underworld.

Some of the most significant trends in fashion design include:

- **Cultural and caring** – from our outrage at sweatshops to preference for sustainable materials, supporting local brands, reducing carbon, adapting and swapping, hand-made and vintage.
- **Fast and efficient** – from 'ready-baked' catwalk designs to low priced imitations, ranges that change weekly and clothes that are seen as disposable, a thirst for shopping, for fads and hyper-cool fashions.
- **Smart and intelligent** – from nano-tech and ultra-light to spray on and biodegradable, clothing does more, as do the body scanners and 3D printers that customize it to perfection.
- **Communal and collaborative** – building a fanbase, driven by a love of similar fashions or applications, from crowd-sourced design around competitions, to a shared love of sports and participation.

At the same time, fashion brands are about more than the products. Brands achieve relevance through more niche focus, and then by enabling people to do better; what the products enable them to do. Ashmei is about runners who love the freedom of outdoors, and wants to share that love with them. Desigual is a love of vibrant culture, challenging our senses and normalities. Gucci is about statement, stylish and sophisticated, for those who feel the need to state it.

Rapha, the British-made brand of luxury cycling gear, is a great example of the changing nature of fashion. At the heart of the brand is not Lycra or Goretex, but coffee and croissants. Rapha 'Cycle Club' cafés, also known as shops, replicate the nostalgic cafés along the route of the Tour de France – where enthusiasts share tales of past glories and personal experiences, talking bikes and repairs, horrific accidents and crowning glories – and being in the very best gear too.

GAMECHANGERS

Here are some of the businesses worldwide, from fabric technologies to retail experiences, who are shaking up the world of fashion:

FUTUREFASHION
Toms

Toms ... A pair for kids with every pair you buy

Toms is a brand with purpose, and a dual business model – inspired by the simple canvas shoes of Argentina – it gives away a free pair away to street kids for every pair it sells. 'One to One' has become a worldwide movement, and now stretches beyond shoes.

Blake Mycoskie spent 2006 doing volunteer work in Buenos Aires, when he noticed that most young people wore simple canvas slip-on shoes called *alpargatas*. The shoes have also been worn by Argentine farmers for hundreds of years, and he decided to start exporting them to his native North America. As he explored more of the city, he also realized that many children wore nothing on their feet, unable even to afford the $5–10 for alpargatas.

Shoes for Tomorrow (shortened to Toms) was born, a for-profit company, making cool shoes in an Argentine factory for Santa Monica beach, but also donating a second pair to its not-for-profit sister company Friends of Toms. 'One for one' took off, with 10,000 pairs sold, and given away, in the first six months. By 2012, 2 million pairs of shoes had been made, and an equal number given away to children in developing countries around the world.

Pivot points for Toms in 'changing the game' of fashion have been:

THINK Driven by a higher purpose, to make life better for poor kids

DESIGN Creating a dual business model, where profit enables non-profit

MOBILIZE Building a global movement, an inspiring model of caring capitalism

IMPACT Working with manufacturers and charities in developing markets

The brand has extended its 'one for one' business model into eyewear and clothing, primarily through word-of-mouth advocacy. In the case of eyeware, Toms provides eye surgery or prescription glasses for every pair of sunglasses sold. Beyond charity, the Toms brand has become a movement for more caring capitalism, including volunteering, education and support for entrepreneurs in development markets.

Ashmei ... designing for runners without compromize

Focusing on designing the very best apparel for serious runners, Ashmei refuses to compromize. Combining the best fabric and production from around the globe, focusing on niche audiences who are prepared to pay more for their passion, it outplays the mainstream brands.

Stuart Brooke started running five years ago and was appalled at the poor quality of all the major brands. Having founded his own business 15 years ago making high specification products for other manufacturers, he knew that there were much better solutions.

'The market is full of average running clothes that all perform to mediocre standards, have similar features, made from identical fibres and look exactly the same' says Brooke. 'These are then sold in the same bargain driven environment that offers poor brand promotion'. Other sports, such as cycling and skiing had far better technical products, and enthusiasts were prepared to pay more for them.

Brooke started life as a fabric designer, but quickly focused on sport, joining Pentland with brands like Reebok and Speedo. But he soon became disenchanted with the endless meeting culture of companies, and the lack of ambition. He wanted to create a brand that was fresh and distinctive. Ashmei was born, a name inspired by his Chinese wife, and an anagram of his daughter Meisha's name. The Chinese lettering, interestingly also used in Japanese, means 'ultimate'. He wanted to create the ultimate running apparel, the best fabrics, using the latest manufacturing technologies.

Ashmei focused on design, specifying requirements and then sourcing from the best suppliers and manufacturers around the world. Fabrics from France, Italy and India are combined in China then shipped to stockists, mainly in Europe. The design is functional, but includes distinctive styling which echoes the Asian name. Initially using selective retailers, Ashmei carefully avoids working with competing retailers and thereby discounting. It creates enduring collections, rather than cosmetic seasonal derivatives, so there are no sales, and it can increase volumes quickly because of the large factories of its suppliers.

Ashmei is a brand for enthusiasts who are willing to pay more, and also likely to become ardent loyal fans. Marketing is about building connections with core users, using social media and inspirational events like the Ashmei Mud Race. Word spread rapidly by PR and word of mouth within established communities. Partnering with a complementary shoe brand is likely, alongside growth into adjacent categories like triathlon.

Pivot points for Ashmei in 'changing the game' of sports apparel have been:

DISRUPT   Believing in better; that people will pay more for premium products

DESIGN   Focusing on product design, then bringing together the best partners

INSPIRE   Articulating a brand that captures the aspirations of serious runners

MOBILIZE   Building a community that shares their passion, enabled by the brand

The niche and premium focused business model is working. 'We believe in three words' says Brooke 'performance, quality and style. Of these performance matters most. It's why we started, and it's why people love us.'

Threadless ... the community-based t-shirt company

Threadless was one of the first crowd-sourced brands, recognizing the power and passion of user-generated designs. Voting and limited availability keeps people coming back to the site, from which a vibrant community has developed, engaging people physically and online.

T-shirts are supposed to be cool, and the coolest t-shirts are not made by big companies with corporate logos, but designed and selected by cool people like you. Threadless was founded in 2000 by Jake Nickell and Jake DeHart, investing $1000 of their own money in a website that encouraged people to submit designs, vote for the best ones each week, from which they would then make the limited editions.

Around 1000 designs are submitted each week and, after an initial filter, put up for public votes. The winning designs are sold online, and through the brand's stores and vending machines. Winning designers receive either $2000 in cash, a $500 Threadless voucher or $200 cash. Whilst every design has a time limit, with sufficient requests for reprints, the winner could get another $500.

The combination of crowd-sourcing, frequent competitions and new editions creates a 2.5 million-strong community who become actively involved in the brand and with each other.

They are supported by four 'community ambassadors' who sustain the buzz and interaction, but also the specific groups. The 'Threadless 12 Club' is a subscription-based VIP network with their own ultra-limited editions, the annual 'Family Reunion' brings people together physically. 'Bestee Awards' recognize the best designers by category whilst the 'Alumni Club' is for winners to stay in touch. Added to this are customers' own networks ranging from local groups who meet to share their love of design, through cake-baking and clothes-making based on submitted designs.

Pivot points for Threadless in 'changing the game' of clothing retail have been:

DESIGN Crowd-sourced designs through monthly competitions and prizes

RESONATE Staying cool and topical through unique designs, with limited life

ENABLE People take part in submitting, selecting, buying and sharing

MOBILIZE Establishing a movement of young designers and brand partners

Gilan ... Ottoman treasures inspire modern luxury

Gilan uses inspirations of Istanbul's past to create some of the world's most beautiful and expensive jewellery. The Turkish brand's hand-made and unique designs are examples of how heritage can be reinterpreted in the modern world to be more interesting and individual.

Hagia Sophia towered above the city of Constantinople when it was built in 537. It stood as the world's largest cathedral for nearly a thousand years, before becoming Istanbul's most impressive mosque, and now a still incredible secular museum. Facing the Byzantine masterpiece is the equally impressive Blue Mosque, still in use, and most famous for its incredible tiles. Just around the corner is the Topkapi Palace, home of the Ottoman sultans for four centuries. In fact, Istanbul is one of the world's most awe-inspiring cities of culture and design.

Recreating this rich history for the 21st century is Gilan, a family owned Istanbul-based jewellery brand that creates one-off pieces inspired by the Byzantine and Ottoman eras. Jewels pay homage to Topkapi Palace's gardens (with tulip-cut stones and rose-cut diamonds), reflect the dominant Bosphorus (ocean-blue chalcedony and waves of sapphire represent the water between Europe and Asia). One ring, selling in Gilan's Fifth Avenue store in New York, is priced at $34,500, with a 14-carat rubellite inspired by the pink and purple tones of the Hagia Sophia. Other pieces, worn by Nicole Kidman and Penelope Cruz, are valued at more than $2 million.

Osman Gilan now leads the business founded by his father 35 years ago, and inspired by his great-great-grandmother who hand-made clothes for the Ottoman pashas. He remains committed to the individuality of his craft, creating exquisite pieces of high perceived value. In an interview with *The National* he says 'Increasingly, it is the one-of-a-kind that wealthy people demand, because that to them is what true luxury is about. In fact, some pieces are only ever seen by the craftspeople and the client.'

Desigual ... Spanish clothing with flamenco passion

The brand is not about clothes, but about the vibrant and fun lifestyle of a Spanish holiday. Think of sun and sea, sangria and Spanish dance, and you start to feel Desigual. Flamboyant promotions and partnerships add to the eclectic, distinctive experience.

Desigual is the colourful, patchwork, grafitti fashion brand from Barcelona that inspires thousands of its fans to run semi-naked through the cities of the world. 'We dress people, not bodies' proclaims Thomas Meyer, the Swiss designer who created the brand as a 20-year-old whilst enjoying a Spanish holiday in 1984. Now with a diverse team of 2900 made up 72 nationalities, Desigual seeks to be different.

The brand seeks to be about an attitude rather than fashion. 'We design in Barcelona very close to the sea so it's very Mediterranean, very chic and happy' says Meyer on the Desigual website. The brand's motto 'La Vida ed Chula' means 'Life is Cool' and seeks to project positivity, tolerance, innovation and fun. 'We communicate with kisses, music and cinema', putting an emphasis on being human and real, to resonate more deeply with cultural values and emotions.

The design team of 25 seek inspiration from real life concepts – handmade, me and you, magic, luxury feelings, being cool, all together – and in 2011 formed a partnership with Cirque du Soleil to inspire new collections whilst also extending the entertainment brand. Similar partnerships have extended the brand points of sale, always a place of vibrant colours and flamenco music. The approach to marketing is electic and eye-catching too. 'Come in undressed and go out dressed' ran one promotion, rewarding the first 200 people to arrive only in their underwear – in cities from Berlin to New York – with a new Desigual wardrobe.

Editd ... big data adds to the creativity of fashion

Trends are dynamic and diverse, individual and ambiguous. Data analytics makes sense of what next through behavioural and predictive analytics to design next season's, or next week's, fashions with less risk and more imagination.

Fashion trends are ever more eclectic and fast changing. As markets fragment, global trends spread contagiously, whilst local trends add twists and meaning and anticipating fashion becomes a complex science. It becomes a big data challenge, crunching together hard and soft data from social media, trackable behaviours and media coverage, to make sense of ever changing fashion.

Editd has emerged in this new world as a champion of predictive analytics, and in doing so helps companies from Asos to Gap to sense and track the latest moods. As well as tracking colours and styles, the analysis also covers the ever-shifting segmentation of consumers, price elasticity and sales channels, and competitive perceptions. Insights are enhanced with catwalk coverage and industry experts. The business model is built around per-user subscriptions, Asos for example providing access for its 200 fashion buyers.

Retail, particularly online, is all about matching audiences and products at the right price, at the right moment. Whilst anticipating and responding to trends has always mattered, digital consumers are much more influential amongst friends in shaping collective behaviour and advocacy. With speed and focus, relevance and advocacy, a trend can become contagious, as can the most on-trend items and brands. At the same time, Editd's data enables brands to forecast much more accurately, speeding up time to market, optimizing price points and optimizing stock.

Kering ... portfolio profits from the home of Gucci

Kering owns one of the world's leading luxury brand portfolios. After years of growing bigger, it eventually realized that smaller is often better – focusing on profit rather than sales, to develop a sharper, more coherent and more effective brand portfolio.

You may not know Kering, or even its previous name Pinault-Printemps-Redoute (PPK), but you will certainly know many of its luxury brands, ranging from Gucci and Balenciaga, to Stella McCartney and Alexander McQueen, and Puma. The Breton business was founded in 1962 by Francois Pinault, at the time focused on wood trading, which evolved over 30 years into furniture and paper-making. Retail acquisitions, such as La Redoute and Fnac, saw the group grow rapidly, but mainly in France. When his son took over the reins in 2001, he felt the group needed more balance geographically and focus in its brands. The acquisition of Gucci, followed by a succession of other luxury brands transformed the business. In 2007 Puma added a sporting-lifestyle component.

However Kering recognizes that a portfolio of acquisitions needs to do more than sit on the same balance sheet. Each brand needs help from the portfolio to grow in ways in which it couldn't alone. This might be in the form of investment and expertize, or in shared innovation, technology, logistics, finance and retailing. At the same time, luxury brands are like delicate masterpieces, with their own values and culture, which contribute to their artistic differences and premium reputations.

However the real skill in managing a portfolio of brands is also to know what not to do. Whilst focus can be achieved through financial analytics – putting resources into the brands which can generate best return – it is also about having a coherence of logic. One of Kering's most significant insights has been to focus much more on profit than scale, eliminating many of its peripheral businesses, or those that had scale but lower margins. In a decade the business has shrunk from €24.4 billion to €9.7 billion, whilst profits have grown by 40%. It is also a truly international business, in five years seeing the proportion of its revenues from France fall from 41% to 4%.

Rapha ... Cycle clubs with coffee and Paul Smith

Cycling is a sport of connoisseurs. They love their coffee, in France they love their pastis, and they love their bikes and gear. Riding in the heart of a Sunday morning pelaton is as much social as physical, and so Rapha decided to create premium cycling gear, and coffee shops – or Cycle Clubs – where enthusiasts can meet.

The brand name comes from the 1960s cycling team Rapha, famous for its love of drinking St Raphaël after a long ride, whilst the logo is inspired by that of Citroën's H Van. Founded by Simon Mottram, a Chartered Accountant who got creative at Interbrand, and Luke Scheybeler, a digital designer with Sapient who preferred to design fashion, Rapha makes luxury cycling clothing fusing high tech fabrics with sporting nostalgia.

Walk into a Rapha Cycle Club – in London or New York, Sydney or Osaka – and you can see, smell and touch a love of cycling.

The business has grown rapidly, building a direct relationship with consumers, through events and online community, as well as its coffee-shop stores. There are also line extensions into luggage, skincare, books and travel. Tour de France and Olympic champion Bradley Wiggins and his Team Sky wear Rapha, whilst there is a co-branded range with designer and cycling enthusiast Paul Smith.

Rapha is a brand that polarizes opinion. For some it has created the ultimate in high performance equipment, dedicated to a sport that breeds passion and perspiration. For others, it is over-priced and over-designed vanity wear for middle-aged men who have taken up weekend cycling in recent years. Whichever your view, it gets talked about. Especially items such as the $450 pair of yak-leather cycling shoes, or the $150 pro-glide coffee tamper to flatten your coffee like the best baristas after your run.

Patagonia ... clothing to community, caring for the outdoors

Clothing brand Patagonia puts care for the environment not just as a slogan, or mission, but as a priority. So much so that it even suggests 'Don't buy this jacket' to consumers, preferring them to hang on to their existing Patagonias for longer. Good for the consumer, the environment, and ultimately the brand too.

'Don't buy this jacket' shouted the poster campaign, slightly confusing some consumers, but then making them think harder about effect of consumerism on the environment. Whilst it might sound like a questionable advertising concept, it was really saying 'if you are going to buy less, then buy what you really need'. It was a masterstroke that captured the far sighted purpose of Patagonia.

The outdoor clothing brand was founded by climbing enthusiast Yvon Chouinard in 1973 and uses a marketing strategy which could be thought of as being part nudge, part shock tactics. The company initially made climbing equipment but changed its philosophy to include a wider range of environmentally-sound products after Chouinard realized his climbing tools were causing damage to rocky cliff faces.

Patagonia has since grown into a $600m company whilst staying true to its eco-friendly ethos by using organic cotton and recycled polyester in its products and by urging consumers to consider the environmental effect of their purchases. The company commits 1% of their total sales, or 10% of their profit, whichever is more, to environmental groups. Since 1985 it has donated $46 million in cash and in-kind donations to domestic and international environmental groups.

The brand encourages people to support its environmental efforts by signing up to 'The Common Threads Initiative', a scheme set up by Patagonia that asks people to buy only what they need, repair what breaks, and re-use or recycle everything else. Compared to the disposable nature of some fashion, this brand is about products designed to last forever, and with a lifetime warranty just to prove it.

Shang Xai ... Hermès rebrands luxury for the Chinese

China's new affluent consumers love luxury brands. Western brands like Hermès have recognized the market, but also the need for more local brands and locally-relevant fashions. It therefore created China's first premium brand, and is now bring Chinese luxury to the Western world too.

Walk through Shanghai's opulent Plaza 66 shopping mall, and you will find more luxury brands than in Beverly Hills, but few of them Chinese. Whilst Burberry, Louis Vuitton and the like have all seen exponential growth in recent years, and diverted most of their attention to Asia, there are few options to support local businesses. Shang Xai changes that, launched in 2010 with the financial backing and brand expertize of Hermès.

Shang Xai's store is a futuristic zen-like setting filled with unusually beautiful products. Minimalist clothing, home furnishings, shoes and tableware — Chinese inspired, hand crafted, but contemporary and muted. No red dragons and gold embroidery. The brand aims to revive Chinese crafts that were nearly destroyed by China's Cultural Revolution, including ancient styles of porcelain, cashmere felt and bamboo furniture.

Shang Xai, whose name means 'up down' in Mandarin, is growing rapidly, with branches in Hong Kong, Macau and Taiwan. Its growth is outpacing luxury brands from the West, including Hermès. In 2014, the brand came full circle, opening its first Shang Xai store in Paris, the standard bearer of a new generation of Asian brand entrepreneurs looking to capture the sophistication of Chinese history and culture in the luxury world.

20 FUTURETRAVEL

CHANGING THE GAME OF TRAVEL AND HOTELS

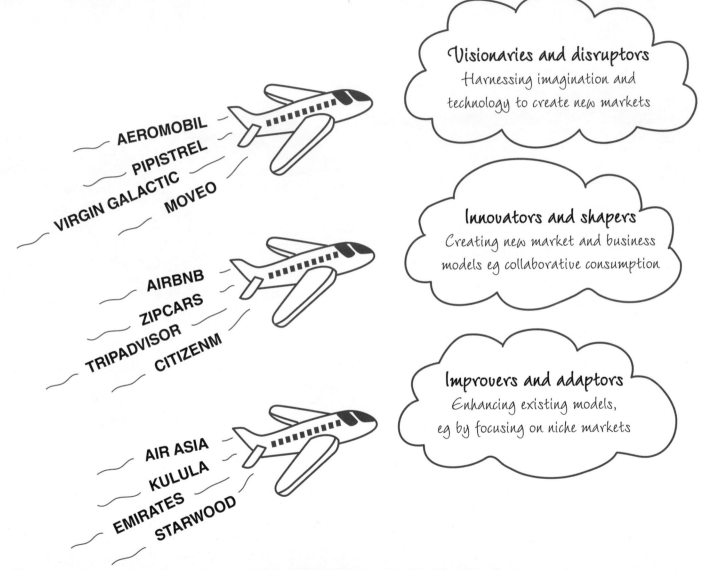

Visionaries and disruptors
Harnessing imagination and technology to create new markets

AEROMOBIL
PIPISTREL
VIRGIN GALACTIC
MOVEO

Innovators and shapers
Creating new market and business models eg collaborative consumption

AIRBNB
ZIPCARS
TRIPADVISOR
CITIZENM

Improvers and adaptors
Enhancing existing models, eg by focusing on niche markets

AIR ASIA
KULULA
EMIRATES
STARWOOD

Futuretravel, Rethinking the World of Travel and Hotels

In a more **connected** world, we want and need to travel more. Whilst the world has shrunk through communications, **intimacy** drives the lust for more distant adventure and the interconnectedness of business.

ASIAN TRAVEL BOOM

The most significant growth in air travel will be in Asia. The past dominance of North American, and transatlantic routes, has been replaced by the rapid growth of **intra-Asian**, African–Asian, and North–South American traffic flows. Beijing and Mumbai will replace Atlanta and Chicago as the world's busiest airports. Seoul to Jeju is already the world's busiest route, followed by Sao Paulo to Rio de Janiero, and Beijing to Shanghai.

Whilst most millennials will expect to travel the world, and live in at least **three different countries** during their lives, there is huge wanderlust too in the over 60s market. Vacations become more frequent, with shorter trips to more exotic destinations, whilst dispersed populations make more flights home to visit family and friends.

The growth in the business travel market will be even more significant, with its much higher margins. Companies in the West and North seek the growth markets and the East and South, exporting or entering the markets, competing or collaborating. Whilst tele-conferencing becomes an everyday norm, rising early for Eastern partners, staying late for Westerners, there is still no substitute for meeting people, understanding culture and building human relationships.

MAKING IT REAL AND EASY

As travel democratizes we spend more time on-board or in-room, driving airlines and hotels to adapt their **formats**, business models and service styles to the needs of the modern traveller.

For airlines, the on-ground experience will matter as much as the in-flight experience, particularly as airlines like **Emirates** build new global hub and spoke networks. Travellers want to be in control, with personal itineraries that can easily be flexed, and real-time alerts rather than relying on boarding announcements. Luggage companies like **Tumi**, for example, seek to make the fast-track security channels even faster with fast-pass bags.

On-board the experience will be more like home entertainment fused with a great coffee shop. Several hours immersed in your own world is a rare opportunity, and so calls for the best music or movies, or precious time to work or learn. In a world where attention is rare, it is also the ultimate brand showcase, to sample new gadgets, to browse a digital mall, to experience a brand more deeply.

For hotels, few people aspire to the staid opulence of Ritz Carlton, or the oppressive sameness of a Marriott anywhere in the world. More casual and comfortable, healthy dining and free wi-fi, modern art and a good movie, or even more sociable areas rather than unnecessary atriums. When it comes to service, relax and smile, and stop calling me sir. Relevant benefits are far more important than yet another plastic loyalty card to carry around, and throw away your brochure, I only trust Tripadvisor.

TRANSFORMING TRAVEL

More dramatic innovations will transform travel over time – from the customization of experiences around the traveller, to **business models** with new revenue streams from subscription to sponsorship – from the biological sequencing of body clocks and time zones, to the

hypersonic, intercontinental space hops promised by **Virgin Galactic**.

GAMECHANGERS

Here are some of the brands and businesses who are changing the game of travel and hospitality, each with ideas and innovations to apply to your own business.

**FUTURETRAVEL
Zipcars**

 # Zipcars ... why own a car when you can hire a cooler one?

Collaborative consumption drives the better use of assets, and often a better deal for customers. Better products at a fraction of the price. The subscription model builds community and loyalty.

Becoming a 'zipster' takes seconds – register your details online for a $50 membership fee, and then whenever you need a car, for a quick 15 minute trip across town, or a two week vacation, just search your mobile phone to find the nearest cars to you, by GPS. Walk along the street of most cities and you will see Z spaces, reserved for Zipcars to be dropped off or picked up. Zap the door with your Bluetooth phone, turn the key and it's yours for as long as you want, paying per minute.

Compare that to the cost of owning a car, particularly in cities where it might stand unused most days, depreciating in value with every day, and you suddenly have a good business case. It can even be cheaper than a taxi ride.

Zipcar was born in Berlin by Antje Danielson where 'mitfahr' car-sharing had long been common, and then launched in Boston in 2000 in partnership with Robin Chase. Soon the concept spread across many cities. Early adopters were students, who in the past had dreamt of owning a car but usually ended up with a one on its last legs, and were far more attracted by a cool Mini Cooper for the

weekend, at much less overall cost. As customers grew, the network was able to grow, becoming an even more attractive option.

Pivot points for Zipcars in 'changing the game' of car ownership and rental were:

EXPLORE   Observing a trend in one market, and taking it to a bigger potential market

DESIGN   Designing a better business model, attractive to customers, and business

RESONATE   Targeting a niche audience to make the case in relevant, emotional ways

MOBILIZE   Unlocking the 'network effect' of more customers and more cars

The car-sharing concept grew rapidly. Many imitators emerged; some like Flexcar were acquired by Zipcar. Car manufacturers also woke up to the challenge, and launched their own versions like Daimler's Car2Go. Car rental companies, too, realized that their future wasn't in weekly airport hires, extending their business model with concepts like Hertz on Demand. In 2013 Zipcar, with over 800,000 members sharing 10,000 cars, was acquired by Avis Budget for $500m. In the meantime Robin Chase moved on to her next venture, Buzzcar, which is a car sharing network where people with cars offer their spare seat to others.

Airbnb ... connecting the world of spare bedrooms

Airbnb is a great example of collaborative consumption, making more of under-utilized assets whilst also enjoying the social experience of sharing. All built around a sustaining community.

Airbnb started out as the result of lack of accommodation for a major design conference in SanFrancisco. Brian Chesky and Joe Gebbia launched AirBed and Breakfast to help people who couldn't find a hotel room – first in their own spare room with a couple of airbeds, and a tasty breakfast, and then with friends too. They spotted the potential, but needed to raise some money to develop a website. Obama was fighting McCain in the US election of 2008, so the pair quickly designed and launched two new breakfast cereals, 'Obama O's' and 'Capn McCains' raising $30,000 to get started. The site quickly became a social movement helping people rent out their spare bedrooms for a little extra cash, and others to find a great place to stay.

Tired of standard hotel rooms? Airbnb helps you discover real places, and get closer to culture and normality. What began with two guys and a few airbeds now offers nights in everything from crusader forts to private islands. It is now a global marketplace with over 500,000 locations in 33,000 cities, and over 10 million booked nights. It has also become a serious rival to the leading hotel chains and travel companies.

Christopher Lukezic, CMO, speaking at The Marketing Society annual conference in 2013, says 'Airbnb has pioneered social travel and set the stage for the emergence of the sharing economy.

The main reason for our success is that we've taken a very long-term vision and approach to building a brand – to build a company and community. If building a brand takes a few years, building a community takes decades. Early on we knew that the ultimate success of our business would come from building a community, not merely a brand. That would take a decade, without being distracted by short-term gains.'

Pivot points for Airbnb in 'changing the game' of travel accommodation were:

DISCOVER   Identifying a niche market with a trend away from standardized hotels

DESIGN   Designing an attractive business model and online booking experience

RESONATE   Articulating the proposition through PR and contagious social media

MOBILIZE   Building a community of travellers and people with spare rooms

Airbnb think and act differently. 'The business always puts our users forward, often doing things that don't scale and don't have immediate returns' says Lukezic. 'It wasn't about putting up billboards to get lots of users very quickly, because we had to build trust with each member one-by-one. Not long ago, people wouldn't have dreamed of staying at somebody else's house, now they see it as positive experience.'

Virgin Galactic ... astronauts all, but the goal is long-haul

The space race is on, to provide regular affordable flights for business, research and tourism. Virgin's innovative launch and spacecraft design promises to achieve even more.

Richard Branson was looking for a new challenge. Having conquered music and flight, retail and banking, he pondered where next. 'To the moon?' suggested a helpful waitress. Like most new ventures, Virgin had little idea how to enter the market, but finding the right partners has always been a strength. And in particular, partners who can help do things differently, better for customers and ultimately for business too.

'Space travel is absolutely, unbelievably exciting' Branson told me when I interviewed him at the London Business Forum. 'For a British company to be preparing to be the first to take fare-paying customers into space is phenomenal. We registered the name Virgin Galactic in 1991 and then spent a decade looking for potential engineers to build a reusable spaceship.'

'We explored mad, zany ideas, and then found Burt Rutan who's the absolute genius in this area. He'd come up with the idea of turning the spaceship into a massive shuttle cock, to slow the vehicle on its dangerous re-entry phase. The whole project is almost carbon neutral. Each space flight will generate fewer emissions than a flight to New York, whereas NASA use the power of New York City to spend up the Space Shuttle' he said.

The spaceship takes off on the back of a larger 'carrier' rising to around 50,000 feet, the cruising altitude of Concorde, where it is then launched horizontally into space requiring much less power (Branson's vision is to use biofuels from his Caribbean algae farms). Accelerating from 170 knots in gliding mode to four times the speed of sound in six seconds, you are suddenly weightless. The cabin is designed with huge windows to look down on our planet, and space to jump around, and enjoy the thrill of weightlessness. Branson says he wants to turn an experience of only 540 people in the last 50 years into one shared by millions, and already has a long waitlist.

Pivot points for Virgin Galactic in 'changing the game' of space travel were:

THINK Imagining new markets and shaping them in your own vision

DESIGN Designing launch and flight solutions that enabled new experiences

INSPIRE Building a brand that reinvigorates Virgin, and inspires a waiting list

IMPACT Finding more efficient and less damaging ways to make it work

Watching the test flights from Spaceport America, deep in the New Mexico desert, it's easy to dream of flights to Mars, or even jumping on-board for a one-hour tourist flight to circle Earth. But the real ambition of Virgin is more terrestrial. The ability to launch and land efficiently makes frequent flights and fast turnarounds possible. Between continents, rather than just into space and back. Imagine flying from LA to Sydney, or Shanghai to London, in one hour ... that is the real gamechanging vision of Virgin Galactic.

Aeromobil ... the incredible flying cars from Bratislava

The flying car has long captured the imagination of the futurist. For Stefan Klein it was his life's passion. When he retired from designing cars, the inventor set his mind to adding wings.

In 1940 Henry Ford predicted that one day somebody would combine the car and aeroplane to create a flying car. In 1982, Hollywood captured that vision in Bladerunner. Now in the Slovakia, cars really can fly.

Stefan Klein is a quiet unassuming guy, with degrees in both mechanical engineering and fine arts. He wanted to be a sculptor but studied design, going on to work for Audi, BMW and Volkswagen. But flying has always been in his family ... 'My father and grandfather were both pilots, and soon I learnt to fly too. This has always been my passion.' Since 1990 he has pursued his dream of building a flying car, 'To me it is something at the intersection of technology and art' he said.

'Aeromobil' is a car and a plane ... the wings fold straight back along the fuselage and the engine drives the front wheels. 'There is room for two people, both with a steering wheel and flight-yoke, for the navigation you can use built-in Garmin autopilot or iPad,' he told me. Small enough to fit in the urban parking space, when Klein hits the road it is more sci-fi. Then as he drives onto the airport runway, it's all James Bond ... a **propeller emerges** at the front, and the 8.2m **wings spread out** to the sides. Down the runway he accelerates and into the air. Yes really.

'Whilst I have various prototypes being tested, the plan is to have a plane that can fly 700 km at 200 kph and more. We have just returned from North America where we are exploring potential agreements with several institutions and companies to become our partners in making Aeromobil happen full scale.' His co-founder Juray Vaculik, an ad agency man by background, says 'We don't need purposeless investment, it's about finding the right partners to make this happen commercially'. He imagines an initial selling price of around $200,000, similar to supercars.

Air Asia ... low cost, premium service, virtual airline

Air Asia's focus on high volume, fast growing routes and its virtual business model have combined to create a profitable airline, where a premium customer experience is possible at low prices.

In 2001, when CEO Tony Fernandes bought AirAsia for a token 1 Malaysian rinngit (plus $12.5 million debt), it was a failed, state-owned regional airline with only two aircraft. In just a decade, the Kuala Lumpur-based low-cost airline has grown to serve 75 destinations with a fleet of over 100 aircraft. It also has a long-haul brand, AirAsiaX, a joint venture with Virgin, and local subsidiaries in Indonesia, Philippines and other countries.

Inspired by what CK Pralahad termed the 'bottom of the pyramid', a billion people emerging out of poverty representing a $5 trillion opportunity, AirAsia's growth has been underpinned by the emerging regional economies, a new middle class and large families dispersed across the region.

Whilst AirAsia's goal is to be 'the lowest cost airline in every market they serve', it is a premium experience – with the best cabin crew attracted from nearby Singapore Airlines, and the leather seats equipped with 35 satellite TV channels. Most significant has been its virtual business model, leasing everything from aircraft to offices, and focused route strategy, rather than a few profitable routes subsidizing a global network like many competitors.

Innovations include a Red Carpet service which offers business-style check in and lounges for just $35, a wide range of auxillary services driving around 20% of revenues, and even an on-board immigration process to save time at the destination.

Emirates ... world's best airline with the desert hub

Dubai has become the new world's travel hub, connecting west and east, north and south, with limitless space for growth. Emirates has innovated with technology and service to lead the world's airlines.

In 1985, Dubai was still a small desert town and a new airline, Emirates, flew its first routes with just two aircraft. Emirates has evolved into a global network, and one of the most respected and profitable airlines in the world. Whilst still state-owned it has grown through innovation and become a global leader, carrying 40 million passengers and 2 million tonnes of cargo, making Dubai one of the world's leading hubs, and delivering an award-winning inflight service preferred by many travellers. In fact the airline has remained profitable for 25 years, incredibly rare in the industry.

Emirates now flies to over 125 cities in 80 countries. In 1985 Dubai's royal family provided $10 million start-up capital, and has since operated the airline separately from the government. Led by Ahmed bin Saeed Al Maktoum, Emirates has become one of the world's fastest growing airlines with revenues increasing by around $100 million each year. With a huge, young fleet, the largest operator of Boeing 777 in the world, and innovative entertainment, it is now firmly established as the world's best airline by Skytrax, well ahead of old favourites like Singapore Airlines and Cathay Pacific.

Kulula ... the South African airline that has more fun

The low-cost airline uses humour to stand out from the crowd, creating outrageous ads that spread without cost, and everyday funny to make the travel experience more human and fun.

When South Africa's President Jacob Zuma married for the sixth time, the quick-thinking Kulula Airlines offered free flights to the fourth wife in big families, the country's new number of official first ladies. People loved the joke, and jibe. It was typical of Kulula, a small low-cost airline owned by Comair.

On one flight to Port Elizabeth from Cape Town, just before landing, an announcement said 'Welcome to Zimbabwe' which was met by silence followed by laughter. On another flight, the pilot

after a rather hard landing asked if any passengers would like to have a go landing the plane instead.

CMO of 'the world's funniest airline', Heidi Brauer, says each plane is painted in its own livery, based on a brainstorm of crazy ideas and humour. Not surprisingly PR and advocacy lie at the heart of the brand's marketing efforts.

When South Africa hosted the FIFA World Cup in 2010, Kulula, in an audacious form of gorilla marketing, declared itself as the 'Unofficial National Carrier of the You-Know-What' which took place 'Not next year, or last year, but somewhere in between'. When FIFA took action it offered free seats to anybody called Sepp Blatter, the FIFA president. Only a renamed dog came forward, and became an internet star.

Pipistrel ... Slovenia's electric planes ready to soar

The carbon emissions of today's aircraft are far more than cars, yet few airlines have explored electric engines, ideally powered by the sun. In southern Europe, Pipistrel is creating the future of flight.

Slovenia leads the world in making ultra-light electric aircraft. Secretly founded in 1987 by Ivo Boscarol, at a time when the communist Yugoslav government banned such aircraft, he tested his first aircraft under the cover of darkness. The quietness of the engines, and hang-glider style wings, made them resemble huge bats flying in the sky above Ajdovščina, a small town in the Vipava Valley, and ultimately inspired the name Pipistrel.

The company leads the market in light sport aircraft and motor gliders. Pipistrel's Panthera is a sleek four-seat

electric-powered aircraft developed in collaboration with Penn State University. In 2011 it won the NASA/Google 'Green Flight Challenge' to find the world's most efficient aircaft. 'I think we're sort of in the dawn of electric flight, maybe compared to the times after the First World War' said the plane's young designer Tine Tomazic in an interview with *Wired* magazine.

Airlines are working hard to reduce their huge carbon emissions, so a switch to electric is much anticipated, particularly for the short-hop commuter routes around the world which are fast growing. Once electric motors are perfected for flight, the next step is to cover the wings in solar power-generating panels. The bat that likes sunlight.

Red Bus ... Making sense of India's chaotic bus routes

India's cities are clogged full of thousands of buses. Finding a way to coordinate the many operators, and provide a single online booking platform across the country, was a profitable vision.

In India buses matter. Red Bus is the nation's leading bus ticketing platform, connecting 1500 bus operators and 80,000 routes which previously lacked any form of coordinated schedules, or integrated booking system. It was founded in 2005 by a small group of friends who had studied together at India's leading engineering school, BITS Pilani.

As the festival of Diwali approached, Phani Sama was trying to find a ticket home from his new job with Texas Instruments in Bangalore to his family in Hyderabad. He ran around the city visiting many different bus stations and travel agents trying to find a ticket with one of the many operators. He failed. So he stayed in his flat with his friends, thinking how crazy it was to search for hours for any unsold tickets. Whilst nobody in India currently sold tickets online, mobile penetration was mushrooming and it seemed so obvious.

Creating a website was relatively easy, building relationships with all the different bus companies and encouraging them to integrate their schedules and accept self-printed tickets was much harder. It required a fundamental change in behaviour. They needed consumers to trust them too. Using word of mouth and social networks, the simple new approach took off. So much so that many imitators quickly followed. However Sama and his team had the strongest relationships with operators and came to define the market. Eight years later, with a 65% market share they found themselves $138m wealthier, acquired by IbiboGroup, a venture between South Africa's Naspers and China's Tencent.

Starwood ... hip brands, urban spaces and heavenly beds

Starwood has reinvented its hotel portfolio – from Aloft to W Hotels – recognizing the changing needs of different travellers and creating distinctive destinations worth talking about.

Starwood Hotels was only founded in 1999, by Barry Sternlicht, a youthful property entrepreneur who ran a Connecticut-based firm called Starwood Capital. It brought together his recent acquisitions, fading prestigious brands like Sheraton and Westin.

With properties in over 100 counties, Starwood became a leading network, combining great brands with financial flexibility and global scale. It focused 80% of future growth on emerging markets, mostly in the Asia Pacific, and is now the second largest hotel group by market value, despite being only eighth largest by total bedrooms, reflecting investor confidence in the portfolio.

However Starwood stands apart from other hotel groups because of its innovation. In traditional brands like Westin, the concept of the 'Heavenly Bed' ingredient brand has transformed perceptions of luxury and what matters most. Recent concepts like W Hotel went further, creating a hip experiences for travellers and locals. At the same time, brands need to deliver better customer experiences – encouraging staff to show their own personalities rather than being corporate stereotypes, to smile and have fun.

Most disruptive has been Starwood's Aloft concept. Research showed that both business and leisure travellers sought a fresh, relaxed hotel experience at reasonable prices. People hated the frills and conservatism of premium hotels. Aloft was designed as a highly sociable, millennial-minded destination. The loft-like rooms and 'urban' spaces for eating and meeting are fun and inspiring. Interesting modern art, clean-lined furnishings and chilled out music are brought together with a vibrant bar.

21 FUTUREFOOD

CHANGING THE GAME OF FOOD AND DRINK

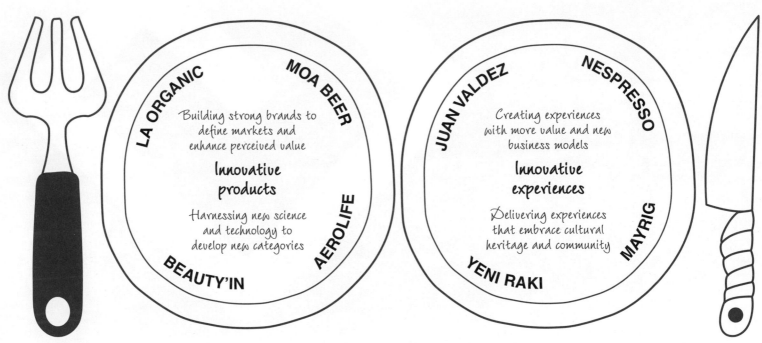

LA ORGANIC **MOA BEER**

Building strong brands to
define markets and
enhance perceived value

Innovative
products

Harnessing new science
and technology to
develop new categories

BEAUTY'IN **AEROLIFE**

JUAN VALDEZ **NESPRESSO**

Creating experiences
with more value and new
business models

Innovative
experiences

Delivering experiences
that embrace cultural
heritage and community

YENI RAKI **MAYRIG**

Futurefood, Rethinking the World of Food and Drink

The future of food is about **authenticity** and **relevance** – traceability of supply chains, natural and organic ingredients, convenient and well designed packaging, and fantastic, inspiring taste.

CATERPILLARS, SEAWEED AND iPODS

Splash out on dinner at Heston Blumenthal's Fat Duck restaurant, and you might find an iPod accompanies your seafood risotto. Sounds of the sea enhance the perceived freshness and flavours, and can also affect our sense of sweetness and saltiness.

Caterpillars, already popular in Africa, contain 28 mg of protein per 100 g, more than minced beef, and add 35 mg of iron too. If you're in search of a calcium boost, try grasshoppers.

Rising food prices, the growing population and environmental concerns make food one of the big debates for governments and interest areas for investors. Meat production takes up huge amounts of land, consumes water, diverts crops from humans and adds to carbon emissions.

Insects, perhaps rebranded as **micro protein**, could become a staple of our diets – low cost, requiring little space or water. With 1500 edible species, we could soon be tucking into nutrititous crickets and grasshoppers, ground into burgers. Wasps are a delicacy in Japan.

If you still want meat, your next steak could be sourced from a test-tube. Strips of muscle tissue using stem cells taken from cows, a little like calamari to look at, are grown in a lab, and then shaped to expectation, similar to existing meat substitutes such as Quorn.

Of course you could just become vegetarian, and still get a balanced diet.

Another source of improved eating is **sensory-engineering**. Scientists have shown that look and smell affect what we taste. Condiment Junkie, a sonic-branding company, is exploring how certain frequencies can compensate for sugar in foods, thereby improving health as well as enhancing the whole cooking and eating experience.

However the most significant source of future food is likely to come from **algae**: 145 species of green, red and brown seaweed are already eaten in huge quantities across Asia, often as a delicacy. Ground into other foods, its strong flavour can dramatically reduce the amount of salt used, for example in bread or prepared meals. Algae farming, for food as well as energy, could become the world's largest crop industry by 2030.

251

GAMECHANGERS

'Gamechangers' in the world of food range from those who are delivering science fiction, like Aerolife's breathable pizza, to more profitable business models like Nespresso, to others who are turning commodities into brands like Zespri and richer experiences like Juan Valdez.

Juan Valdez Café ... Colombian coffee grower cafés

Most coffee growers make a few cents on every bag sold to consumers, even less for every cup drunk. Colombia's farmers decided to create their own branded experience.

Imagine if the barista making your macchiato started explaining that he and his colleague pick and select every grain of coffee themselves, from tree to cup, in the pursuit of the best taste you will find. Wearing his ethnic poncho he waves to his donkey tied up outside, and the pan pipes float over the chatter. Juan Valdez coffee, and its extension into cafés, is a sensorial and cultural experience straight from the Andes mountains.

In 1959, the National Federation of Coffee Growers of Colombia wanted to capture the spirit of more than 500,000 coffee growers and small local producers who made '100% Colombian coffee'. The federation set out to create a mascot, a character based on many of its members – they called him Juan Valdez, always with his mule called Conchita, and carrying a sack of coffee beans. The character became the stamp of authentic Colombian coffee around the world He is played by a real person, selected from more than 360,000 coffee growers, most recently Carlos Castañeda from the small town of Antioquia in the Andes.

However the grower's federation became concerned that Colombian coffee was increasingly regarded as a commodity, marketed by many brands, and they needed to give Juan a stronger identity. In 2002, they launched Procafecol SA, a company to build the Juan Valdez brand. They started by branding their own coffee through an online star, which was quickly also stocked by supermarkets locally and across the Americas. Small brand extensions included coffee makers, cups and flasks, coffee-flavoured foods, and replicas of Conchita the mule. Sign up to Juan's coffee-lovers club, and you can receive discounts and exclusive products. With the increasing penetration of cafés like Starbucks, Procafecol recognized the opportunity to do more. By 2007, there were 100 Juan Valdez Cafés in Colombia, and Starbucks retreated.

Pivot points for Juan Valdez Café in 'changing the game' of coffee growing were:

INSPIRE   Creating a brand from a commodity, with personality and humour

DESIGN   Developing a rich portfolio of branded coffees and accessories

ENABLE   Delivering a branded experience with a hundred times the margins

MOBILIZE   Connecting the nation's growers to represent and promote the brand

Growth outside Latin America has been slower, as the company focuses on establishing a local stronghold. At the same time, the Colombian economy is growing more strongly than most of the world, so it is proving an effective strategy. Juan Valdez has remained a local and authentic brand, in Bogata it is everywhere, making the most of its authenticity and local roots, riding on the growth wave of the Colombian economy.

Zespri … Putting the zest into the world's kiwifruit

Kiwifruit are a great example of market creation. Zespri, owned by New Zealand growers, shows how to build premium brands that increase the market size, whilst also capturing disproportionate value.

'Yang tao' or 'Chinese gooseberries' as they were initially known, were taken from China to New Zealand in the early 20th century, by a Wanganui school mistress called Mary Isabel Fraser. In the 1950s they evolved into the green, furry 'Kiwifruit' which we know today and became New Zealand's largest export. Today, Kiwis are still the second largest grower of their fruit (after Italy), and it is Lain Jager, CEO of Zespri, who continues to shape the market.

'Fresh produce is a marketplace cluttered with commodities, where earning a price premium and sustaining customer loyalty is a significant challenge' says Jager. Recognizing that overcoming this commodity trap is critical to building a profitable livelihood for growers, Zespri has focused on establishing meaningful brand reputation through sophisticated marketing.

This commitment to sophisticated marketing is backed by a consistency of supply of a high-quality, high-taste product, a market-based payment method where growers are paid according to meeting demand and driving innovation. Most successful amongst the different branded varieties is Zespri Gold.

'Zespri became the world's leading brand by capturing two third's of the global market in value terms, from one their of the volume' explains Jager. 'Despite kiwifruit only accounting for less than half a percent of the global fruit bowl, in markets where Zespri has invested, kiwifruit has become one of the top ten fruits consumed, with a large base of regular and loyal consumers.'

The brand is owned by New Zealand kiwifruit growers, who fiercely protect their ability to capture value from the supply chain.

'Unlike most fruit producers the shared brand commands a price premium, supported by sophisticated marketing programmes to trade and consumers.'

New product development in the fruit business takes time. Through critical selection of kiwifruit plant varieties and natural plant breeding methods, Zespri has the largest global selection of new kiwifruit varieties. It launched the immensely popular 'Zespri Gold' to the market in 2000; and is working now on the next generation of sweeter, flavourful varieties for Asia and Europe. New variety breeding and selection can take up to 15 years through to commercialization. Kiwifruit is also celebrated for its health benefits 'twice the vitamin C of an orange, low glycemic index for diabetics, accelerates digestion of proteins, and a natural source of folate'.

Zespri is also an advanced user of social media. These include a game application developed in China and launched globally where you grow your own Zespri kiwifruit, the 14 day Zespri challenge to feel healthier, and online competitions particularly seeking to promote the health benefits to older people.

Pivot points for Zespri in 'changing the game' of kiwifruit were:

DISRUPT   Creating a new market space, built around a new type of fruit

INSPIRE   Building a premium brand, Zespri Gold, that defines the market

DESIGN   Product innovation that constantly evolves varieties, flavours and process

AMPLIFY   Promoting the fruit (not just the brand) globally for its nutrition and taste

Mayrig ... Cooking up a passion for Armenian culture

Whilst most of Armenia is long gone, the culture lives on through traditional recipes and delicious food that brings people together to explore the stories that sustained a nation and now still inspire a global tribe.

'There is no love more sincere than the love of food' said George Bernard Shaw, and that love echoes in Mayrig's Armenian cuisine. It is the love of a full table, the Mediterranean sun that transforms vegetables into beauty and fragrance, and most importantly, of people.

Aline Kamakian, cook and co-owner of Mayrig restaurant, is passionate about Armenian culture. She created her first restaurant in the Beirut suburbs, using the finely-tuned recipes of her mother and grandmother. At the same time she learnt much about her heritage – when Armenia was a much greater nation, the impact of genocide, and how Armenian people still thrive on their history and traditions, despite now being spread across the world. Mayrig is about the culture, not just the food.

Kamakian and her cousin now have a thriving business, franchising into new markets, and a second brand, Batchig. There is also a new 'boutique' foods-to-go business, selling everything from sandwiches to ready-to-cook traditional dishes. Behind these brands is an industrial kitchen, with over 100 employees following her family recipes then distributing them to the different restaurants and stores.

'Mayrig was born on a Sunday lunchtime, when our extended family sat around the table for hours enjoying the our food' says Kamakian. 'That was the moment when our brand was born. For this we went back to the recipes of our grandmother. Besides our language and heritage it is this practice of gathering at mealtimes that gives us a sense of belonging, of identity. In Mayrig we do not only want to share delicious, healthy food, we also want to tell the world who we are and where we come from.'

'The Mayrig experience is about storytelling, about people together creating memorable moments. Our passion is for the distant land of Armenia that we lost and recreate in every meal. Our cooks are Armenian mothers, those who do not have a place on the job market and still have so much to give. They are the core of our story, of who we are.'

Her book *Armenian Cuisine* creates a platform to share recipes and heritage, whilst social media actively builds community. Franchising authentically has required a more thoughtful approach, recently opening next to the Burj Khalifa in Dubai. 'We started to work differently with investors who are more than just investing money. From different backgrounds (construction, banking, finance) they share with us their expertise. Next stops are Paris and New York, as well as un-thought-of locations such as Irbil.'

Pivot points for Mayrig in 'changing the game' of the restaurant experience were:

THINK   Inspired by a vision beyond food that brings a culture back to life

DESIGN   Recipes to dishes, interiors and ambience that reflect Armenian life

RESONATE   Stories from her grandmother add humanity and relevance to each dish

MOBILIZE   Tapping into a global tribe of Armenians, and those who enjoy their world

Yeni Raki ... Turkish heritage, much more than a drink

The national drink of Turkey is much more about the culture, the way you drink it and what you do, rather than the alcohol. Since the Ottomans, raki has defined Turkish life. Yeni Raki is the leading brand, and is recognized across the world as a premium brand. Of culture.

Raki is an unsweetened, aniseed flavoured alcoholic drink, popular in Turkey and across Greece and the Balkans. It emerged during the Ottoman Empire, served with meze in the many 'meyhanes' or taverns, particularly of Istanbul. The Muslim Sultans sought to restrict the practice, but the drink had become instilled in culture. A good night out in Istanbul, to this day is raki drunk whilst enjoying 'fasel' song and dance accompanied by a motley band of violin, lyre and clarinet playing classic Turkish music, often with a slightly funky arabesque drum beat.

In modern-day Turkey, grape-based raki has its origins in the state owned distillery of Tekel, based in Izmir. It distilled alcohol from the molasses of sugar beat. Unlike other aniseed-flavoured spirits, this created a unique flavour which became known as 'new' raki, or Yeni Raki. It is strong stuff, 90 proof (meaning 45% alcohol by volume), and is consumed chilled with a little water. The water turns the drink cloudy, resulting in its nickname 'Lion's Milk' (Aslan, or lion in Turkish, means a strong courageous man). In 2004 Tekel was privatized, handing the brand to Mey Alkol, now part of Diageo.

Today it remains the national drink of Turkey, not least becase it was the favourite drink of Kemal Ataturk, the secularist founder of the Turkish Republic. Yeni Raki is increasingly found in bars across the world as a premium brand. However, given its strength, it is wise to remember that the brand is about the culture as much as the alcohol. Drink it slowly with friends, enjoying good food and music, and your mind will soon be floating along the Bosphorus.

Aerolife ... inhalable pizza and martinis, but no calories

A quick squirt puff on Aerolife's Energy will keep you going through the toughest days. A quick puff could equally give you a great tasting pizza, or a chill out martini at the end of the day. Just breathe it in. All of the taste and nutrients, but none of the calories.

David Edwards is a Harvard professor who likes to play in the real world. So much so, that he is revolutionizing not only what we eat, but how we eat too. In the world of Aerolife, all you need to do is breathe. His growing range of powdered foods each comes in a small plastic tube, ready to hold to your mouth and inhale. They include all the taste and nutrients you seek, but none of the calories.

Aerolife's most successful line is Energy, pure inhalable caffeine. Just keep a tiny tube of 100 mg caffeine plus a healthy boost of vitamin B, and its ready whenever tiredness kicks in. In fact, each

tube contains enough for six hits to get you through the busiest days. Chocolate is also popular, whilst everything from breathable pizza and alcoholic drinks are under development.

Aerolife was launched in 2011 at Le Laboratoire in Paris, one of a network of creative labs set up by Edwards. They believe in the 'mash-up' of art and design with science and technology. The goal is to generate ideas that are educational first (students and others working in the lab learn from them), cultural second (inspiring the public's imagination as word spreads) and commercial third (consumers are able to buy real products). Edwards focuses his teams on aspirational designs, or rather new whitespaces that don't yet exist. At a recent Wired event he said 'Disruptive change does not usually emerge from analysis of what is not working, but by moving to unoccupied spaces and asking what if?'

Beauty'In ... eat and drink yourself beautiful in Brazil

'Almetics' is a self-styled fusion of two categories, food and cosmetics, to create a bold and bright range of new products that are supported by the founder's personality whilst carefully choosing international markets.

Christiana Arcangeli is the dentist specializing in homeopathy, who became a fashion and beauty entrepreneur, radio show host and was voted the most influential woman in Brazil. In 2010 she launched a new category of products calling them 'almetics', a range of food and drinks with cosmetic properties. She describes them as healthy drinks and nutritious snacks that supplement the body's essential nutrients, with no added sugar, preservatives or trans fats. 'Enjoy them anytime, anywhere' she says sitting back

in her Sao Paulo office talking to brand anthropologist Anouk Pappers, 'They are good for you inside and out!'

'Even though I trained as a dentist, beauty was always my passion' she says. 'The different companies and businesses I established all focused on beauty and cosmetics.' Beauty'In is a unique innovation, combining the pleasure of food, the healthy aspects of vitamins and new cosmetic technologies. According to the marketing, nutrients in the candy provide for 'renewal, hydration, cellular protection, an increase in energy' and, less expectedly, 'willingness'. 'So far, we've launched seven product lines including drinks, candy bars, tea and chocolate, which all contain unique ingredients that have cosmetic and health benefits'.

Graze ... healthy snack boxes by subscription

Healthy snacks are not always easy to find. Sign up to Graze, and it will deliver a regular snack box to your door, with the contents individually selected to what you like most, through artificial intelligence.

Graze offers subscription-based healthy snacks delivered to your door, ideal for frenetic lifestyles that seek wellbeing that is convenient, whilst watching the latest movie on demand. Co-founder Ben Jones says that when he and a bunch of friends started exploring the idea, everybody said it was not wanted and not possible. Snacks are treats, impulsive and unhealthy, came the response.

Based in West London, Graze delivers small boxes of healthy snacks – costing around £4, with over 90 optional ingredients, ranging from sesame crackers to pumpkin seeds, chilli dips, dark chocolate, cranberries and dried fruit – anywhere, by first-class post. All options are either low calorie, a good source of protein or provide essential vitamins and minerals.

In 2013 Graze launched in the USA, securing 25,000 'grazers' in the first two weeks and $65 million sales in the first year. The real magic behind the proposition is Darwin, an artificial-intelligence algorithm developed in house, that chooses snacks that it thinks each customer will like based on each individual's stated preferences and feedback, allergies, diet concerns and previous selections. According to Jones, it's possible to get 4.9 million different combinations of snacks in a Graze box.

LA Organic ... Starck transforms Spanish olive oil

The most beautiful olive oils from Andalucia just wouldn't sell. Until a touch of design magic by Philippe Starck turned La Amarilla into LA, ensured everything was organic, and created funky cans to sell it in.

Two hundred years ago, an order of Spanish nuns started producing olive oil from the La Amarilla country estate near Ronda. The oils from the gnarled and twisted trees, some a thousand years old, located in one of the most beautiful parts of Andalucia, had always been famous locally for their exceptional quality. In recent times, the Gómez de Baeza family acquired the estate and sought to revive the olive oil-making tradition commercially. As sales grew beyond La Amarilla's capacity, the family turned to 'pagos asociados' a form of licensing where other growers collaborate under strict controls. Fifty-six different pagos asociados came together to create an exceptional range of extra virgin organic olive oils.

The problem was Spain just did not have the same reputation for premium olive oil as Italy, for example, yet often produced superior products. The family knew they had to change perceptions, and branding would be key. Looking for a touch of magic, they called on Philippe Starck, the 'enfant terrible' of the design world, who has added his own style to everything from hotels to orange squeezers.

The emerging design focused on rebranding and distinctive packaging. The estate's name was recast as 'LA', he insisted that all oils had to be organic, and then focused on distinctive packaging design, a chunky shaped tin with the LA Organic logo bold against a bright olive background. 'A creation of Philippe Starck and Michel Rolland' is added at the base. Starck, interviewed by *The Times*, says his motivation was to 'give back the justice for Spanish olive oil', whilst on shortening the name he says it was simple: 'In French we say "Oh là là" and that's how good the oil is.'

Moa Beer ... super premium beer, super sexy investment

New Zealanders like to do things a little different. Moa is the premium beer for breakfast, made by the finest winemakers, named after a prehistoric bird, and even adds a touch of sex to their financial reports.

Rise and shine to a Moa Breakfast beer. New Zealand brewer Moa, likes to do things differently, so why not a cherry-flavoured wheat lager to get your day off to a better start? The brand's founder, Josh Scott, grew up in Marlborough, world-famous for its great wines, and spent his youth learning from his father, Allan, one of New Zealand's most famous winemakers. 'It takes a lot of beer to make a good wine' says Josh in his blog, referring to his personal needs and preferences. Having qualified as a master grower, Josh went travelling, but returned a year later to set up his own brewery amidst the vineyards.

Moa Beer combines traditional beer and winemaking techniques – local hops and labour intensive, barrel aged and bottle fermented like champagne. A chance meeting with ex Heineken brewer David Nicholls led to improved branding and portfolio innovation – blanc and noir beer, apple and pear cider. The 'Moa' is New Zealand's giant dinosaur bird, and the brand has spread rapidly across the world, found in the best bars from Seattle to Singapore. When some Moa bones were found locally, Josh was straight there with refreshments. Indeed the partners like to do things differently. Their 2012 IPO prospectus featured a rather glamorous female, black mini dress and fishnet stockings, recommending beers for every hour of the day.

Nespresso ... the business model with a daily kick

You might credit George Clooney with much of Nespresso's brand appeal. But the money is in the pods. Whilst the coffee machines are sold at minimal prices, it is the addiction – or subscription – to the refills that drives profits.

'Nespresso. What else?' ask George Clooney, as if you were to question his taste in coffee. In 1976, Eric Favre of Switzerland's largest business, Nestle, invented the Nespresso system. Ten years later, Nestle remembered that it was the coffee that people really wanted, not just a great machine. It licensed out manufacturing of the hardware and created 'Le Club'. Whilst the machines are now made by others, from Alessi to Krups, the coffee is made by Nestle, with drinkers subscribing to pod refills sent directly to their homes. Over the decades, coffee culture came to dominate our towns, and people demanded better at home. Nestle, as Nespresso, was waiting.

Nespresso's success lies in two factors – its business model, and its market strategy. The low cost machines and premium coffee is an echo of the 'shaver and blades' model used so successfully by Gillette, whilst the direct to consumer channel allows the brand to build a deep understanding and relationship with its drinkers. Nestle targeted two primary markets for growth – the USA and China. However it realized it would need different strategies from what had worked in Europe. In the USA, Nespresso sought to differentiate itself by targeting women, with a more sophisticated approach, endorsed by Penelope Cruz. In China, growth is slower, taking time for people to consider the alternative to tea. Slow, with huge potential. But Nestle is playing a long-term game. 'Relax, it will happen' as Clooney might say.

22 FUTURETECH

CHANGING THE GAME OF TECHNOLOGY AND NETWORKS

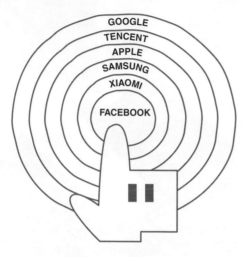

Consumer brands and networks

Engaging people in new applications of technology, trusted as navigators, best devices to best content

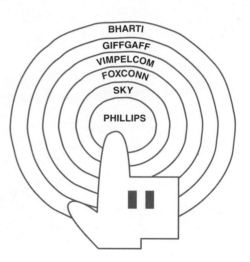

Enabling networks and assemblers

Functional brands that provide the solutions and platforms with new tech, but less engaging, increasingly squeezed

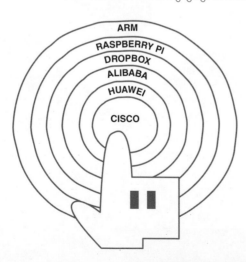

Infrastructure and components

Provide the global connectivity, resources and basic technologies that enable everything else.

Futuretech, Rethinking the World of Technology

The future of **technology** lies in the ability to create relevant and useful applications for people. It is about fusing technical capabilities and relevant partners to create infrastructures and platforms that enable brands and people to **do more**.

A recent survey of 16–30 year olds by *The Drum* showed that 85% believe that technology brands will have the most influence on their futures. The question is which ones. Some tech brands will evolve into **lifestyle brands** – the new Cokes and Nikes by which we live our lives – whilst others will become **invisible**, technical ingredients inside other branded experiences.

The difference between commercial success and failure for the brands that embrace these opportunities will be the same as the value drivers of today's technologies. They are:

- **Design** … designed around the customer, enabling people to practically achieve more, whilst also adding emotional resonance.
- **Connectivity** … being social and connected, technology works together and enables people to be more effective, and more human.
- **Intelligence** … harnessing the potential to capture and apply big data through more personal, responsive and intuitive behaviours.

In the near future, the **smartphone** – in new formats – will evolve into our personal controller – for everything from health to work, shopping and entertainment. It will make payments, order food, turn on cars, control temperatures, and occasionally make calls.

In many ways technology is not a category of its own, but an enabler of every other type of business. The more that tech companies realize that they are **part of** other categories (multiple not just singular), certainly from a customer's perspective, then the more impact they are likely to have.

Whilst we obsess about 'the next big thing' to be found at the Consumer Electronics Show, the reality is that most tech innovations are really inventions that don't change people's lives or turn into commercial success. It is the innovations that address a real or latent consumer need, that have a relevant and realistic business model and long-term commitment, that succeed.

GAMECHANGERS

These are the 10 technologies that are proving most disruptive and commercial:

Mobile	$400 for an iPhone, compared to $5m for an equivalent 'supercomputer' 40 years ago	6 times growth in smartphones and tablets since launched in 2007
Cloud	Server performance doubles every 18 months	Costs 3 times more to own a server than rent in the cloud
Connectivity	300% increase in device to device connectivity in the last 5 years	90% decline in cost of sensors in last 5 years
Robotics	80% lower price for Baxter than a typical industrial robot	170% growth in sales of industrial robots in the last 3 years
Energy storage	40% decline in price for lithium-ion battery in last 4 years	2000 times increase in power of lithium-ion batteries in last year
3D printing	90% decline in price of home 3D printer in last 4 years	4 times increase in additive manufacturing revenues in last 10 years
Advanced materials	$1000 to $50 price per gram of nanotubes over last 10 years	Carbon nanotubes 115 times stronger than steel
Renewable energy	85% fall in price of PV cells in last 10 years	19 times growth in solar and wind energy generation in last 10 years
Driverless cars	200 times increase in driverless cars produced in last year	500,000 km by Google's driverless cars with only one accident
Genomics	Genetic sequencing speed doubles every 10 months	100 times increase in GM crop growth over the last 15 years

Sources: Forbes, McKinsey, NASA

McKinsey estimates the potential economic impact of these 'disruptive technologies' as between $14 trillion and $33 trillion a year by 2025 – a combination of people prepared to pay more for better products, cost efficiencies in operations, a cleaner environment and better health.

GAMECHANGERS

Here are some of the 'gamechangers' who are harnessing the potential of disruptive technologies to achieve disruptive change in their markets.

Samsung ... South Korea puts the tae kuk into the Galaxy

Samsung has always focused on innovation, however it was only by embracing the power of design that they were able to engage people in objects of desire, rather than products quickly imitated.

Samsung's 'the next big thing is already here' advertising theme promises to keep you ahead of the game, but does the future really look Korean rather than Californian (with a bit of Chinese)? The ad's defining moment came when it showed parents queuing to buy an iPhone, the ultimate suggestion of uncool.

In Korean the word *Samsung* (三星) means 'three stars', where 'three' represents something big, numerous and powerful, and 'stars' means eternity. Samsung's current vision is to 'inspire the world, create the future'.

Samsung leads the mainstream smartphone market though collaborations with Google and Microsoft that enable it to develop quickly and broadly, whilst its product includes tablets to televisions and even washing machines.

Visit Samsung Town, just outside Seoul, and you will quickly experience the distinctive business culture, based on five elements of innovation:

1. Developing a 'creative elite' based around ideas and innovation, attitude and talent, rather than a hierarchy based on status and experience.
2. Relentless competitiveness, tracking the patents of other brands, seeking to out-play them, or simply create something better.
3. Adopting a consistent, replicable innovation methodology across the business, which enables collaboration and rotational working.
4. Maintaining focus and agility, by partnering with academia and specialist external companies, not getting locked into specific research.
5. Staying small whilst being big, by adopting a conglomerate organizational structure, a reflection of the traditional Korean 'chaebol' model.

The Value Innovation Programme has been crucial to its emergence. Six design labs, each with 450 people, focus on exploring consumers and their emerging needs, rather than the technologies to deliver this. It believes that success in consumer electronics can only ever be short term, requiring continuous innovation in order to develop new technology platforms and innovative products.

Samsung realized that people have incredibly emotional relationships with tech devices based around aspiration and desire more than function and reliability. It turned to the South Korean flag for inspiration, and to the circle at the centre of the yin yang symbol, known as the tae kuk, that seeks to positively combine the opposing forces of male and female, hard and soft, or more practically, human and technology. Samsung turned to art for new inspiration, to combine emotion with rationality, searching the world for new ideas and inspiration. Software engineers attended Seoul's school of performing arts, learning to fuse logic with intuition, performance with expression.

Pivot points for Samsung in 'changing the game' of digital devices have been:

THINK   Recognizing 'ideas' as intangible assets, for competitiveness and growth

DESIGN   Creating devices as objects of desire through aesthetics and ergonomics

RESONATE   Use of sport and music sponsorship to connect with people culturally

ENABLE   Focusing innovation on the connectivity of devices, e.g. wearable tech

An example of tae-kuk is Samsung's collaborated with Bang & Olufsen to create the Sereno phone, described by one review as 'cooler than an Eskimo in an Armani anorak'.

ARM ... licensed chipmaker for Apple and Samsung

ARM designs the chips inside most of the world's smartphones, creating an ecosystem of research and innovation with its partners, and most of the world's device brands as licensee customers.

Invisible to most of us, ARM is the 20 year old software design company from Cambridge, UK, that is responsible for many of the components inside our tablets and mobile phones. What is unique about ARM's business model is that it doesn't actually make anything.

Ian Drew, ARM's executive vice president for marketing and business development, says 'we make the knitting patterns for technology manufacturers. You'll find us in 95% of smartphones, 70% of laptops. Partnerships are at the heart of ARM's business model, or ecosystem as we call it'.

The model works for ARM and its customers. Investing over a third of revenues on R&D with an expert team of 1200 chip designers, ARM is able to keep pushing the boundaries of chip design forward and the intellectual property that will drive the next generation of products. ARM licenses these reference designs to manufacturers through up-front payments to use the design and ongoing royalty fees. The whole industry therefore shares in relatively low-cost R&D, whilst ARM has sustainable revenue streams.

The business specializes in low power consumption processors, chips better suited to phones than high-powered computers, claiming that over 90% of all chips used in mobile phones originate on the drawing boards of Cambridge. However ARM also aims it will be in 50% of all tablets and laptops by 2015.

Drew says 'The internet of things – switching motors on and off, smart metering, healthcare, gaming and toys – are all opportunities. As an example, our partner Enlighten which controls street lighting will be able to save millions of tonnes of CO_2 because of our intelligence inside.' He sees ARM playing a major role in reducing the cost of devices. ARM-based chips for PCs will likely cost a bit more than the $20 for a chip, compared to $80 to $200 for Intel's Core line of PC processors.

Drew argues that ARM is different from Intel in every way 'We don't go around saying "You have to build a product that looks like this". Our partners who come to us and say, "This is what we want to do, how can we work together"'. As part of this collaboration, ARM established Linaro, a not-for-profit network of over 120 engineers from the world's leading tech companies.

ARM is riding the wave of a smartphone market growing at around 20% per year. At the same time smartphones keep getting smarter, requiring more chips to support increased functionality, and premium chips that do more, faster, and with higher royalties to ARM.

Drew estimates that ARM's partners are using its licensed designs to produce over 7 billion chips per year.

Pivot Points for ARM in 'changing the game' of software design were:

THINK   Value is in the idea, the design, rather than the manufacturing

EXPLORE   Focus on a different space, low power for small devices

DESIGN   Business model based around IP access and royalties

AMPLIFY   Ecosystem of partners who develop new concepts together

Raspberry Pi ... build your own computer gadgets for $25

Eben Upton wants to inspire kids about the potential of computing. With an incredibly simple $25 computer, a cool brand and social movement, he is inspiring the next generation of entrepreneurs.

Over one million Raspberry Pi computers have been sold since launched in 2012. The credit-card sized computers have been used in a huge variety of DIY computing projects. One reached an altitude of 25 miles (40 km) attached to a high-altitude balloon.

The Raspberry Pi is a simple, small, single-board computer developed at Cambridge University by a team of research scientists led by Eben Upton. In 2009, he and his colleagues, frustrated by the dwindling number of students in Computer Sciences, founded the not-for-profit Raspberry Pi Foundation to promote the teaching of basic programming skills in schools. In the early days of computing, kids would dismantle their Commodore 64 or ZX Spectrum to learn how it worked, tinker around, and hopefully make it better. Nowadays, laptops are too complex for such antics.

The incredibly simple, yet powerful, single-board computer is manufactured through license with Premier Farnell and RS Components, both selling the Raspberry Pi to schools and kids, amateur enthusiasts and entrepreneurs for around $25. It includes an ARM-designed processor and 256 MB of memory, but no built-in hard disk, instead using an SD card. In 2013, a cheaper version, with less memory, and using less power was added, but still good enough to support solar-powered robotics and sensors. An online Pi Store now stocks a diverse range of components to enhance and extend the initial platform.

Upton thinks Raspberry Pi is a gamechanger. 'We bring a low-end desktop computing (and high-end multimedia) experience to a previously unachievable price point, with a business model that permits us to scale into the million-unit-per-year range without working capital issues.'

He says there have been three essential components to the venture's success. 'Firstly, technology. We have a great board design using a great chip. Secondly, our business model is efficient and scalable, working through IP licensing rather than manufacturing ourselves. Third, there is zero marketing spend, yet we have incredible awareness through social media, that has led to press coverage worldwide, and particularly the development of Raspberry Pi clubs in schools and online through social media.'

Pivot points for Raspberry Pi in 'changing the game' of computing were:

THINK   Clear purpose, driven by societal need, a shared passion

EXPLORE   Targeting kids with the curiosity to create and innovate

DESIGN   Virtual business model, simple and scalable, and non-profit

AMPLIFY   Inspiring a movement, people enthused to do more together

Upton is a reluctant hero, claiming he just wanted to get kids excited about the potential of computers to make life better, rather than just playing games on them. His own hero is Elon Musk at Space X. 'Doing a lot of the things we're trying to do, particularly in technology-driven value innovation, but on a much vaster and more impressive scale.'

Alibaba ... Connecting the world's businesses together

Alibaba is a trading platform for the new world order, enabling a small business in remote China to deal directly with a large corporate, for any entrepreneur to access a global marketplace.

Jack Ma grew up in Hangzhou, China. As a yound boy he was desperate to learn English, often riding his bike for an hour each morning to meeting foreigners in the city's hotel. Having failed his college entrance exams twice, he was eventually able to train as an English teacher. However he soon found himself intrigued by business, and at 25 was lecturing in international trade. Friends in the USA helped him develop his first website, China Yellow Pages, which friends back home were amazed by. But Jack had bigger ambitions, for himself, and Chinese business.

In 1999, Ma was back in the USA, sitting in a San Francisco coffee shop thinking about the name Alibaba. He asked a waitress what she thought of the name. 'Open sesame' she replied. He found 30 more people in the street and asked them the same. 'Alibaba is a kind, smart business person, and he helped his village' concluded Ma (with no mention of thieves). The name fitted his website that he believed would open up a world of possibilities to thousands of small and medium Chinese businesses. It is now a global business exchange, with 80 million companies using the online platform to buy and sell anything across the world.

Alibaba.com is the only publicly traded part of the Alibaba Group, the other major businesses being Taobao, an online consumer shopping mall with 370 million users. The Group has also extended in North America, acquiring Vendio, an online retailer similar to Taobao, and Auctiva, a database and digital marketing business.

Alibaba.com has three versions. The company's English language international marketplace (www.alibaba.com) serves to bring together importers and exporters from more than 240 countries and regions. The China marketplace (www.1688.com) is developed for domestic business-to-business trade in China. In addition, Alibaba.com offers a transaction-based wholesale platform, AliExpress (www.aliexpress.com), which allows smaller buyers to buy small quantities of goods at wholesale prices.

Taobao Marketplace, or simply Taobao, is the biggest consumer to consumer shopping platform in China, launched in 2003. Tmall.com was introduced in April 2008 and is now a major online shopping destination for quality, brand name goods in China. eTao is an independent engine, particularly focused on comparison shopping, whilst Alipay is an online payment platform, similar to but significantly bigger than Paypal.

Alipay has been particularly important in a market where consumer trust in online payments is low, consumer protection laws are weak, and there is limited credit card penetration. Alipay is an escrow payment, meaning that consumers only release their payment if they are happy with goods received.

Bharti Airtel ... Indian mobile phones move into Africa

Airtel has grown rapidly in India, leapfrogging the need for fixed lines with mobiles at very low prices. It has then taken this simple model to other developing markets, most significantly in Africa.

There were only 1 million fixed line phones in India, spread amongst 950 million people, when Bharti first launched its Airtel brand in Mumbai back in 1995. Today, there are 50% more people, and every one of them wants a mobile phone.

Bharti Airtel is India's largest mobile operator, with over 250 million subscribers, whilst also the second player in fixed line, broadband and television. It is also the world's largest mobile network reaching across 20 countries in Asia and Africa. It offers fixed line telephone, broadbrand and satellite TV services to over 100 Indian cities.

Founded by Sunil Bharti Mittal, the business strategy is based around a high volume 'minutes factory' to drive usage, whilst costs are minimized with the outsourcing of all operations except marketing, sales and finance. This included a deal with Ericsson, its infrastructure partner, to be paid per use rather than upfront, further reducing costs and risks. The result is prices as low as $0.02 per minute.

Airtel Africa is a booming business, and the Indian company is learning to transfer their expertize and business model for success in developing markets to an even faster growing region. In 2010, Bharti acquired the Kuwaiti operator Zain in a $10.7 billion deal, giving it access to an additional 50 million customers in 15 local markets. Airtel is now regarded as one of the most loved brands in Africa, and has the potential to offer many more services.

GiffGaff ... customers do more in order to get free calls

Developed by O2, part of Telefonica, GiffGaff encourages customers to do the work for them – design products, promote the brand, recruit new customers – in return for free calls.

The GiffGaff manifesto goes like this ...

'Typical. Just as the caring, sharing attitude of the 90s exited the swing-doors of the millennium, in came the mass-market mobile phone network on the other side. So we never really got to see how the two of them would hit it off together. (You're probably anticipating an "until now .." line. Here it is!) ... Until now We're GiffGaff, a David amongst Goliaths in Mobile-land. We may be sort-of-small but we're big on that caring, sharing thing. We believe in community; in people; in the person but specifically, that the power should rest with them.'

Giffgaff is an ancient Scottish word that means 'mutual giving' and that summarizes the ethos of O2/Telefonica's virtual mobile network launched in 2009. The more customers get involved in the business, the more they get back – help solve other customer problems, help recruit new customers or create content for marketing – and will soon find that your calls are free. Of course this doesn't appeal to everyone, but for its target segment of (largely youthful) consumers, it adds value through being part of the business, a perceived community, and getting far better quality connections than on Skype. Founded by Gavin Thompson, O2's head of brand strategy, 'the mobile network run by you' soon started winning awards for innovation and customer excellence.

Google <X> ... augmented reality in the moonshot factory

Just around the corner from the Googleplex is a secret, anonymous – yet far more inspiring – building. It is the home of Google's really big ideas, to solve the biggest problems, to create bigger solutions. Mostly driven by data, they go far beyond search, even to the moon.

Google Glass is a wearable, head-mounted computer with its display embedded within the lens of specially made eyewear. Interaction is through voice commands, but eventually through movement of the eye. Project Glass is one of a number of futuristic innovations emerging from Google <X> Lab, including data-driven healthcare and driverless cars, global wi-fi and space elevators, as the search engine giant continues to develop new services and devices to 'organize the world's information'.

Babak Parviz leads Project Glass; an electrical engineer by training, he recognizes that head-worn displays for augmented reality are not a new idea: 'Google's designs are smaller and slimmer than previous concepts, resembling a normal pair of glasses where one lens is replaced by the display, lighter than the lens itself.'

Google co-founder, Sergey Brin, wore a prototype version in 2012, demonstrating its use when skydiving and mountain biking. The 'Explorer' pre-launch edition was subsequently made available to market influencers, people who could enrich the pre-launch stories of the product through their innovative uses of Google Glass – from baseball stars to intrepid explorers, as well as journalists and potential retailers. Whilst testing the product, they would also build a rich storybook of interesting applications to inspire the future mass market.

Google's innovation has evolved from its relaxed 20% of time 'bootlegging' for wild ideas, into a more structured approach which builds platforms and explores business models beyond advertising. In particular, the innovation process focuses on adjacencies, i.e. similar needs but in different markets, and applying existing concepts in new places. Customer-centricity and design thinking have become core principles, rather than an obsession with technological possibility.

Competitively, Google is also bringing together hardware and software, partly in response to the challenge of Apple and others. In the past it outsourced most hardware development, but this was quickly copied, requiring a more integrated approach through in-house collaboration and 'fusion' thinking.

Huawei ... China, making the world's networks work

From local reseller to global researcher, the Shenzen-based, employee-owned business learnt from the most difficult situations to create better infrastructure solutions for a connected world.

Founded by Ren Zhengfei in 1987, Huawei started off as a reseller of networking equipment into the Chinese market, with particular focus on rural communities. It learnt quickly to adapt to local conditions – limited infrastructure, power shortages and rats chewing cables. Based in Shenzen, Huawei grew quickly, now focusing on its own products and local customers in mid-size cities, region by region, and won its first international contract with Hutchison Whampoa in 1997. In 2000 it formed a consulting partnership with IBM allowing it to build much more strategic partnerships with global customers.

Huawei has become a leader in networking and telecoms equipment, overtaking Ericsson in recent years, and supporting 90% of the world's leading telecom operators. It is owned entirely by employees, with around 60% of the 140,000 staff holding non-tradable shares that are allocated according to position and performance: 46% of its people are engaged in R&D, spread across 22 countries, and filing around 49,000 patents.

Tencent ... building the world's largest social network and more

The Chinese internet giant with ambitions to be much more, and on course to make QQ the world's largest social network, with a broad range of revenue generating content and services.

Tencent dominates China's internet. From search and messaging, social networks and gaming, it comes with a mission to 'enhance the quality of human life through internet services'.

Founded in 1998 by Huateng Ma, Tencent now offers a diverse yet connected range of online and mobile applications that seek to create a 'one-stop online lifestyle experience' with brands including QQ (messaging, networking and gaming), WeChat (messaging) and Tenpay (virtual currency). With over 800 million users, QQ is now one of the world's largest networks and on course to outsize Facebook by 2016.

The business also created one of China's largest charities, gongyi.qq.com, which focuses on youth education and providing care for disadvantaged young people.

The business is growing rapidly internationally too, initially focused on connecting the world's immigrant Chinese populations. We Chat, having seen the $19bn flotation of WhatsApp, is proving to be most effective in reaching new markets, and keeping customers engaging in and between its other services. Now that the world has adopted search, networking, online retailing and gaming, it is the one that connects them that is likely to succeed.

Xiaomi ... China's Apple-like phones with Jobs-like leader

Chinese consumers cannot get enough of Xiaomi's MiPhones. With excitement and desire whipped up by rockstar CEO Lei Jun, it is building a lifestyle brand, at affordable prices, for a huge new generation.

Xiaomi is best known for its iPhone-like smartphone, and Steve Jobs-imitating CEO. Within 18 months of launch, Xiaomi had become China's fifth largest brand, largely due to the high profile of its leader, Lei Jun. With faded jeans and black turtle necks, he bounds onto stage, with rock music and dry ice, adored by the young Chinese, proclaiming his latest innovation. Or should that be imitation.

Of course Xiaomi maintains that it is different. It has no stores, and only sells direct, online. Whilst its phones may be similar in style, their customizable software is distinctive, and there is a growing range of Chinese apps. The product range is expanding too, including a tablet – not surprisingly. With sales approaching 20 million in 2013, it is still only 15% of Apple's size, or 3% of Samsung, but with a huge market potential. India and Indonesia, Russia and Brazil are already on Jun's travel plans.

Jun has said that his priorities are innovation, iteration and image. Perhaps most impressive is the boldness and speed of Xiaomi's growth. In fast growing, still emerging markets, the ability to imitate a premium and proven business model makes sense, particularly if the cost base makes it accessible to the new audiences. The ability to build a personality leader and cult-like following is a powerful strategy for any brand.

23 FUTUREMAKERS

CHANGING THE GAME OF MANUFACTURING

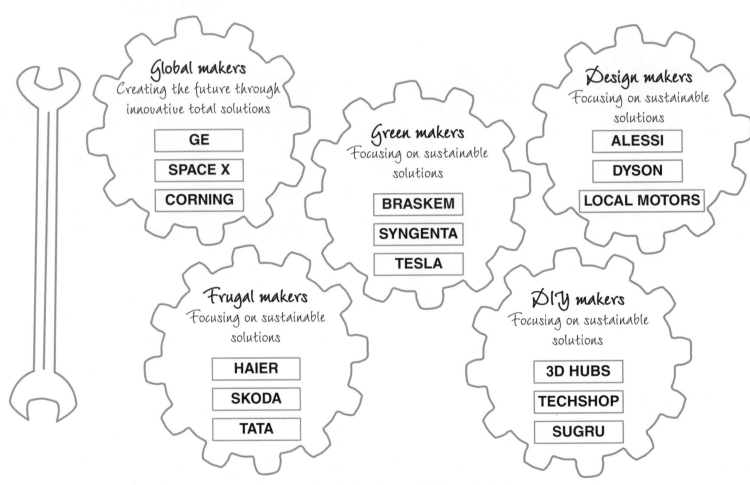

Global makers
Creating the future through innovative total solutions

- GE
- SPACE X
- CORNING

Green makers
Focusing on sustainable solutions

- BRASKEM
- SYNGENTA
- TESLA

Design makers
Focusing on sustainable solutions

- ALESSI
- DYSON
- LOCAL MOTORS

Frugal makers
Focusing on sustainable solutions

- HAIER
- SKODA
- TATA

DIY makers
Focusing on sustainable solutions

- 3D HUBS
- TECHSHOP
- SUGRU

Futuremakers, Rethinking the World of Manufacturing

The future of **manufacturing** is more about science than production; built around specialist research and technical innovation, **decentralized** across the world, balancing focus and efficiency to manufacture on **demand** and to order.

Manufacturing has been through a turbulent decade – choked by economic crisis, challenged by global shifts in supply and demand, transformed through automation, redesigned through **virtual ecosystems**. Whilst the car-making heartland of Detroit lies in ruins, and the industrial heartlands of Europe are green again, manufacturing is on the rise. But in new places and with new models. It remains a driving force of both advanced and developing economies, a pathway from subsistence farming to material wealth.

Whilst the huge industrial complexes surrounding cities like Jakarta and Mumbai, Nairobi and Sao Paulo, signify productive nations, manufacturing has also reinvented itself in small and quiet ways. The factories of Seoul hum with the sound of high tech engineering, whilst 500 **3D Hubs** scattered across Amsterdam signify a maker city. Gone are the huge factories and workforces, smoking chimneys and hard hats. Manufacturing today is much more about science and **technology, design and innovation**.

Far from the stereotypes of long production lines, today's manufacturing takes on a variety of different forms:

- **Global makers** – chemicals, transport, appliances – defining consistent quality and progress to their high volume categories, leveraging economies of scale, distributing them worldwide with global brands.

- **Knowledge innovators** – electronics, education, pharmaceuticals – driven by ideas and research, data and technology, their value is in intellectual property, with products often assembled under license.

- **Regional processers** – food and drink, printing, clothing – local companies or subsidiaries adding cultural relevance and speed of delivery to consumables, fast fashion, daily news, and local tastes.

However the blur of categories means that manufacturing is less of a sector, more of a process. Every product demands a wide range of services and support, delivered through many different related products and partners. The best way for a manufacturer to grow, sustainably and profitably, is to enhance their **service experience**, enabling customers to solve problems, standing out from competitors and adding new revenue streams.

GAMECHANGERS

The future of manufacturing is about focusing less on products and more on customers, adding more value to their experiences. In global markets, where distance is irrelevant but still exists, it is also about efficiency, of borderless supply networks and on demand delivery speed. It is about innovation, creating and making, of products and business models, finding ways where less is more in a resource-constrained world.

Tesla ... faster than a Ferrari, powered by the sun

Tesla is the fastest, sexiest, most-hyped car of its generation. It can drive 500 km on a solar powered battery, with zero carbon emissions, whilst also becoming the must-have luxury accessory in Hollywood.

'Don't take from the earth, accept from the sun, untold memories for a gallon of light' goes the voice over as Tesla's incredibly sexy Model S pulls up at a beautiful sun-setting Californian beach.

Tesla, named after the Serbian physicist who invented the AC induction motor, started as a Silicon Valley dream. To create the world's leading electric car company, believing that, unlike the Toyota Prius, being good didn't need to compromize great performance. Having burnt through their start-up capital, Elon Musk took over the company, investing much of his fortune made at PayPal. The company now has 6000 workers producing 100 cars every week.

The challenge, however, is not just to build great cars, but to grow and shape the market. More cars mean more charging points, crucial to overcome the fear of your lithium oxide battery running flat. Musk established Solar City, his own solar energy company, and now provides almost 100 charge stations, reaching 98% of the US population. He also recognized the need to grow the overall market for electric vehicles. It needed more competitors, in order to gain many more customers. In 2014 he decided to open source all of his IP, allowing competitors to use his patents.

Pivot points for Tesla in 'changing the game' of automotives include:

THINK   Tesla has a bold vision, shaping its market to its advantage

DISRUPT   Breaking the paradox, cars can be fast and sexy and good for the world

INSPIRE   Tesla's is the most hyped car in history, using PR to build the brand

DESIGN   From batteries to stores and charging, Tesla designs a better experience

'When I was at college I wanted to be involved in things that change the world' says Musk in a recent interview with '60 Minutes'. Whilst the journey hasn't been smooth, the cars are now the fastest, coolest, most hyped sports cars in California, and with zero carbon emissions, no guilt either. Walk through the designer shopping mall of LA's Century City, and you come across a Tesla boutique store. Just two incredibly shiny cars with spot lights and chilled music. No dealers, no forecourts, no discounts. You buy it like the most exclusive luxury goods, with prices starting at $49,900. As Musk believes, 'life is too short for compromizes'.

GE ... becoming market makers with better machines

GE is leading an industrial revolution in applying the 'internet of things' to business processes and equipment. The challenge is to do this in ways that capture the imagination of businesses and consumers.

Tommy Lee Jones, dressed all in black, describes how GE is providing hospitals with software that invisibly connects patients to nurses to doctors to machines, reducing down time and improving care ... GE has become a storyteller, helping businesses and consumers to understand the potential of new technologies to make life better.

CMO, Beth Comstock, says she connects the dots between products and people, whilst also making sense of fast changing markets, looking for new patterns and opportunities. In an interview with *McKinsey Quarterly*, Comstock says a great marketer 'translates observations into insights that can move a business or product forwards'. However that is not just about brand and communicating what exists: 'Marketing is now about creating and developing new markets; not just identifying opportunities but also making them happen.'

Speaking at a Google *Think* event, she describes herself as a market maker. 'To be an effective marketer, you have to go outside, you have to see what's happening and be a translator. You have to immerse yourself in the customer world.'

Customer innovation centres across the world drive this innovation within markets. In Chengdu, China, for example, local and global marketers and researchers collaborate on new initiatives in mobile, affordable healthcare and green energy. Others sources of ideas come from new types of open partnerships and innovation competitions.

Communicating ideas in more human, intuitive ways is important to GE. Whilst advertising still matters, it is the integrated use of videos, social media and events that engage people more deeply. 'The idea of an ad as a separate entity is gone' says Comstock. Facebook is used as GE's social 'hub' for engaging both business customers and end consumers. There are over 30 GE pages including social health and fitness apps. Google+ is used more to reach technical audiences with videos and articles, whilst Pinterest is more female focused, with lifestyle photos, stories and quotes. Twitter is for business users, keeping stories topical and drawing people in. Youtube is more of a background library complementing TV ads.

Pivot points for GE in 'changing the game' of industrial products include:

EXPLORE   Being a market maker, finding and defining markets in your own vision

DISRUPT   Creating new ways in which markets work, products and people connect

RESONATE   Harnessing the power of storytelling for both business and consumers

ENABLE   Focusing on how the brand helps people to live better lives

One of the company's biggest growth strategies is based on the 'industrial internet' or to most of us, the 'internet of things,' applying digital and social technologies to machines – from brain scanners to wind turbines – to improve their effectiveness. The emerging data helps GE and its clients to design and operate the machines. But to communicate these new opportunities requires stories – as powerful for business customers as for consumers. GE's new storyline about 'Brilliant Machines' features, for example, Night Rider's KIT supercar getting a 21st century upgrade thanks to GE.

Syngenta … biochemists of the world's future food

As populations rise, and farmland diminishes, Syngenta is applying science to every aspect of food production, finding better ways to feed the changing world and also improve health.

Every day our planet wakes with 200,000 more mouths to feed and more farmland lost to erosion. Many people who produce the world's food live themselves in poverty. At the same time sea levels rise, deserts replace farmland, biodiversity declines and we continue to use the Earth's resources 50% faster than we replace them.

Syngenta applies science to nature to address these formidable challenges. Formed in 2000 by a merger of Novartis and AstraZeneca's agrichemical businesses, it defines a purpose 'to bring plant potential to life'. This might be in creating new types of seed that can thrive in harsh environments, providing more nutrition to more people, or in protecting existing crops from disease and damage.

Of course 'genetically modified' crops can often draw a negative reaction from consumers who seek authenticity, and fear the disruption of natural processes. Yet it is a scientific response to an unnatural, polluted environment which people have created. It also establishes a creative tension, to balance innovation and sustainabiliy, but Syngenta seeks scientific solutions that promote healthiness, and could rescue billions of people from malnutrition. Food security will become a huge global issue as populations grow, sea levels rise, and agricultural land turns to desert. Syngenta's first priority is therefore to make farms more productive. As well as crop nutrients, this also includes new growth techniques and distribution models, improving yields, reducing waste and reaching new markets.

Syngenta's Good Growth Plan commits by 2020 to make crops more efficient, increasing crop productivity by 20% without using more resources. It seeks to rescue more farmland, improving the fertility of 10 million hectares, and to enhance biodiversity on 5 million hectares. To achieve this it will particularly focus on small farms, where it believes it can make much bigger improvements, whilst also improving farming skills and processes, particularly in developing markets.

Pivot points for Syngenta in 'changing the game' of agriculture were:

EXPLORE   Focus on solving the biggest problems, like feeding the future world

DISRUPT   Be bold and persistent in applying science, despite people's fears

DESIGN   Not just better seeds, but educate farmers with new process and skills

IMPACT   Build a brand that makes the world better, far beyond bags of fertilizer

Whilst the business operates in 90 countries, product development is consolidated in one place, and then tested in different environments. New hybrid seeds produce crops more resistant to disease and hot weather, whilst new bio-friendly sprays protect crops from pests. In the last five years revenues have growth by 45% to $15bn, doubling net income. New products now account for around 10% of sales, and are growing fastest.

Corning ... Envisioning a better world made out of glass

We live in a world of glass – from tablets to televisions, high rise buildings to Google Glass. But glass breaks. Not if it's made for gorillas. Corning has turned itself into an ingredient brand that even adds value to Apple.

Corning's 'Gorilla Glass' is the ultra-strong, highly-flexible, scratch-resistant material that is used in the screen of over 1 billion devices including iPhones and iPads, flat screen TVs and in outdoor displays. The drive to create thinner, lighter, more perfect devices is as much dependant on screen materials as computing power or energy management. Corning's glass has therefore become a crucial part of making digital visions a reality.

Once an almost invisible manufacturer, Corning has seized on its new role to engage consumers in its brand and innovations. 'A Day Made of Glass' became a Youtube sensation with over 25 million views. The company spent $1.5 million on the ad, only released on Youtube, not on TV. In the video, a narrator takes you inside a world made of Gorilla Glass, where edge-to-edge displays make nearly every surface interactive: windows, a car's dashboard, walls, tables. Everything is touch sensitive and transparent. 'How close are we to this?' the narrator asks. 'Well, it's do-able now, but not to this scale and not at an affordable price. Further innovation in manufacturing is needed to get us there on a broad scale.'

'We spent far less than we would have for a Super Bowl spot', says Corning CFO Jim Flaws, talking to Fast Company. He believes the viral nature of the clip makes it more powerful than conventional marketing. 'We've found this to be incredibly effective.' With every audience, he might add. Brands like Apple and Samsung mention Corning as an added value part of their proposition, whilst for investors it shows how the business is not just a manufacturer but part of a digital revolution in entertainment, healthcare and lifestyles. Investors immediately look to different growth trajectories, and profit potential, transforming the perceived and real value of the business.

Tata ... India's portfolio of Tetley Tea and Range Rovers

Tata is the Indian super group, actually a charitable trust, that is reaching across the world, combining basic industries with luxury brands to shape markets in its own vision, primarily to make life better.

Walk through the streets of New Dehli and you will see Tata everywhere. Buses and trucks, mobile phones to energy supply, airlines and hotels, a proliferation of food and drinks. The Indian giant is now going global, acquiring well-known brands, and also building its own in new markets. With nearly 100 companies in the group, and a combined market cap over $100 billion, Tata has come a long way since 1868.

Tata, with its 350,000 employees spread across 80 countries, works differently – it is much more diversified than most Western firms, more engaged in the life of its communities, and with a focus on creating and sustaining long-term success. As corporate biographer Morgan Witzel told me: 'Their companies are loosely unified as a confederation under the Tata brand. All of them have their own strategies and cultures, and almost every one is profitable.'

Tata Motors gained much attention for its $2500 Nano car, a great example of frugal innovation to be affordable in local markets. Its acquisition of Europe's leading steel maker combined low cost sourcing in Asia with the added value of Corus, enabling it to migrate the advanced innovations and skills to its growth markets. The same model is working with Jaguar Land Rover, now profitable again, and demonstrating that M&A activity can work well.

Jamshedpur is the home of Tata Steel in India. Unlike most steel towns it has clean streets, green parks and good amenities. Tata even provides the local hospital, the zoo and sports stadium. This is because Tata is ultimately here to make the world a better place, with the holding company Tata Sons two-thirds owned by a charitable trust. This is not just nice words, it really does drive the culture. As I discuss business priorities and performance with business leaders it is both surprising, but impressive, that doing more for employees, customers and society really does matter more than making money.

3D Hubs ... print your product, anytime, anywhere

3D Hubs is the new Kinko's, establishing 5000 print locations in 80 countries, in just 9 months, to ensure that you can 3D print your products within minutes wherever you are.

3D printing went from fiction to fad in 2013, but it was difficult to imagine everyone with a printer in their kitchens, producing Gaudi-esque versions of vases, car parts and ice cream. However Dutchman Bram de Zwart thought differently, believing that a distributed network of printers would work better than personal ownership. Nobody knew how the market would evolve, but de Zwart didn't wait. Within nine months of launch he had set up 5000 'hubs' across the world, reaching 10% of the global population within 15 km of their homes.

The growth model is similar to Kinkos, but with a social franchise model based on people becoming their local 'mayor'. Local communities of makers rapidly emerge, disrupting old supply chains, and providing on-demand, personalized manufacturing using the state of the art printers. This revolutionizes the cost models of manufacturing, in particular for small businesses who themselves seek to offer personalized solutions – classic cars to home builders, doctors to chefs.

Braskem ... the Brazilian bottles made out of plants

Braskem makes plastics out of sugarcane, embraced by brands across the world in search of more sustainable packaging solutions. The Brazilian company uses a process that actually reduces greenhouse gases.

Our oceans are littered with plastic bottles, made from petroleum and difficult to recycle. In 2010 Coca-Cola committed to using only 100% sustainable packaging, and turned to $19b Brazilian petrochemical giant, Braskem, for help. The innovation was to use HDPE plastic created using ethylene, derived 100% from sugarcane. The fully-recyclable, zero carbon PlantBottle was born, and 2.5 million were produced in the first year. The process actually reduced greenhouse gases, absorbing 2 tonnes of carbon dioxide for every tonne of plastic produced.

The Sao Paulo business, established in 2002, has now transformed its entire business to focus on the global demand for renewables, and is now the world's largest producer of biopolymers: 200,000 tonnes of green plastics are produced each year, although there is still 80 million tonnes of traditional plastic in the world to replace. Braskem's 'I'm Green' stamp can now be found on the packaging of 23 different brands, from Johnson and Johnson to Walmart, helping them to achieve sustainability goals, whilst also building an ingredient brand.

Space X ... delivery service for satellites and spacemen

Whilst some have described Elon Musk as the new Thomas Edison, his own inspiration is just to have fun. When you've got his money, why not create a space business? Which might just change our world, and others too.

We already know Elon Musk for the fortune he made creating PayPal, part of which he spent developing electric cars with Tesla, and a solar-powered charging network to support it. He spent most of his remaining money on developing a space transport company. As you do.

Space X started work in 2002 developing a range of Falcon reusable launch vehicles, followed by a spacecraft called Dragon which launches off their back. In 2012, it became the first private company to send a cargo payload on the Dragon, destination the International Space Station. With NASA having retired its own Space Shuttle it is looking to people like Musk to outsource its transportation services to. Space X won the $10bn contract.

Human travel in the Dragon, a small cone-shaped vehicle, will start from 2015, shuttling astronauts back and forth between the International Space Station. Private companies, governments and the military have also signed contracts for taking satellites into space. Most ambitious is the NASA-funded project to send Dragon on a Mars landing mission in 2018. Indeed Musk's stated ambition for Space X is to create a permanent human presence on Mars.

Dyson ... bagless cleaners to bladeless fans

A vacuum cleaner used to be called a Hoover. Now it's called a Dyson. The industrial design business is intent on making things better, with a relentless focus on creativity, design and engineering to keep breaking rules.

After 5126 attempts to create a better vaccum cleaner, James Dyson eventually smiled. He had learnt the value of persistence when running up sand dunes time after time in Norfolk, England, as training for his cross country races. Five years of getting it wrong, resulted in a disruption that changed the world ... of vacuum cleaners at least. There was no bag. Just a dual cyclone fan with a centrifugal force of 100,000 G. A lot of suction.

Dyson explains that his innovation came out of personal frustration with having to fit and empty bags of dust when seeking to clean his home. 'Anger is a great motivator' he says in his autobiography *Against the Odds*, 'design is just problem solving'.

He told a recent *Wired* audience: 'I'm a designer and an engineer, I get angry about things that don't work, like hand dryers, endless paper towels, what a huge waste.' Try solving problems by thinking differently, he said, 'What if you could scrape water off your hands with a blade of air?' The AirBlade, like the vacuum, uses a high-speed digital motor, scrapes water off your hands like a windshield wiper, but with air. Simple, better, cheaper, faster: three times as environmentally friendly as regular hand dryers, using one-sixth of the amount of energy, taking 12 seconds instead of 40.

Whilst Dyson's products are manufactured across the world, his ideas factory remains in the heart of the countryside, employing a mix of local people and the brightest youth 'I want people who haven't done something before and will find a new way of doing it, and that aren't afraid of failure,' said Dyson. 'If you always succeed, you're learning nothing. Failure is terribly important.'

Local Motors ... crowd-sourced cars not normal

Most industries become incredibly predictable about what a product looks like, and how it's made. Products become indistinguishable and innovation is incremental. Local Motors changed that with a community of 35,000 fanatics wanting better.

John 'Jay' Rogers is CEO of Local Motors, a small car factory in Phoenix Arizona with the tagline World of Vehicle Innovations. Rogers, still in his 30s, is passionate about co-creation, taking designs and suggestions from the thousands of car geeks who spend time on his online discussion boards, collaborating with those who propose the best ideas, and putting them to work. Local Motors designs and builds cars in collaboration with thousands of supporters.

His first crowd-sourced car emerged in 2009 as the off-road Rally Fighter chosen from 35,000 designs submitted from across 100 countries. The winner was a design student who based his sketches on a P-51 Mustang fighter plane. The car was designed and manufactured in 14 weeks, compared to the normal 24 months time to market for most new models of car. Thousands of participants were ready to pledge deposits for the car they helped create.

Local Motors now holds regular contests, turning to the collective creativity and intelligence of its community to design everything from door handles to dashboards. Clients use the process to solve problems with new thinking – a new delivery truck for Dominos Pizza, an off-road jeep for the US military, and a new urban electric car for BMW. Rogers hasn't worked out how to crowd-source the manufacturing yet, however he does let designers and buyers come into the factory and support his team in making their dream machines.

PART 4
GAMECHANGER LABS

Now it's your time...to see and seize the future...to think bigger and better...to define your real purpose, and make it real, through ideas and innovation, brands and business...to make life better, and the world a better place...Everything you need is already inside you. Be bold. Be brave. Be brilliant. Get started.

Market scenarios

How are existing and new markets likely to evolve, in terms of customers, channels, competitors, and ways of working?

New possibilities

What are the potential new opportunities for customers, their articulated and unarticulated needs and aspirations?

Change drivers

How will the most relevant drivers of change in markets –social, economic, technological –shape emerging trends?

Future vision

What is our inspiring vision of the future? How will life be better for people?

Future space

So what kind of business are we? What market are we really in? How can we articulate our business in a better, more inspiring and distinctive way?

Business purpose

Why do we exist? What is our contribution to the world? What do we distinctively do?

Business ambition

Given this business purpose, and future vision, what do we want to achieve as a business?

Profitable segments

Evaluate existing customer segments (defined by type, need, motivation) by existing and potential profit.

Potential segments

Explore 'adjacent' customer segments (eg similar needs, attitudes) as potential new markets.

Potential for profitable growth

Evaluate existing and potential markets in terms of their attractiveness (ability to add value to customers, profit and growth potential), and accessibility (competitiveness, ease of entry, available partners).

Profitable geographies

Evaluate existing customer geographies (defined by region, culture distance) by existing and potential profit.

Potential geographies

Explore 'adjacent' geographic regions (eg nearby, similar culture, structures) as potential new markets.

Target markets

Profitable categories

Evaluate existing customer geographies (defined by sector, product, application) by existing and potential profit.

Potential categories

Explore 'adjacent' categories(eg similar products, complimentary benefits) as potential new markets.

Prioritize your markets based on current and future potential, including the relative Importance of growth by segment, geography or category to your business, or a mix of all.

Change the 'why'

How could you change (redefine, extend, etc) the purpose or ambition of your business and brand? eg business goals, benefits, applications.

Change the 'who'

How could you change (refocus, extend, etc) the core audience? eg a new segment, different influencers or decision makers.

Change the 'what'

How could you change (reinvent, extend etc) your products and services? eg additional services, price positioning, and customer experience.

Change the 'how'

How could you change (reconfigure, simplify etc) the way you work? eg business model, partners, organisation, channels, rewards.

Change the game

How will you combine a number of these factors, to change the way the market works? What are the differences (structures, processes, behaviours) between the old and new 'game'? Which will be most significant? What will be the benefit for customers and business?

Market space

What is your distinctive space in the world – how will you define it, the business that you are in?

Where to focus

Making the strategic choices about where you will focus, to shape the future in your own vision.

Target markets

What are the potential new opportunities for customers, and the benefits they would deliver?

Change the game

How will you play a different "game" in the market, disruptively and distinctively?

How to compete

Making the strategic choices about how you will compete and succeed in this space.

Distinctive assets

What do you have (ideas, partners, brands, networks etc) that enables you to do this better?

Pivot points

What are the big moments on this journey, the most dramatic shifts, the key deliverables?

What to do to win

Making the strategic choices about what you will need to change, develop and deliver over time.

Horizon planning

What are the big (typically 3) phases (over the next 1–5 years) to deliver this strategy?

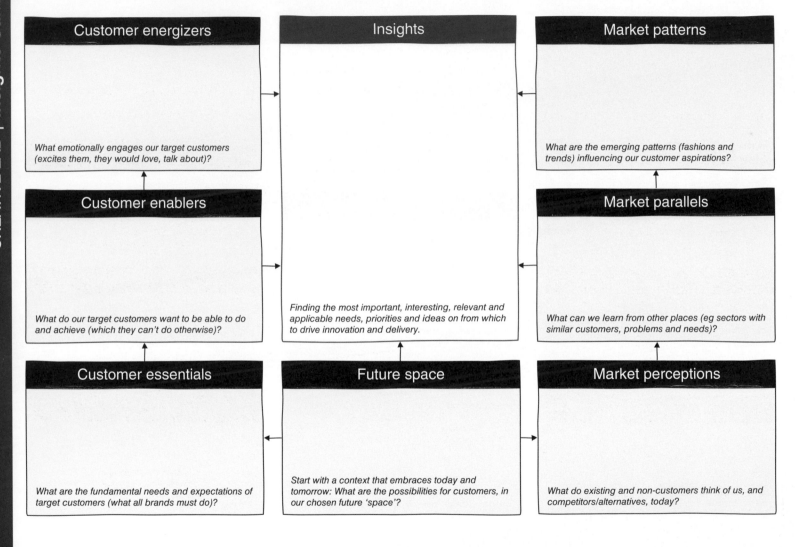

CREATIVE LAB | Insights Canvas

Customer energizers

What emotionally engages our target customers (excites them, they would love, talk about)?

Customer enablers

What do our target customers want to be able to do and achieve (which they can't do otherwise)?

Customer essentials

What are the fundamental needs and expectations of target customers (what all brands must do)?

Insights

Finding the most important, interesting, relevant and applicable needs, priorities and ideas on from which to drive innovation and delivery.

Future space

Start with a context that embraces today and tomorrow: What are the possibilities for customers, in our chosen future 'space'?

Market patterns

What are the emerging patterns (fashions and trends) influencing our customer aspirations?

Market parallels

What can we learn from other places (eg sectors with similar customers, problems and needs)?

Market perceptions

What do existing and non-customers think of us, and competitors/alternatives, today?

Customers

How will you encourage customers to collaborate with the business? And even more powerfully between themselves, enabled by the brand?

Employees

How will you encourage employees to collaborate between each other? Particularly across functions and distance?

Partners

How will you encourage partners to collaborate (eg suppliers, distributors, complinementors), facilitating a business ecosystem?

Experts

How will you encourage experts to collaborate with your business (eg tech specialists, experienced retirees, creative agencies)?

Collaborative business

Building an 'ideas and networks' business that is sustained through smart collaborations that bring people together. Creating the infrastructure and incentives to enable this (eg open forums, competitions, and communities), and business model to capture the benefits for collaborators and the business (faster, cheaper, better).

Co-design

How to facilitate shared ideas and design, that embraces different perspectives and priorities? (eg ARM's business ecosystem, Nike's ID Studio)

Co-develop

How to facilitate shared build and delivery, that taps into other capabilities and networks? (eg Threadless t-shirts, P&G's Connect+Develop)

Co-consume

How to facilitate shared purchase and usage, that is good for customers and the environment (eg Airbnb's rooms to rent, Zipcars's car sharing)

Co-support

How to facilitate shared support and selling, that is built around community and advocacy? (eg Avon's network selling, Apple's help forums)

CREATIVE LAB | Innovation Canvas

Possibilities

Stimulating creativity through, what is possible – technological capability, best in class solutions, ideas from other places, and random catalysts.

Idea fusion

Divergent … generating lots of ideas, using each 'wave' spark more … and in particular through "unusual combinations" (fusions).

Concept design

Convergent … Clustering together the best ideas into themes with similar customer benefits … shaping small number of molecules (concepts).

Insights

Finding the 'right question' to answer through innovation, based on a prioritization of the most important customer and broader insights.

Evaluation

Evaluating each of the emerging concepts in terms of customer and business attractiveness (high medium low – impact, cost, time, risk etc).

Business innovation

Innovating the total business concept – from product and service, business model and customer experience, partnerships and relationships … Accelerating the 'best few' evaluated concepts to shape further through in-market testing and adaption … to innovate the market and application, as well as business and solution.

Resources

What are the business requirements, from raw materials that is responsibly sourced, to business infrastructure to deliver in each market?

Proposition

What are the value propositions (based around distinctive benefits, supported by the brand) to engage each customer segment?

Customers

Who are the target customers (consumers), and what defines them (eg needs, attitudes, location etc). There may be multiple segments?

Partners

Who are the right partners to deliver our vision better eg with the right capabilities, connections, investment, and talent to make it happen?

Products and Services

How will we deliver each of the propositions to each customer – through configurations of products or customized solutions?

Networks

What are the networks (communities, social media, distributors, licensees etc) which amplify the potential of our brands and market reach?

Costs

What are the significant cost streams involved in creating and delivering our propositions?

Profit

Adapting the configuration of each aspect of this business model in order to find the best combinations for sustainable, profitable growth.

Revenues

What are the significant revenue streams we can create through our propositions and networks?

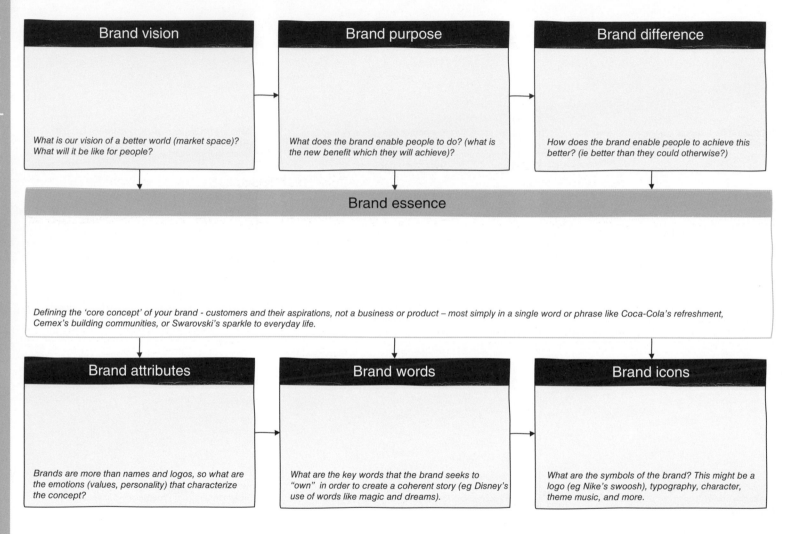

Brand vision

What is our vision of a better world (market space)? What will it be like for people?

Brand purpose

What does the brand enable people to do? (what is the new benefit which they will achieve)?

Brand difference

How does the brand enable people to achieve this better? (ie better than they could otherwise?)

Brand essence

Defining the 'core concept' of your brand - customers and their aspirations, not a business or product – most simply in a single word or phrase like Coca-Cola's refreshment, Cemex's building communities, or Swarovski's sparkle to everyday life.

Brand attributes

Brands are more than names and logos, so what are the emotions (values, personality) that characterize the concept?

Brand words

What are the key words that the brand seeks to "own" in order to create a coherent story (eg Disney's use of words like magic and dreams).

Brand icons

What are the symbols of the brand? This might be a logo (eg Nike's swoosh), typography, character, theme music, and more.

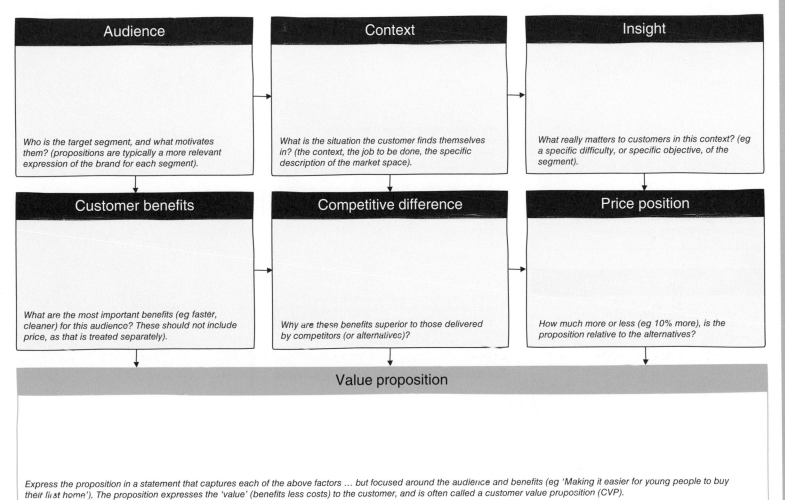

Audience

Who is the target segment, and what motivates them? (propositions are typically a more relevant expression of the brand for each segment).

Context

What is the situation the customer finds themselves in? (the context, the job to be done, the specific description of the market space).

Insight

What really matters to customers in this context? (eg a specific difficulty, or specific objective, of the segment).

Customer benefits

What are the most important benefits (eg faster, cleaner) for this audience? These should not include price, as that is treated separately).

Competitive difference

Why are these benefits superior to those delivered by competitors (or alternatives)?

Price position

How much more or less (eg 10% more), is the proposition relative to the alternatives?

Value proposition

Express the proposition in a statement that captures each of the above factors ... but focused around the audience and benefits (eg 'Making it easier for young people to buy their first home'). The proposition expresses the 'value' (benefits less costs) to the customer, and is often called a customer value proposition (CVP).

Brand storytelling

What are the storylines that bring the brand to life in a human and memorable way, and make the propositions relevant for each customer?

Engaging customers

How will you engage people in your brand, driving consideration and preference, as they explore their needs, aspirations and options?

Customer's experience

What is the experience that you seek customers to have through purchase and application? What will they 'see feel think do' at each point? How can you streamline the negative and elaborate the positive aspects of their experience?

Enhancing sales

How will you drive more effective sales, better influence selection, improve perceived value to maximize price, and sell more?

Realtime marketing

How to communicate in a fast, personal and topical way, using the most relevant media, analytics and creativity, to engage people now?

Enabling more

How will you help customers to, get more out of their purchase, to realize its full value to them, and also repurchase and recommend others?

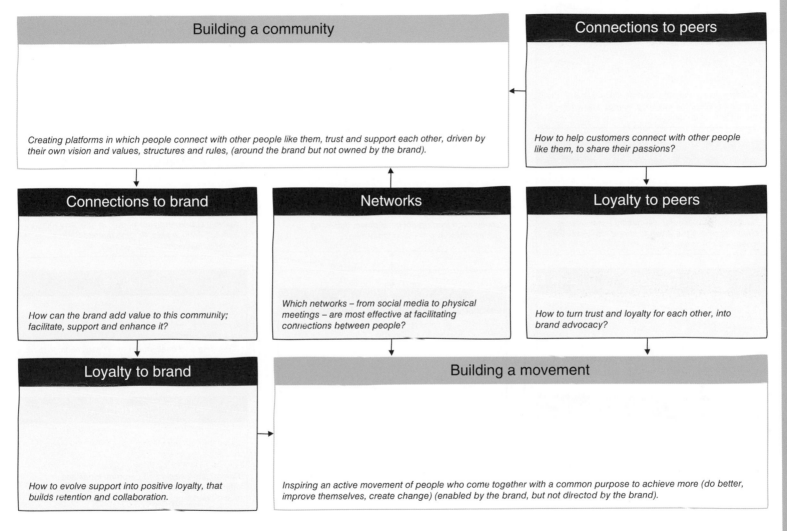

Building a community

Creating platforms in which people connect with other people like them, trust and support each other, driven by their own vision and values, structures and rules, (around the brand but not owned by the brand).

Connections to peers

How to help customers connect with other people like them, to share their passions?

Connections to brand

How can the brand add value to this community; facilitate, support and enhance it?

Networks

Which networks – from social media to physical meetings – are most effective at facilitating connections between people?

Loyalty to peers

How to turn trust and loyalty for each other, into brand advocacy?

Loyalty to brand

How to evolve support into positive loyalty, that builds retention and collaboration.

Building a movement

Inspiring an active movement of people who come together with a common purpose to achieve more (do better, improve themselves, create change) (enabled by the brand, but not directed by the brand).

PERFORMANCE LAB | Leadership Canvas

Fit
Building your personal and professional fitness, the physical and mental capacity, energy and agility, to be a leader of change.

Future
Having a future orientation, making sense of a changing world, the vision to shape the future, and to leave a positive legacy.

Focused
Combining creative flexibility with the disciplined focus to define clear priorities and deliver against business and personal targets.

Financial
Balancing the short and long-term demands and performance of the business financially, whilst staying true to the purpose and vision.

Gamechanger leader
Changing your own 'game' whilst inspiring the organization to do likewise – a change agent and innovator. Head up not head down, delivering today whilst also creating tomorrow.

Amplify potential
Increasing the capacity of your people and partners, brands and business to achieve more through more creative and diverse connections, bigger thinking in a bigger space.

Communicate
Articulating a clear vision that inspires followers, goals and priorities that creates effective focus, whilst listening and engaging all stakeholders.

Coach
Actively supporting your people in how they think and act, on their side, helping them to perform better individually and as teams.

Catalyse
Stretching and challenging the organization, to think bigger and better, disrupting the culture, exploring new ideas, encouraging participation.

Connect
Connecting people and partners, ideas and innovations, to create more novel solutions, break down boundaries and improve innovativeness.

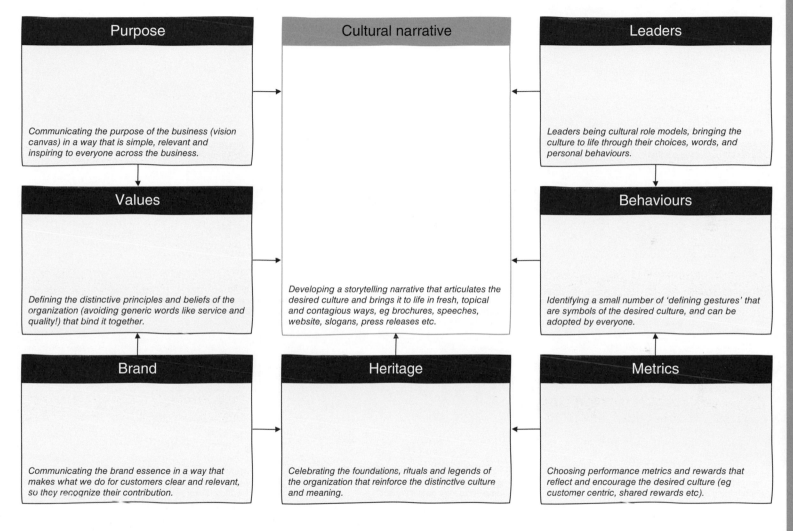

Purpose

Communicating the purpose of the business (vision canvas) in a way that is simple, relevant and inspiring to everyone across the business.

Cultural narrative

Developing a storytelling narrative that articulates the desired culture and brings it to life in fresh, topical and contagious ways, eg brochures, speeches, website, slogans, press releases etc.

Leaders

Leaders being cultural role models, bringing the culture to life through their choices, words, and personal behaviours.

Values

Defining the distinctive principles and beliefs of the organization (avoiding generic words like service and quality!) that bind it together.

Behaviours

Identifying a small number of 'defining gestures' that are symbols of the desired culture, and can be adopted by everyone.

Brand

Communicating the brand essence in a way that makes what we do for customers clear and relevant, so they recognize their contribution.

Heritage

Celebrating the foundations, rituals and legends of the organization that reinforce the distinctive culture and meaning.

Metrics

Choosing performance metrics and rewards that reflect and encourage the desired culture (eg customer centric, shared rewards etc).

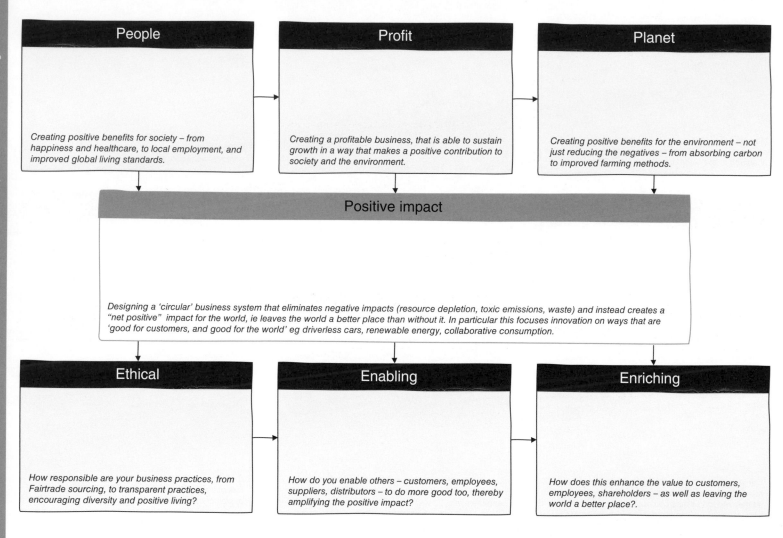

People

Creating positive benefits for society – from happiness and healthcare, to local employment, and improved global living standards.

Profit

Creating a profitable business, that is able to sustain growth in a way that makes a positive contribution to society and the environment.

Planet

Creating positive benefits for the environment – not just reducing the negatives – from absorbing carbon to improved farming methods.

Positive impact

Designing a 'circular' business system that eliminates negative impacts (resource depletion, toxic emissions, waste) and instead creates a "net positive" impact for the world, ie leaves the world a better place than without it. In particular this focuses innovation on ways that are 'good for customers, and good for the world' eg driverless cars, renewable energy, collaborative consumption.

Ethical

How responsible are your business practices, from Fairtrade sourcing, to transparent practices, encouraging diversity and positive living?

Enabling

How do you enable others – customers, employees, suppliers, distributors – to do more good too, thereby amplifying the positive impact?

Enriching

How does this enhance the value to customers, employees, shareholders – as well as leaving the world a better place?.

Market drivers

What are the factors that determine success in the market eg the relative importance of scale, choice provenance, innovation, growth etc?

Customer drivers

What are the factors that create perceived value, retention and advocacy for customers eg the relative importance of brand, price, service,etc?

Business drivers

What are the factors that determine success financially eg capital, operating costs, risks, speed, time, accessibility, licenses etc?

Market mix

Optimizing your choice of markets and segments to balance short and long-term success.

Product mix

Optimizing your portfolio of brands and products to balance short and long-term success.

Revenue

What are the revenue streams, ideally from sources that are profitable and growing? How can you enhance and accelerate these revenues?

Profit

How profitable is the revenue generation, driven through adding value as well as efficiency? How can you enhance this profitability?

Value creation

What is the economic value of the business, based on current and future performance? How is the value shared for sustained growth?

APPENDIX: DOING MORE

THE AUTHOR

Peter Fisk is a bestselling author, inspirational keynote speaker and has 25 years experience as an expert consultant helping business leaders to develop innovative strategies for business and brands.

He leads his own company, GeniusWorks, a boutique consulting firm, that helps companies around the world to build better brands, drive innovation and accelerate growth. He is also a visiting professor of strategy, innovation and marketing at IE Business School, one of the world's top ranked business schools. He features on the Thinkers 50 "Guru Radar" as one of the best new business thinkers.

Having grown up in the rural countryside of northern England, he studied physics across Europe, exploring new types of materials and their superconductivity. In a change of direction, Peter moved to the business world, managing brands like Concorde at British Airways, helping Microsoft to adopt a value-based marketing model, American Express to develop digital services, and Virgin to launch into new markets. He has worked in every sector and region of the world. As CEO of the world's largest marketing organisation, the Chartered Institute of Marketing, he became a global authority on what's best and next in business and markets.

Finding his own space, he founded GeniusWorks, with offices in London and Istanbul. He now works with leadership teams, facilitating new strategy development, innovation projects,

and executive development - in companies as diverse as Accenture and Aeroflot, Apotex and Arcelik, Canon and Coca Cola, Deloitte and DSM, Eczacibasi and GSK, Mars and Nestle, Philosophy and Pinar, Phillips and Raiffeisen, Red Bull and Sabre, Santander and SAP, Savola and Skanska, Swedbank and Tata, Teliasonera and Turkcell, Unilever and Virgin, Visa and Vodafone — helping them to think bigger and smarter, develop innovative strategies, bolder brands, and accelerate growth.

Peter's best-selling book "Marketing Genius" explores the left and right-brain challenges of success in today's markets, and is translated into 35 languages. It was followed by five others — "Business Genius" on leadership and strategy, "Customer Genius" on customers and experiences, "People Planet Profit" on sustainable innovation - and most recently "Creative Genius" defining what it takes to be Leonardo da Vinci in the 21 Century.

Peter was described by Business Strategy Journal as "one of the best new business thinkers". He is thoughtful and practical, combining high-energy keynotes with high-impact workshops. Each one is uniquely designed for the specific audience, their issues and aspirations. Helping people to find their own space, to be leaders of change - to be bold, brave and brilliant.

Email: peterfisk@peterfisk.com
Twitter: @geniusworks
Website: www.theGeniusWorks.com

THE BOOK

My inspiration for *Gamechangers* came from the many fascinating companies I have come across, in places like Buenos Aires and Bratislava, Istanbul and Jakarta, who have incredible ideas and innovations, yet often lack the vision and confidence to make them happen in a bigger way. They intuitively embrace the many new approaches of business today – from business models to experience design, social media and sustainability – but in more creative and joined up ways.

Entrepreneurs like Aeromobil's Stefan Klein to Positive Luxury's Diana Verde Nieto, have become friends and continued inspirations. Indeed every one of the 100 case studies offers a different and practical view on how to challenge yourself as well as your market, to see things differently, and do things nobody else has thought of. My thanks to all of them for their stories and support.

The book has evolved with the encouragement and helpful challenges of many colleagues – in particular Des Dearlove and Stuart Crainer at Thinkers 50 – plus a diverse range of other expert friends such as Kevin Roberts, Philip Kotler, Shaun Smith, Andy Milligan and Dave Ulrich; and business partners including Cosimo Turruturro and Eithne Jones, Enrique Vessuri and Brendan Barns, Tanyer Sonmezer and Hany Mwafy, Charles Nixon and Hugh Birkett. I also want to thank the faculty at IE Business School in Madrid, editorial teams at Fast Company and Wired, and my publisher John Wiley and Sons.

Most of all my inspiration comes from, and thanks go to my family – my wonderful wife, Alison, who is always there with a smile and support, and my two amazing daughters Anna and Clara who keep me real in today's world - with a millenial mindset, embracing the latest gadgets, reminding me what's cool and what's not – and that the future is full of unlimited possibilities and incredible opportunities for those with the vision and determination to realise it.

WHAT'S NEW?

Change never stops … the possibilities and players, the ideas and innovations – keeping in touch, even ahead of what's happening is tough, but exciting. To stay up to date with the Gamechangers, the progress of our case studies, and new insights from around the world, go to any of the dedicated resources that accompany this book:

- **Ideas and insights**: Explore all of the Gamechangers, including new award-winners around the world, updates on the book's case studies, digital tools and resources, videos and free downloads, plus news of all the latest events: www.Gamechangers.pro

- **Awards and accreditation**: Working with local partners to find the Gamechangers who are shaking up your local markets, through profiling and interactive voting, followed by accreditation and global showcase. Examples videos at www.youtube.com/thegeniusworks

- **Live updates**: Daily updates on the progress of the Gamechangers, together with more ideas for your strategy, brands and innovation, on Twitter @geniusworks.

- **Newsletter**: Sign-up to Peter Fisk's MASH+UP newsletter with the best new ideas in business, sent to you quarterly by email. Go to the website or request from peterfisk@peterfisk.com

WHAT'S MORE?

Read more books from Peter Fisk … all published by Wiley and Capstone, exploring new ideas from around the business world. All books are available in hardback and digital formats from Amazon, and all other good book retailers. Special orders, individual or with volume discounts, can also be ordered direct from the publisher at www.wiley.com

- **Marketing Genius**: How would Einstein and Picasso do business today? Explore the left and right-brain world of marketing that combines creativity and analysis, future strategy and operational delivery.

- **Customer Genius**: What does it take to be a customer-centric business – from a vision for making life better, through customer insights and value propositions, to brand experiences and customer relationships.

- **Business Genius**: A more inspired approach to leadership, business strategy and organization change. Turning ideas into action, brand promises into distinctive cultures, customer advocacy into accelerating growth.

- **Creative Genius**: Could you be the next Leonardo da Vinci? From radical creativity to design fusion, strategic innovation and market impact, how to make better ideas happen faster.

WHAT'S NEXT?

So, are you ready to change your world? … Beyond the ideas and insights in this book are a wide selection of resources and events to help you individually and as a team. Sometimes it requires more than a concept or process to spark your imagination, it needs energy and inspiration, asking the right questions, making new connections, helping you to harness you capability, realize your potential.

- **Inspiring events**: Inspiring keynotes and interactive seminars, customised to your objectives and audiences, delivered by Peter Fisk, and also bringing together some of the world's leading experts and entrepreneurs. See the event schedule at www.Gamechangers.pro

- **Executive masterclass**: Develop your own gamechanging strategies for business and brands, marketing and innovation, working with other leading executives workshops over 3 days at IE Business School. Download the Gamechangers brochure at www.ie.edu

- **Practical workshops**: A portfolio of leading-edge workshops on strategy, brands, marketing and innovation that can be customized to your business goals, embrace real issues and project work, and delivered anywhere in the world. More details at www.theGeniusWorks.com

- **Making it happen**: Bring together your people, issues and ideas, and let's make your best ideas happen faster and better using Innolab … an accelerated process for developing new strategies, brands and propositions, ready for implementation. www.theGeniusWorks.com

Time to get started. Time to change your game, and change your world …

Good luck!

INDEX

GAMECHANGERS